Marriage, Work, and Family Life

in Comparative Perspective

Marriage, Work,

and Family Life in

Comparative Perspective

Japan, South Korea, and the United States

Edited by Noriko O. Tsuya and Larry L. Bumpass

University of Hawai'i Press *Honolulu*

Library of Congress Cataloging-in-Publication Data

Marriage, work, and family life in comparative perspective :
Japan, South Korea, and the United States / edited by
Noriko O. Tsuya and Larry L. Bumpass
      p. cm
Includes bibliographical references and index.
   ISBN 0-8248-2508-X (Hardcover : alk. paper) —
ISBN 0-8248-2775-9 (Paperback : alk. paper)
   1. Family—Cross-cultural studies. 2. Work and family—
Cross-cultural studies. 3. Family—Japan. 4. Work and family—Japan.
5. Family—Korea (South) 6. Work and family—Korea (South)
7. Family—United States. 8. Work and family—United States.
I. Tsuya, Noriko O. II. Bumpass, Larry L.
HQ519.M37 2004
306.85—dc22

                                        2003019690

Designed by Deborah Hodgdon

Printed by Maple-Vail Book Manufacturing Group

Contents

Figures

Tables

This volume has grown out of our long-standing concern with comparing family patterns in East Asia to those in the U.S. and other Western societies. Similarities and differences across countries with such different cultural heritages and histories may provide essential clues about underlying processes. Most Western societies have undergone profound changes in family life affecting marriage, childbearing, female employment, and intergenerational relationships. Recently, marriage and fertility rates have plunged, first in Japan and then in South Korea. While descriptive analysis is only a first step, it is an essential step toward an increased understanding of family change in cultural and economic context. Such descriptive analysis is the explicit goal of this volume.

This work builds on a long collaboration among the authors of the chapters, in various combinations, based largely at the East-West Center in Honolulu. By the early 1990s, we realized that new data collection would be necessary if we were to continue our agenda. There were virtually no individual-level data with comparable measures of critical outcome and analytic variables across the three countries. At that time, Bumpass was a principal investigator on the National Survey of Families and Households (NSFH), the primary national study in the U.S. devoted to family issues. Taking advantage of this, and under the leadership of Tsuya, the team designed the National Survey of Work and Family Life (NSWFL), which was directed by Tsuya in Japan in 1994. A number of question sequences from the NSFH were included in this survey to facilitate comparisons between Japan and the U.S. In order to include South Korea in these comparisons, Choe and Tsuya approached the Korea Institute for Health and Social Affairs (KIHASA) to initiate a national survey on families. This survey, in turn, was very comparable to the Japanese survey, facilitating comparisons across all three countries. This volume is thus a product of the design and collection of comparable data across three countries, created by a close-knit network of researchers from both sides of the Pacific.

The volume occupies a somewhat unusual niche in that it falls between an edited volume and a monograph. Different combinations of authors took responsibility for designing and writing the various chapters, using procedures and modes of presentation that they deemed most appropriate to the subject they were addressing. Hence, each chapter was allowed to have its own voice in the mode of an edited volume. At the same time, during this process, drafts of each chapter were read by almost all of the authors of the other chapters and discussed collectively in the process of revision.

We could not have carried out this project without the help and support of many individuals and organizations in Japan, South Korea, and the U.S. First of all, we thank Karen Oppenheim Mason for her contributions and support. She not only co-authored a chapter of the volume, but also participated actively in the design of the 1994 Japanese survey and edited, together with Tsuya and Choe, a volume based on papers presented at an international symposium on family held in 1996 in Tokyo. Some of the analyses included in this volume are extensions of the materials presented in the symposium.

Our appreciation also goes to the East-West Center for facilitating our collaboration over many years, before and including this project, and for providing many forms of support and assistance over the course of the data analyses and manuscript preparation for the volume. We are especially grateful to Ann Takayesu, who spent many hours formatting tables and checking references. Judith Tom, Yoke Yun Bauer, and Gayle Yamashita provided expert programming assistance.

The 1994 National Survey of Work and Family Life in Japan was funded by Nihon University in Tokyo, and the University Research Center (URC) of Nihon University made it possible to conduct this survey by offering invaluable administrative and logistical support. We especially thank Fukuji Kawarazaki, the URC's former director of research administration, whose steadfast support and encouragement made possible the survey and the ensuing international collaboration.

Thanks are also due to the KIHASA for funding the 1994 National Survey on the Quality of Life in the Republic of Korea. We especially thank Nam-Hoon Cho for being instrumental in making this survey possible, Moon-Sik Hong and Hyun-Sop Chang for directing the survey in the field, and Yong-Chan Byun for collaborating with us in the preparation of the volume.

The NSFH was funded by the U.S. National Institute of Child Health and Human Development and the National Institute on Aging. The Center for Demography and Ecology of the University of Wisconsin–Madison provided the essential context for the design and execution of the NSFH, and the leadership role of James A. Sweet as co-principal investigator of this study is gratefully acknowledged.

The Center for Global Partnership of the Japan Foundation provided the funding that made it possible to continue our comparative analyses of the three surveys beyond the initial phases of data collection. The University of North Carolina's Kenan Fund is also acknowledged: Rindfuss was on leave with the fund's support when one of the chapters of the volume was written.

Finally, many colleagues read or heard our presentations of earlier versions of the chapters and provided useful comments and suggestions. They include Makoto Atoh, Cameron Campbell, Robert Hauser, Albert Hermalin, Hiroshi Kojima, Shigemi Kono, James Z. Lee, Takako Sodei, James Sweet, Wang Feng, and Kazuo Yamaguchi. We also thank Lee-Jay Cho, for originally bringing us together, and Toshio Kuroda for his support and encouragement over many years.

Chapter One

Introduction

Noriko O. Tsuya and Larry L. Bumpass

In preindustrial economies, families and households were the primary units of both production and consumption, and economic activities were organized around family and kinship. Under the primacy of the family as a social institution, marriage and childbearing were imperative for subsistence and protection. Women and, to a lesser degree, men depended on the ensuing family relations and kin network, and conjugal and parent-child relations were considered unbreakable, lifelong commitments.

The expansion of market economies increased global interactions, thus restructuring societies internally and leading to profound changes in many aspects of family life (Caldwell 1976; Freedman 1975; Goode 1963). The transition from agrarian to industrial economies resulted in the separation of work and home, along with an increasing division of labor in economic activities, with men becoming the primary breadwinners and women adopting the role of full-time homemakers (Oakley 1976; Rindfuss, Brewster, and Kavee 1996). As the macroeconomic structural change proceeded, however, paid employment of women outside the home increased dramatically after World War II in much of the industrialized world (Oppenheimer 1994; Rindfuss, Brewster, and Kavee 1996; Shimada and Higuchi 1985). These changes made the combination of market and family roles increasingly more difficult. This was particularly so for married women, given the persistence of cultural expectations regarding the gender division of labor, resulting in a "double shift" among women employed full-time (Hochschild 1991; Tsuya and Bumpass 1998).

The growth of market economies was also accompanied by changes in views toward marriage and family. The transition from family-based production to individual wage earning eroded the once sacred notions of marriage as lifelong commitment and obligations to one's family, emphasizing instead individual well-being and self-satisfaction (Lesthaeghe 1983). To be sure, societies have different preexisting family values and systems, and these cultural differences and differing histories have left unique imprints on family life, serving as filters through which market economies have altered family life. Nonetheless, family systems in societies with distinctively different familial-cultural backgrounds are being pushed in similar directions, even while each retains certain aspects of its unique cultural history.

Objectives

In the context of these transformations, this volume compares marriage, work, and family life in Japan, South Korea (referred to as "Korea" hereafter in the volume for linguistic simplicity), and the U.S. The comparative perspective taken in this volume draws on major differences among the three countries in cultural heritage and in the timing and rapidity of industrial development. The dominance of family obligations inherent in the Confucian background of Japan and Korea contrasts dramatically with the individualistic orientation of the U.S., thus presenting a strong test of the influence on family life of modern market economies. Industrialization occurred very early in the U.S., though at a much slower pace than in Japan and Korea. In Japan it developed more recently and at a more rapid pace, and in Korea development has occurred most recently and at an extremely rapid pace. The project on which this volume is based was undertaken precisely because the contrast between the two East Asian countries (with similar cultural backgrounds) and the U.S., combined with differences in the timing and pace of economic development, is of central theoretical importance. It was also for this reason that we undertook the large-scale national data collections in Japan and Korea that permit comparisons with the major data source on American family life. With only three countries, we are clearly unable to analyze statistically the relationship between economic and cultural transformations and family change. Instead, the volume offers descriptive accounts of similarities and differences in aspects of family life that have been changing rapidly but remain underexplored. Our examination of the three countries illustrates the potential effects cultural and industrial-structural factors may have on family processes, as well as gender differences in the impacts of these factors.

Based on the value principles of familism, Japan and Korea have two of the most patriarchal family and gender role systems found in modern history (Lee 1978; Smith 1987; Tsuya and Choe 1991). This is not to say that family culture is identical in Japan and Korea—it clearly is not. Nonetheless, this distinctive cultural tradition in the two East Asian countries poses a clear contrast to the more individualistic and egalitarian cultural heritage in the U.S. (Lesthaeghe and Wilson 1986; Steinhoff 1994). On the other hand, viewed from the economic-structural perspective, the U.S. and Japan—the world's largest and second largest economies—share a number of features of advanced industrial development. By contrast, much of the economic growth in Korea has occurred over the last two decades.

The timing and rapidity of demographic changes that have accompanied industrial development have both reflected and influenced family life and relationships. The demographic transition from high fertility and mortality was completed earlier in the U.S. and Japan than in Korea. Further, these declines were much faster in the two East Asian countries than in the U.S. The Total

Fertility Rates (TFR) declined from more than four to two children per woman in one decade in Japan from the late 1940s and in Korea from the early 1970s.[1] By contrast, the U.S. was one of the first countries of the world to begin the demographic transition—in the early nineteenth century—and its fertility and mortality declined gradually over a period of more than a century (Oppenheimer 1994; Preston 1976).

Three major domains of family life are examined in this volume. We first compare the three countries with respect to attitudes toward marriage and the family. Although the causal relationship between attitude and behavior is complex and reciprocal, accumulating evidence suggests the importance of ideational change that accompanies industrial development as a factor in changing family relations and demographic behavior (e.g., Lesthaeghe 1983; Oppenheimer 1994; Pagnini and Rindfuss 1993; Rindfuss, Brewster, and Kavee 1996).

We then look at the intergenerational aspects of family life from the perspective of the middle generation's relationships with its parents and its children. Comparing differences in intergenerational relations in the three countries, we seek to sort out the relative importance of cultural, socioeconomic, and demographic influences on family relations across generations.

Finally, we examine the "work-family interface." The relationship between work and family reflects the joint influences of economic structure and family culture. In this context, we compare the relationship between employment and housework among married men and women. Based on these comparisons of views on marriage and family, intergenerational relations, and relationship between work and family, the concluding chapter synthesizes findings and presents an assessment of changes in the nature and stability of family relations in the three countries.

Cultural Backgrounds in the Three Societies

To better establish the context of the comparisons explored in this volume, we briefly review relevant aspects of historical and cultural backgrounds in Japan, Korea, and the U.S. Alternative pairs of these three countries provide contrasts with respect to traditional family value orientations and levels and pace of industrial development and demographic transition.

The traditional family systems and values in Japan and Korea resemble each other, reflecting their common roots in the culture of Confucian China. The traditional family system in the two countries—called the *"ie"* in Japan and the *"jib"* in Korea—is the patrilineal, patrilocal, and patriarchal stem family (Taeuber 1958: 100–104; Tsuya and Choe 1991).[2] Under this system, in principle, the eldest son, who was the heir presumptive, brought his bride into his parental home and lived with his parents while other offspring formed their own households upon marriage or shortly afterward. Upon the father's death, the eldest son inherited a major portion (or almost all) of the family property and succeeded to the family headship. While the Korean *jib* system placed an almost absolute primacy on the paternal bloodline, the adoption of a son or son-in-law as heir presumptive was easily accomplished under the Japanese *ie* system when the usual process of biological reproduction failed.[3] Thus, the *ie* and the *jib* were consanguineous or pseudo-consanguineous systems whose primary purpose was to preserve biological and cultural continuity of the family based on patrilineal rules of descent.[4]

Since the ultimate goal of the two systems was the biological and social continuation of the family line, the most important obligation for men and women was to marry and produce an heir (Tsuya and Choe 1991). Marriage and procreation were especially important for women because they were excluded both from opportunities of paid employment outside the home and from their natal family upon marriage, so their only viable option was to marry and provide an heir to their family of marriage.[5] From the viewpoint of the extended family (i.e., for the continuity of the family as a whole), it was also important and necessary that decisions pertaining to marriage and divorce not be left to individual men and women; rather, such decisions were the prerogative of the family head (Taeuber 1958: 101; Tsuya and Choe 1991).

In summary, the traditional family systems in the two East Asian countries involved a complex set of well-defined hierarchical relations among family members according to the ascribed supremacy regarding gender (males over females), generation (parents over children), and birth order (first-born over later-born).[6] The idealized principles of the systems provided the bases for cultural and social stability. At the same time, the systems constrained the lives of individuals, especially those of women, leaving few opportunities for life outside the matrix of family relationships. Though many aspects of the traditional family system have been drastically altered or disappeared altogether in the postwar years, its influences still persist both in intergenerational relationships and in inequality between men and women in Japanese and Korean homes (see chapters 4 and 7; also see Lee 1972; Smith 1987; Steinhoff 1994; Tsuya and Bumpass 1998; Tsuya and Choe 1991).

In contrast to the patrilineal stem family systems in Japan and Korea, the bilateral system in the U.S. advantages neither paternal nor maternal lines. Each generation is expected to establish and maintain an independent household, and intergenerational coresidence of adult children and their parents is expected only during times of special need (Bumpass 1994). In clear contrast to the tradition in Japan and Korea, the family is seen in the U.S. as an institution for the protection and support of individual family members, rather than as an enduring entity above and beyond those individuals (Gecas 1987). By the same token, a strong cultural emphasis is also placed, in principle, on equality among family members, with an obligation to justify differences in power by gender, generation, or birth order (Bernard 1973; Steinhoff 1994). Nevertheless, women continue to bear a greater burden in child care and household tasks, while their options are more constrained in the labor market compared to those of men.

To be sure, individuals do not always behave according to culturally prescribed expectations. Some actively resist those expectations or ignore them altogether. Further, both cultural expectations and patterns of interaction are changing in response to changing economic and social environments, including both internal economic development and expanding contact with other societies through the growth of market economies and the mass media. Nonetheless, cultural ideals and expectations are important for our understanding of variations in family-related attitudes and behaviors in what appear to be objectively similar circumstances.

Fertility and Marriage

It is also important for our comparisons with respect to attitudes, intergenerational relations, and work and family that they be set in the context of changes in fertility and marriage patterns.

Fertility Decline

Both Japan and Korea experienced a dramatic downturn in fertility after World War II (see figure 1.1). In Japan the TFR declined from 4.5 per woman in 1947 to 2.0 in 1957 (National Institute of Population and Social Security Research 2002: 50–51). After this rapid decline, fertility stabilized until it started to decline again in the mid-1970s and reached an all-time low of 1.3 per woman in 1999. High fertility persisted in Korea until rapid economic development began in the early 1960s. The TFR dropped by almost three-fourths in twenty-four years—from 5.9 per woman in 1963 to 1.6 in 1987 (Choe and Park 1989; Tsuya and Choe 1991). This remarkable decline was followed by a modest upturn in the early 1990s and then by a resumption of decline in the late 1990s, resulting in a TFR of 1.4 per woman in 1999 (National Statistical Office 2000: 106).

In clear contrast to the two East Asian countries, the U.S. started its gradual fertility transition before the twentieth century. After a substantial "baby boom," beginning in the late 1940s, fertility began to decline around 1960 and then increased modestly in the 1970s to reach its current level of around 2.0 children per woman (Ventura et al. 1998). These differences in the onset and pace of fertility decline (charted in figure 1.1) are related to the pace and type of socioeconomic development in each country and in turn have influenced attitudes and behaviors relating to family and gender relations. Declines in fertility are ipso facto an aspect of changing family orientations, and at the same time they alter the context of interactions across generations and between husbands and wives.

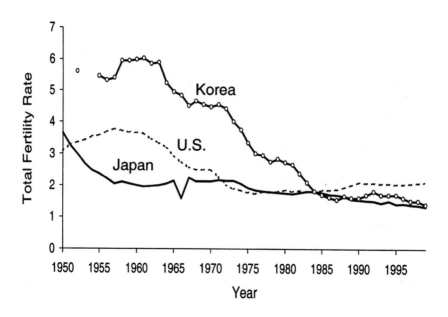

Figure 1.1. *Trends in Total Fertility Rate: Japan, Korea, and the U.S., 1950–1999*

Delayed Marriage and Nonmarriage

The increasing delay of marriage is one of the most prominent features of family change in all three countries after World War II (Bumpass 1990; Tsuya and Choe 1994). Because out-of-wedlock childbearing has been minimal in the two East Asian countries, the delay of women's first marriage has been a major factor in the fertility decline to very low levels in recent decades. In Japan, the proportion never-married among women in their twenties and thirties has increased precipitously since the mid-1970s. For example, from 1975 to 1995, it more than doubled: from 21 to 48 percent for women aged 25–29 and from 8 to 20 percent for women aged 30–34 (National Institute of Population and Social Security Research 2002: 113). The proportion single also increased dramatically among men in their late twenties and thirties in the same period. This phenomenal delay of marriage suggests a possible future increase in permanent nonmarriage. By 2010, it is estimated that the proportion single at ages 45–49 will reach 10 percent for women and 20 percent for men (Retherford, Ogawa, and Matsukura 2001). This is remarkable in light of the East Asian tradition of universal marriage and the normative expectation that women should marry "on schedule" in their early to mid-twenties (e.g., Brinton 1992).[7]

Korean women are also marrying later, though almost all marry by their mid-thirties. The proportion of never-married women aged 20–24 has increased phenomenally: from 21 percent in 1955 to 83 percent in 1995 (National Statistical Office 1997a: 582; Tsuya and Choe 1991). The percent of single women aged 25–29 also rose from a mere 3 percent to 29 percent between 1955 and 1995. Although almost all Korean men still marry by age 40, the proportions single among men in their late twenties and early thirties have also been increasing rapidly in the last few decades. American women and men are marrying later as well, even though they still marry at younger ages than Japanese or Koreans. For example, the proportion single among women aged 20–24 rose from 40 to 67 percent between 1975 and 1995 (U.S. Bureau of the Census 1980, 1998). Men have experienced similar (or even more rapid) increases in the proportion single.

In sum, young women and men are marrying later in all three countries. The magnitude of the delay is especially notable in Japan, where there also is a sign of increases in permanent nonmarriage. In addition to delayed marriage, the most profound changes in American marriage have been in the declining stability and viability of marital relations, as characterized by high levels of divorce, increased cohabitation, and out-of-wedlock childbearing. We next turn to these issues.

Divorce, Cohabitation, and Nonmarital Childbearing

Although we cannot estimate the probability of divorce equally well in the three countries, it seems clear that divorce has been rising rapidly in all of them. With periodic fluctuations around the trend line, the divorce rate in the U.S. has increased exponentially since the early 1800s (Cherlin 1981). There was a particularly large increase between the mid-1960s and around 1980, after which the rate stabilized at a level at which about one-half of all first marriages end in divorce (Bumpass and Raley 1999).

Though lower than in the U.S., divorce has also increased in both of the East Asian countries. In Japan, the rate of divorce per 1,000 persons rose from around 0.8 in the mid-1960s to 1.6 in 1995 and to 2.3 in 2001 (National Institute of Population and Social Security Research 2002: 100). Period life-table estimates suggest that the proportion of couples expected to divorce within twenty years of marriage rose from 9 percent in 1965 to 19 percent two decades later (Institute of Population Problems 1989a). Though a comparable estimate of the likelihood of divorce is not available for Korea, evidence indicates a similar, or even more rapid, increase in recent years. The crude divorce rate tripled from 0.5 per 1,000 in 1975 to 1.5 in 1995 (National Statistical Office 1998: 121).

Mass changes in family behavior are occurring not only within marriage, but also outside marriage in all three countries. Premarital sex has become nearly universal in the U.S. as the proportion sexually active among American teenagers doubled in just two decades from the late 1960s (Bumpass 1998; Forrest and Singh 1992), and the proportion of first marriages preceded by cohabitation reached about one-half in the late 1980s (Bumpass 1990). Related to these changes in sexual behavior and union formation is a phenomenal increase in nonmarital childbearing in the U.S. The proportion of American babies born to an unwed mother increased from 8 percent in 1965 to 33 percent in 1994 (Ventura 1995; Ventura et al. 1998). While levels are higher among minority women, nonmarital childbearing has become more common among American women of all racial and ethnic groups (DaVanzo and Rahman 1993; Ventura 1995).

By contrast, in both Japan and Korea, out-of-wedlock childbearing has remained extremely low, at about 1–2 percent of all births (S.-K. Kim 1992; National Institute of Population and Social Security Research 2002:69). Cohabitation among young single persons has also remained extremely rare in the two East Asian countries; for example, less than 3 percent of unmarried Japanese under age 35 have ever lived in a cohabiting relationship (Institute of Population Problems 1989b: 71; Kong et al. 1992; National Institute of Population and Social Security Research 1999: 184; Tsuya 1993).

Despite the virtual absence of cohabitation and out-of-wedlock childbearing, however, premarital sex has become increasingly common among young women and men in both East Asian countries. According to national surveys in Japan, 32 percent of single women aged 20–24 in 1987 reported having had sexual intercourse; the percentage had increased to 52 percent by 1997 (Institute of Population Problems 1989b: 70; National Institute of Population and Social Security Research 1999: 184). The prevalence of premarital sex is lower, but clearly increasing, in Korea. According to national surveys of high school students, 3 percent of girls and 12 percent of boys reported having had sexual intercourse in 1988; the corresponding figures in 1998 were 8 and 18 percent respectively (Han et al. 2001).

Thus, we see similar signs of retreat from marriage in the forms of marriage postponement and increasing divorce in all three countries. There are also signs of increasing erosion of the social significance of marriage as an institution, as illustrated by the increases in sex among the unmarried, as well as, in the U.S., the prevalence of cohabitation and out-of-wedlock childbearing. Because childbearing remains almost exclusively within marriage in the two East Asian countries, the increasing retreat from marriage is associated with very low fertility in recent years. This association may reflect the indirect consequence of marriage delay/avoidance on fertility, but it may also reflect desires to delay or forgo childbearing that in turn have resulted in later marriage and increasing nonmarriage.

Economy, Employment, and Education

There have been dramatic changes since World War II in the social and economic structures of all three countries, and these changes have been important factors in the changes in fertility and marriage described above. We briefly review some of the key aspects of macro social-structural changes—economic growth, urbanization, and industrial structural transformations—as well as two very important changes in women's status—employment and educational attainment.

Economic Growth, Urbanization, and Industrial Transformation

Though the timing is different, Japan and Korea both had extremely rapid economic growth after World War II. Starting in the mid-1950s, Japan's per capita Gross National Product (GNP) grew at a phenomenal pace, quadrupling in constant prices every 10–15 years (Tsuya and Choe 1991; World Bank 1991: 2–5, 1997: 6–9). Korea's rapid economic development began in the mid-1960s, with its per capita GNP quadrupling in constant prices every 10–15 years until the mid-1990s. Consequently, the country has been transformed from one of the poorest in the world to one of the newly industrialized economies. In contrast to the two East Asian countries, the U.S. was already the wealthiest country in the world at the end of the war, and its pace of subsequent economic growth has been much slower.

In the course of rapid economic growth, the two East Asian countries also experienced rapid urbanization. In Japan, the proportion living in urban areas increased from 37 to 63 percent from 1950 to 1960, reaching 78 percent in 1995 (National Institute of Population and Social Security Research 2002: 168). Korea experienced even more rapid and continuous urbanization throughout the postwar years, with the proportion urban rising from 21 percent in 1950 to 81 percent in 1995 (World Bank 1997: 114–116; Tsuya and Choe 1991). By contrast, the U.S. was already an urbanized society in the early postwar years, and the pace of urbanization since then has been very gradual: from 64 percent urban in 1950 to 76 percent in 1995 (United Nations 1996).

The rapid economic growth and urbanization in Japan and Korea were concurrent with dramatic changes in industrial structure. In Japan the proportion of the employed population in primary industries shrank from 49 percent in 1950 to 19 percent in 1970 to 6 percent in 1995 (National Institute of Population and Social Security Research 2002, 143). In Korea the proportion of the employed population engaged in agriculture decreased phenomenally from 66 percent in 1960 to 12 percent in 1995 (National Statistical Office 1998: 161; Tsuya and Choe 1991). By contrast, the U.S. had completed much of its transformation from agriculture to a modern industrialized economy before the war. The proportion of employment in agriculture was 12 percent in 1950 and dwindled to 3 percent in 1995 (U.S. Bureau of the Census 1975: 127, 1998: 421).

Women's Employment

With industrial structures shifting rapidly from primary to secondary and then to tertiary industries, employment, especially female employment, also underwent notable changes in all three countries. In Japan, although the overall labor force participation rate of women changed little in the postwar years (remaining at roughly 50 percent, with some fluctuations), the type of female employment changed dramatically. The proportion of employed women who were family workers (worked on a family farm or in family businesses) declined steadily from 43 percent in 1960 to 12 percent in 1995, while the proportion in paid employment increased rapidly from 41 percent to 78 percent during the same period (Rodosho Joseikyoku 1999: appendix 16). Further, although the M-shaped pattern of female labor force participation by age still remains, the drop at the peak ages of women's marriage and childbearing (ages 25–34) has become much less distinctive in recent decades. Especially notable are the increases in the labor force participation rate for women aged 25–29—from 43 percent in 1975 to 66 percent in 1995—suggesting an association with the increasing delay of marriage among women in this age group. The rate for women aged 30–34 also increased steadily—from 44 percent in 1975 to 56 percent in 1995. This in turn suggests that employment of mothers with small children has been on the rise in the country in recent years (nearly one-third of mothers of preschoolers were employed in 1994; see chapter 6 of this volume).

In Korea, the overall female labor force participation rate increased from one-quarter in 1960 to about one-half in 1995; however, the M-shaped age pattern of women's employment remains clear and intact. Whereas the labor force participation rate of women in their early twenties has increased considerably in recent decades, the rates for women at the peak marriage and childbearing ages of 25–34 have been essentially stable. Moreover, the proportion of employed women who are in agriculture is still sizable at older ages—roughly 60 percent of women aged 50 and above in 1995 (National Statistical Office 1997b: 198). All together, these suggest that while employment of young (mostly single) women has been on the rise, opportunities for married women to enter paid employment have remained limited.

While the industrial transformation in the postwar U.S. was not as dramatic as that in Korea and Japan, there have been profound changes in the employment of mothers with small children. The labor force participation rate for all women increased from 38 percent in 1960 to 59 percent in 1995; the corresponding rate for women with children under age six increased even more rapidly: from 31 to 64 percent (U.S. Bureau of the Census 1975: 134, 1998: 408–409). The normative and social "barriers" to the employment of mothers of small children appear to have been overridden by the economic and social needs of women and their families.

Education

Education has a major impact on women's status in society—directly, as well as through associated employment and earnings. Education also affects a number of aspects of family life, including intergenerational relationships and gender relations at home. In Japan, where primary and lower secondary education

Tsuya and Bumpass

had already been prevalent in the prewar years, the most notable educational change was a rapid and continuous increase in the proportion of women with higher education. The percentage of female high school graduates advancing to higher education increased phenomenally from 6 percent in 1960 to 48 percent in 1995, while the corresponding figures for males rose from 15 to 43 percent (Monbusho 1998: 38). It is especially notable that whereas the advancement rate for male high school students has remained around 43 percent during the last two decades, the rate for females has continued to increase, closing the once large gender gap. The proportion with higher education among women aged 25–29 increased from 10 to 49 percent between 1970 and 2000, surpassing that of men in the same age group during the 1990s (National Institute of Population and Social Security Research 2002: 151).

The level of women's educational attainment was much lower in Korea in the early postwar years. Indeed, a sizable proportion of older women had no formal education at all (Tsuya and Choe 1991). Thereafter, however, the education of Korean women (and, to a lesser extent, men) increased remarkably. Only 3 percent of women born in 1936–1940 obtained higher education, compared to 32 percent among women born in 1966–1970 (National Statistical Office 1995: 64–66). The corresponding figures for men increased from 17 to 44 percent; thus, in Korea as well, the once vast gender gap has almost disappeared when we consider postsecondary school attendance. However, the gender gap remains with respect to the completion of college, even though there were very large increases for both men and women: from 14 to 33 percent among men and from 3 to 23 percent among women.

If not as dramatic as in the two East Asian countries, educational attainment also increased substantially in the U.S. after World War II, with a large majority of Americans today having at least a high school education. From 1950 to 1995, the proportion of the population aged 25 and over who had completed at least four years of high school increased from about one-third to 82 percent for both women and men (U.S. Bureau of the Census 1975: 380, 1998: 167). The attainment of higher education in the U.S. is also characterized by a closing gender gap, especially among younger cohorts. For example, from 1970 to 2000, the percentage of the population aged 25–29 with four years of college or more increased from 13 to 30 percent for women and from 19 to 28 percent for men (U.S. Bureau of the Census 1973: 627, 2000: table 1).

Data

All the chapters in this book use data from at least two of these three countries; the data are based on national surveys conducted in the late 1980s and mid-1990s: the National Survey on Work and Family Life (NSWFL) in Japan, the National Survey on the Quality of Life (NSQL) in Korea, and the National Survey of Families and Households (NSFH) in the U.S. As noted above, we included questions in the national surveys in Japan and Korea that could be compared directly with the NSFH. Table 1.1 summarizes the basic characteristics of the surveys.

Japan: NSWFL

The NSWFL is a national probability sample of men and women aged 20–59 and of all marital statuses. The survey was intended to parallel the U.S. NSFH, as well as to collect information on marriage, work, and family life specific to Japanese families. Conducted in January–February 1994, the survey was designed by a research team from Nihon University in Tokyo assisted by researchers from the Korea Institute for Health and Social Affairs, the East-West Center, and several U.S. universities, including the University of Wisconsin–Madison and the University of North Carolina–Chapel Hill. Funding and logistical support were given by the University Research Center of Nihon University.

The NSWFL is based on a national, stratified, two-stage probability sampling of individuals, in which 175 locales were randomly selected based on the 1990 census tract distribution; then twenty individuals aged 20–59 were randomly selected within each locale (potential N=3,500). Information was collected through self-administered questionnaires that were distributed by field workers and then subsequently picked up. A total of 2,447 usable questionnaires was obtained—a response rate of 70 percent. Sample distributions on basic characteristics such as age and sex compositions closely match those of the 1990 population census of Japan. Further information on the survey can be found in Nihon Daigaku Sogo Kagaku Kenkyusho (1994).

Korea: NSQL

The NSQL was conducted in August 1994. Unlike the Japanese and U.S. surveys, however, the NSQL sample was limited to household heads and spouses

Table 1.1. *Characteristics of the National Surveys: Japan, Korea, and the U.S.*

Characteristic	Japan (NSWFL)	Korea (NSQL)	U.S.[a] (NSFH)
Year of survey	1994	1994	1987–88
Sample size	2,447	2,666	13,017
Age range	20–59	n.a.[b]	19+
Marital status	All	All[c]	All
Sexes	Both	Both	Both

[a] Characteristics shown are for the 1987–1988 National Survey of Families and Households (NSFH1) rather than the 1992–1994 followup (NSFH2).

[b] No age constraint was imposed on the sample.

[c] Restricted to heads of household and spouses of heads. Though there are some unmarried heads, this sample restriction results in a high proportion (87 percent) who are currently married.

of heads, and no age limit was imposed. The NSQL thus represents household heads and spouses of heads living in Korea in 1994 rather than the country's general adult population. Given the nature of this sample, although basic characteristics of the subsample of currently married men and women aged 20–59 closely match those found in the 1990 population census of the Republic of Korea, individuals of other marital statuses are acutely underrepresented. The NSQL questionnaire was based on the questionnaire of the Japanese NSWFL. The NSQL was designed and conducted by researchers from the Korea Institute for Health and Social Affairs (KIHASA), with funding provided by KIHASA.

The NSQL is based on a stratified, two-stage probability sampling in which a national probability sample of ninety-nine locales was selected and then thirty household heads or spouses of heads were randomly selected within each locale. Rural areas were selected at twice the rate of urban areas; thus, sample weights are used to produce estimates that are nationally representative. Data were collected by face-to-face interviews in most cases. If a selected respondent could not be interviewed after several visits, however, a questionnaire was left for the respondent and then picked up by the interviewer at a later date. A total of 2,666 usable questionnaires was returned, representing a response rate of 90 percent. Further information on the survey can be found in Chang, Kim, and Bae (1994).

U.S.: NSFH

The NSFH is a large-scale, nationally representative survey of the noninstitutionalized population of the U.S., designed to collect information on a variety of issues pertaining to American family life. The first wave of the NSFH was conducted in 1987–1988 (NSFH1); a followup of the same respondents was conducted in 1992–1994 (NSFH2). The surveys were designed by a team of researchers from a variety of U.S. universities and research institutions directed by the Center for Demography and Ecology, University of Wisconsin–Madison. Funding for NSFH1 was provided by the Center for Population Research of the National Institute of Child Health and Human Development (NICHD); NSFH2 was funded by the NICHD and the National Institute on Aging (NIA).

NSFH1 is based on interviews with 13,007 respondents from a stratified, clustered national probability sample. The sample includes a main cross-section of 9,637 households from which one adult (person aged 19 or older) per household was randomly selected as the primary respondent. This main cross-section was supplemented by an oversampling of a number of important subpopulations, and national estimates are obtained by using appropriate sample weights. Most of the information collected from the primary respondents was obtained through face-to-face interviews, which lasted on the average 100 minutes. Information was also collected from the spouse or cohabiting partner of the primary respondent by a shorter, self-administered questionnaire. Further technical details of NSFH1 can be found in Sweet, Bumpass, and Call (1988).

NSFH2 is the five-year followup of NSFH1, based on reinterviews with 10,007 of the original primary respondents. In addition, interviews were conducted with a number of other family members, including spouses and a selected child and parent. Specifics on NSFH2 can be obtained in Sweet and Bumpass (1996) through the NSFH home page (http://www.ssc.wisc.edu/nsfh/home.htm).

Approach to Differences across the Surveys

By design, the three surveys share a considerable number of identical or similar questions. Nonetheless, differences in the sampling designs across the three surveys require some restrictions to increase comparability. First, all the analyses of the NSFH reported in this volume use data only from non-Hispanic whites in order to avoid compounding cross-cultural comparisons with internal differences in familial cultural backgrounds of various racial and ethnic groups within the U.S. population. Not only do levels of family behavior (such as nonmarital childbearing) differ markedly between minorities and majority whites, but also a large body of research on family issues in the U.S. has found different relationships among variables for minority populations compared to majority whites (e.g., Bumpass and Sweet 1992; Carter 1993). As a consequence, it is often necessary to conduct analyses separately for majority whites and for minority groups, and this would be an unnecessary diversion from our major comparative objective.

Second, all analyses presented here are limited to persons aged 20–59, primarily because the Japanese survey was limited to this age range, and some of the analyses impose a narrower age range as appropriate to the topics being analyzed.

Finally, while many of the comparative analyses presented in this book focus on married couples, information on spouses is collected differently across the surveys. In the NSWFL and NSQL, respondents were asked to provide proxy reports for their spouses on objective information. On the other hand, in the NSFH, information on respondents and on their spouses was collected by self-reports. Thus we have controlled sex of respondent in our multivariate analyses.

Organization of the Book

After this introductory chapter, there are six comparative chapters on marriage, work, and family life in Japan, Korea, and the U.S. Chapters 2 and 3 focus on attitudes toward marriage and family, first from the perspective of the general adult population and then from that of young, never-married persons. The next two chapters focus on intergenerational relations, again from different perspectives: chapter 4 examines the relationship up the generational ladder—that is, between married adults and their parents; the other looks at the relationship downward—that is, between married women and their children. The final two comparative chapters examine work and the family from the perspective of married couples in midlife. The volume concludes with a chapter that discusses the advantages and difficulties of cross-national studies, summarizes major findings of the six comparative chapters, and speculates on the future of the family.

In chapter 2, Bumpass and Choe look at key attitudes relating to the importance of marriage and parenthood, nonmarital sex, gender roles, and intergenerational relations in Japan, Korea, and the U.S. It is important to examine differences in attitudes across these three societies because attitudes, while deeply imbedded in cultural heritage, also change in response to socioeconomic conditions. Paying attention to age and gender differences within each country, as well as to intercountry differences, the authors find many similarities in changes in attitude. In all three countries, traditional orientations toward marriage appear to be eroding rapidly, with the younger cohorts holding less traditional views. These differences may well foreshadow continuing changes in the normative climate with respect to the necessity and importance of marriage and childbearing. Attitudes toward traditional gender roles are also clearly related to age and gender in all three countries, with women holding much less traditional views than men. The authors suggest that these gender differences may, in turn, reinforce the delay as well as the instability of marriage that we have witnessed in all three countries, as men and women bring to marital unions vastly different expectations.

Chapter 3, by Tsuya, Mason, and Bumpass, takes a closer look at views on marriage and the desire to marry among young unmarried adults in Japan and the U.S. Comparing the perceived costs and benefits of marriage among single men and women aged 20–27, the authors find that Japanese women are most skeptical about the benefits of marriage. Although almost everybody thinks his or her personal freedom will not improve by marrying, the sense of loss of freedom associated with marriage is most widespread among Japanese women. In contrast to perceptions in the U.S., a large majority of Japanese women and men also feel that marriage would not improve their living standards. However, the majority of young people in both countries think that marriage will improve their emotional security and overall happiness. Nonetheless, Japanese women are the least optimistic about the psychological benefits of marriage: almost one-half of them do not feel that their happiness would increase were they to marry. While most young adults in both countries say they want to eventually marry, many more persons in Japan than in the U.S. are uncertain about this. These lukewarm views toward the benefits of marriage among young unmarried women (and, to a lesser extent, men) may be an important factor in the delay of marriage in Japan, especially in the context of continuing gender inequality in the home and the increasing employment of wives.

The next two chapters address family relations across generations. In chapter 4, Rindfuss, Choe, Bumpass, and Byun examine relationships between parents and married men and women in midlife (ages 30–59). In particular, they explore patterns of intergenerational coresidence and contact across the three societies. Intergenerational relations are a vital part of family life, especially among East Asian families. As expected, levels of paternal coresidence are similar in Korea and Japan, in clear contrast to the U.S. An analysis of personal and telephone contact also suggests that both structural and cultural factors affect patterns of intergenerational interactions. In the two Asian countries, as culturally prescribed, factors such as urban origin and the husband's being the eldest son have expected effects on the patterns of contact, whereas the effects of sociodemographic factors such as age and education are limited at best. By contrast, in the U.S. socioeconomic and demographic factors affect patterns of contact. Further, evidence suggests that the patrilocal stem family tradition is accommodating to the reality of rapid demographic and socioeconomic changes. In Japan *maternal* coresidence may be increasing, implying that the values placed on coresidence may be leading to a new solution in the face of constraints driven by low fertility and the exigencies of the modern market economy.

Chapter 5, by Tsuya and Choe, examines how investments in children's after-school academic programs in Japan and Korea may be related to fertility desires and mothers' employment. The level of desired fertility among married women at reproductive ages is low in Japan and even lower in Korea, and it is lower among women than among men in both countries. The authors argue that the low level of desired fertility may result, at least in part, from the high costs and pressures felt by parents, especially mothers, to educate their children, requiring heavy investments in children's education in the form of cram schools and private tutoring. Enrollment in after-school programs is especially high in large metropolitan areas, and it increases with parents' socioeconomic status, especially mothers' education. In Japan, children's enrollment in after-school programs is associated with mothers' employment, as the number of hours worked increases with the number of school-aged children a mother has. In Korea, enrollment in after-school programs is not associated with mothers' employment, probably because of the lack of suitable employment opportunities (such as part-time employment, as noted in chapter 6) that enable mothers to combine work and family responsibilities.

The next two chapters look at employment and family life. Chapter 6, by Choe, Bumpass, and Tsuya, examines patterns of employment among married women and men, as well as the preferences of both spouses about whether the wife should be employed. Much of the discussion is focused on wives because of the major changes in gender roles associated with their employment. Levels of employment among husbands and wives both reflect and contribute to gender roles across societies (see also chapters 2 and 7). Men work the most hours in Korea, followed by Japan and then the U.S. These inter-country differences are compounded by similar differences in the amount of commuting time required to get to and from work. Men's time away from home for employment-related reasons is much greater in the East Asian countries than in the U.S. On the other hand, the proportion employed among married women is very similar in Japan and the U.S., but Korean wives are less than half as likely to be employed. Among employed wives, however, Korean wives work the longest hours, followed by Japanese and then U.S. wives. Family factors such as age of children and living with or near parents strongly influence wives' employment status and hours but have little effect on husbands' work hours in all three countries. Therefore, despite the marked differences in cultural backgrounds, the assignment of the breadwinning role primarily to men and domestic obligations primarily to women results in married women's employment being affected by family situations in a way that men's is not. Somewhat surprisingly, in Japan as well as in the U.S., both husbands and wives overwhelmingly prefer wives to work, and this is so even among mothers of small children.

In chapter 7, Tsuya and Bumpass examine the gender division of labor in Japan and the U.S. Recognizing employment and household tasks as joint components of "household production," they begin by examining the combined workload of spouses by including both employment time and time spent on household tasks. When viewed from this perspective, the contributions of husbands and wives are approximately even in both countries. (The available measures, however, exclude the demands of child care on mothers of young children, hence substantially understate the contribution of these mothers.) The apparent gender equality in the average combined workload masks large differences in wives' combined workload by their employment hours. Wives who are employed full-time indeed work a full "second shift" of household chores. The other side of this coin, however, is that housewives without young children carry considerably less of the total household production load than do their husbands.

Both husbands and wives in both countries spend less time on household tasks as their hours of employment increase. However, the contributions of husbands to household tasks in response to wives' employment hours are different in the two countries. This relationship is more linear in the U.S., whereas Japanese husbands contribute more to housework only when wives are employed full-time and earn considerable income. This persistence of traditional gender inequality in the Japanese home very likely contributes to Japanese women's ambivalence about the benefits of marriage.

Marriage, family, and work constitute central aspects of life in modernized economies. As the growth of the market economy creates ever more common economic opportunities and constraints, Japan, Korea, and the U.S. exhibit similar patterns of change in family behavior and attitudes despite their dramatically different cultural heritages. At the same time, however, culture leaves unique imprints in the tempo and timing of family change in the face of economic transformation, structuring the way that economic change affects family relationships. The incongruity between women's employment, on the one hand, and the gender role expectations within the home, on the other, may well have played a major role in behavioral and attitudinal changes toward marriage and family in all three countries, but probably more so in the two East Asian countries, where transitions in men's views and behavior are slowed by the strength of the patriarchal cultural heritage.

Chapter Two

Attitudes Relating to Marriage and Family Life

Larry L. Bumpass and Minja Kim Choe

This chapter examines attitudes relating to marriage, parenthood, nonmarital sex, gender roles, and intergenerational relations. Such attitudes may have deep cultural roots, but they also respond to changing socioeconomic conditions, albeit filtered through the preexisting cultural contexts (Bellah 1964; Lesthaeghe 1983; Lesthaeghe and Meekers 1986; Lesthaeghe and Surkin 1988; Rindfuss, Brewster, and Kavee 1996; Thornton 1989). Attitudes are related to behavior in complex and reciprocal ways. They reflect and reinforce normative contexts about appropriate behavior, and in so doing make specific behaviors more or less likely because of the social costs involved. At the same time, behavioral changes—in particular those in response to changing socioeconomic contexts—often contribute to attitudinal change (Axinn and Thornton 1996; Pagnini and Rindfuss 1993). Even though attitudes often may not predict behavior well at the individual level (Bumpass 2002), they nonetheless are an important component of family change (Thornton 1989; Rindfuss, Brewster, and Kavee 1996). Consequently, it seems an appropriate beginning for our comparison of marriage, work, and family life in Japan, Korea, and the U.S. to overview relevant attitudes about family life on which we have similar measures, with particular attention to differences by age, gender, and country.

The differences in economic development described in chapter 1 may also affect the timing and pace of attitudinal changes. In the U.S., parents and children have shared somewhat similar experiences and values because industrialization and the demographic transition occurred over a number of generations.[1] On the other hand, economic and demographic transformations have been much more rapid in the two East Asian countries, especially in Korea. Although attitudinal change tends to lag behind development (Ogburn 1964; Retherford, Ogawa, and Sakamoto 1996), attitudes most closely tied with modes of production and employment may change more quickly than other family-related attitudes (Inglehart 1990; Kohn 1976; Lesthaeghe and Wilson 1986).

In this context, it is critical to keep in mind the distinct cultural heritages of East Asia and the U.S. as the bases from which such changes may be arising (see chapter 1). Even if the individualizing forces of market economies in production and consumption are similar across industrial societies, the differences in cultural histories may shape differently the effects of industrial economies on family change and related attitudes toward marriage and family life. For example, sons have been highly valued in both East Asian countries (especially in Korea). Hence, gender inequality is more strongly embedded in East Asian than in American families (Deuchler 1977; Lebra 1984), and it is likely to change more slowly. Similarly, the emphasis in Confucian ideology on "proper relations" among family members, such as filial piety, contrasts sharply with the U.S. values of individual choice and achievement (Steinhoff 1994).[2] Consequently, intergenerational ties are more highly valued in the two East Asian countries than in the U.S., even though there are clear obligations to parents and children in the U.S.

The relatively high (but now rapidly declining) level of arranged marriages in East Asia (Retherford, Ogawa, and Sakamoto 1996) reflects this traditional family system, in which marriage was viewed as a more rigid social institution involving the interests of and influences from the extended family and kinship. In contrast, marriage is seen in the U.S. as primarily a matter of individual choice for the happiness and well-being of couples and their children. This difference in institutional focus is also likely to be reflected in the role that "romantic love" plays in gender relationships, which, in turn, may affect attitudes toward both premarital and extramarital sexual relationships.

Measures

The analysis here is limited to respondents of ages 25–59, the youngest and oldest ages in the second phase of the U.S. (NSFH2) survey and the Japanese (NSWFL) survey respectively. The analysis on the U.S. draws from the NSFH1 or the NSFH2, depending on data availability; this limits the sample to the respondents who were successfully followed up (i.e., those who are included in both waves of the survey). There are 1,082 men and 1,094 women at these ages in the NSWFL; 1,111 men and 1,053 women in the Korean (NSQL) survey; and 2,336 men and 3,298 women included in both the NSFH1 and the NSFH2 (for specifics of the surveys, see chapter 1).

We take an explicitly descriptive perspective in our comparison of attitudes about the importance of marriage and parenthood, acceptability of nonmarital sex, gender roles, and intergenerational obligations. Multivariate analysis including age, gender, marital status, and education altered little the bivariate differences. Hence, to facilitate discussion, we present only the bivariate results.

Specifically, we look at eight items for which the same (or similar) questions were asked in all three surveys. We also consider five items concerning the care of elderly parents that were asked only in Korea and Japan, and for these two East Asian countries we distinguish eldest sons in comparison to younger sons and daughters. We also look at one item—unmarried sex—for which comparable questions were asked only in Japan and the U.S. Responses to all of the questions considered here were measured on a five-point scale ranging from "strongly agree" to "strongly disagree." To facilitate interpretation, we structure the analysis in terms of the proportion endorsing the "traditional" position. For example, on items indicating a nontraditional position, such as "A woman can have a full and satisfying life without getting married," we code respondents *disagreeing* as traditional. The middle (noncommittal) response category on a counternormative statement is considered as nontraditional since "traditional" respondents would be expected to disagree. Alternatively, on a traditional value such as "It is better for everyone if the man earns the main living and the woman takes care of home and family," respondents *agreeing* are coded as traditional. Again, those in the middle (noncommittal category) are regarded as nontraditional.

Observed age differences are generally interpreted here as reflecting recent changes in attitude. Whereas it can be argued that age differences in attitudes reflect increasing conservatism with age, previous studies have found that virtually all age groups become less conservative over time during periods of increasing liberalization in a society at large (e.g., Bumpass 1982; Pagnini and Rindfuss 1993; Rindfuss, Brewster, and Kavee 1996; Tsuya and Mason 1995). Intracohort changes away from traditional values may occur in response to changes in the larger social environment, particularly in response to the changed values and behavior of children and grandchildren. When this is the case among the older generation, cohort differences (if they had been measured at the same age) will be understated in cross-sectional age differences. Less traditional orientations among the younger cohorts are likely to presage future changes in aggregate normative environments as these younger cohorts age and become, in time, the senior members of society. In some instances, such as perceived obligations of the younger to the older generation, we find that both life-course and cohort interpretations must be engaged.

Differences between men and women reflect perceptions of relative advantages of traditional positions for each gender, as well as different responses to changes in the economic and social environment. Large gender differences in attitudes have implications for marriage and family life as men and women have to strike marriage bargains in finding partners and deal with their differences as they marry and interact within marriage.

The Normative Obligation to Marry and Have Children

As noted in chapter 1, family changes in the West such as increases in divorce, unmarried sex, out-of-wedlock childbearing, and cohabitation are likely to be interrelated aspects of the erosion of the benefits and obligations associated with marriage (Bumpass 1990, 1998). There has been a remarkable increase in

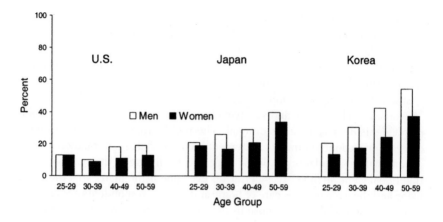

Figure 2.1. *Percent Disagreeing That a Woman Can Have a Full and Satisfying Life without Getting Married, by Age and Sex: U.S. (1992–1994), Japan (1994), and Korea (1994)*

Note: *All three surveys asked respondents whether they strongly agree, agree, are uncertain (neither agree nor disagree in the U.S.), disagree, or strongly disagree with the statement, "A woman can have a full and satisfying life without getting married." Respondents who chose one of the last two categories are classified as disagreeing.*

American society in the "tolerance" of nontraditional behavior regarding marriage and childbearing, even though most people intend to eventually marry and have children (Pagnini and Rindfuss 1993; Thornton 1989). This increase in tolerance reflects the erosion of moral "oughtness" with respect to marriage and family formation. In each of our three national surveys, respondents were asked whether they agreed or disagreed with four items concerning marriage and childbearing, each specific to men or women: whether a woman (man) can have a full and satisfying life without being married or without having children. As noted above, we have coded as traditional those who *disagree* with statements asserting that marriage or children are *not necessary.* Nonetheless, to avoid the confusion that may result from this double negative, we will often describe this variable in terms of low support for the position that marriage and children are *necessary* for a "full and satisfying life."

Concerning whether marriage and childbearing are essential to life satisfaction for women and men, three general patterns appear, as shown in figures 2.1–2.4. First, traditional orientations toward the necessity of marriage and childbearing are highest in Korea and lowest in the U.S. Further, within each country, younger cohorts tend to be less traditional than older cohorts (except among women in the U.S.). Finally, men tend to be more traditional than women.

The percentages disagreeing that a *woman* can have a full and satisfying

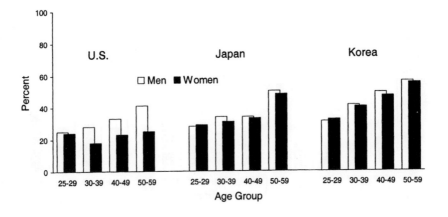

Figure 2.2. *Percent Disagreeing That a Man Can Have a Full and Satisfying Life without Getting Married, by Age and Sex: U.S. (1992–1994), Japan (1994), and Korea (1994)*

Note: *All three surveys asked respondents whether they strongly agree, agree, are uncertain (neither agree nor disagree in the U.S.), disagree, or strongly disagree with the statement, "A man can have a full and satisfying life without getting married." Respondents who chose one of the last two categories are classified as disagreeing.*

life without getting married are presented in figure 2.1. Korea has undergone the most rapid and recent economic transformation—a transformation literally spanned by these cohorts—and it clearly has the largest differences in attitude by both age and gender. The consequence of this rapid change in Korea can be seen in the stark contrast between the oldest men and the youngest women: 54 percent of the former held the traditional position, compared to 13 percent of the latter. In all countries and age groups, females are less likely than males to see marriage as necessary for women's life satisfaction. (The one exception is the seemingly anomalous lack of a gender difference in the youngest cohorts in the U.S.) It is remarkable indeed that only one-sixth to one-fifth of the youngest respondents (ages 25–29) in *any* of the three countries believes that a woman cannot have a full and satisfying life without marriage.

The proportions disagreeing with the same proposition with regard to a *man* are shown in figure 2.2. Age differences are similar in each country, and Korea is again the most traditional and the U.S. the least. Further, age is positively associated with the traditional position in all three countries (again except for the youngest cohort of U.S. women). Only about one-third to one-quarter of the youngest cohort in each of these countries sees marriage as necessary for men's satisfaction in life. Even so, it should be noted that even among the oldest cohort, almost one-half of the Korean population does not endorse the tra-

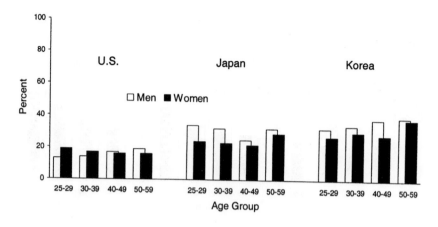

Figure 2.3. *Percent Disagreeing That a Woman Can Have a Full and Satisfying Life without Having Children, by Age and Sex: U.S. (1992–1994), Japan (1994), and Korea (1994)*

Note: *All three surveys asked respondents whether they strongly agree, agree, are uncertain (neither agree nor disagree in the U.S.), disagree, or strongly disagree with the statement, "A woman can have a full and satisfying life without having children." Respondents who chose one of the last two categories are classified as disagreeing.*

ditional value. At the same time, although expectations to marry remain high in all three societies (see chapter 3 for Japan and the U.S.), the normative underpinnings of the necessity of marriage seem to be rapidly weakening. This erosion has been most evident in the U.S., as in most of the West, with increased unmarried cohabitation and childbearing.

In terms of gender contrasts in figure 2.2, it is puzzling that the greatest difference between men and women with respect to men's need to be married is found in the U.S., whereas gender differences on this item are rather small in the two East Asian countries. Perhaps the key question is not why older U.S. men see themselves as more dependent on marriage than younger men, but rather why there are no cohort differences among women. The answer may well be that in the context of changing gender role expectations, the oldest cohort of men is the least willing (and able) to carry out household services for itself, and women of the same age see no reason why men should not be able to do so.

Comparing figures 2.1 and 2.2, we also find that marriage is seen as more essential for men than for women in all three countries. The gender division of household labor has traditionally been viewed, in part, as an exchange of economic security for women with household services for men. In this context, the differences between the two figures suggest that the perceived benefits of marriage are eroding faster for women than for men. This would be

Bumpass and Choe

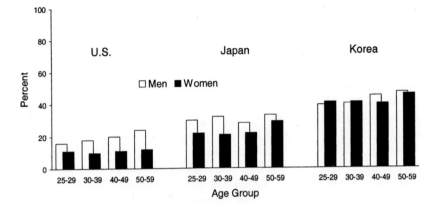

Figure 2.4. *Percent Disagreeing That a Man Can Have a Full and Satisfying Life without Having Children, by Age and Sex: U.S. (1992–1994), Japan (1994), and Korea (1994)*

Note: *All three surveys asked respondents whether they strongly agree, agree, are uncertain (neither agree nor disagree in U.S.), disagree, or strongly disagree with the statement, "A man can have a full and satisfying life without having children." Respondents who chose one of the last two categories are classified as disagreeing.*

consistent with the persisting gender differences in the division of labor documented in chapter 7 and with the marked increase in paid employment among married women in Japan and among mothers of small children in the U.S. (as noted in chapter 1). Employment of married Korean women remains low, however (Choe, Kong, and Mason 1994; also see chapter 6), and this suggests that other factors, such as the ideological impact of the increasing education of women, are also likely to be important factors in the decline in the belief that marriage is essential for women's happiness.

Further, the clearest contrast between figures 2.1 and 2.2 is seen among men at ages 50–59 in the U.S. About twice as many of these men see marriage as necessary for men's happiness than see it as necessary for women's (41 versus 19 percent). We would expect this difference to be the largest among the oldest cohort and for the society in which the transformation of women's attitudes has been under way the longest, and this is exactly what we find. One additional pattern that stands out in both figures 2.1 and 2.2 is that country differences are larger for the oldest than the youngest cohorts, suggesting some convergence across countries with respect to the decreasing necessity of marriage for both sexes.

We turn now to the parallel issues concerning the perceived necessity of having children for life satisfaction of women (figure 2.3) and men (figure 2.4). On this topic, the age and gender patterns are more diverse among the three countries. Korea is again the most traditional and the U.S. the least, but the country differences are smaller than those relating to the necessity of marriage. Furthermore, the patterns of age and gender differences are neither always consistent nor in the expected direction.

In the U.S, there are very small or no differences by either cohort or gender with respect to the necessity of children for *women*. On the other hand, we see the expected pattern in Korea, where the oldest cohorts are the most traditional, especially among women. Although cohort differences are less regular in Japan, the oldest cohort of Japanese women is again the most traditional. In both Japan and Korea, women are less likely than men to feel that women need children for a satisfying life. This is one of the many instances we will note where young Japanese women and men are bringing different expectations to marriage. At the same time, it must be noted that fully two-thirds of the young men in Japan do not hold a pronatalist position on this item. Indeed, the most remarkable finding here is the low proportion, especially in the East Asian societies, of those endorsing what we had regarded as a traditional position. Either changes have occurred among all cohorts in all three countries, or the cultural foundation of the importance of childbearing has been weaker historically than we have thought (Freedman 1975; Jolivet 1997).

In figure 2.4, we find the expected country differences with regard to the necessity of having children for *men's* life satisfaction. The proportion supporting this perspective is highest in Korea (very likely reflecting the exceptional importance assigned to having at least one son) and the lowest in the U.S. Gender differences are substantial in both Japan and the U.S.: men are considerably more likely than women to see children as necessary for men's satisfaction in life. However, gender differences are largest among the oldest cohort in the U.S. and among the younger cohorts in Japan. This parallels the results that we saw in figure 2.2 with respect to the perceived necessity of marriage for men's lives. Again, this may represent a lower responsiveness to secular changes by older men in the U.S; at the same time, it again suggests an increasing divergence between the expectations of Japanese men and women. There are no discernable gender differences on this item in Korea.

We also see the expected age pattern among men in the U.S. and Korea, with younger men somewhat less likely to agree that children are necessary for men's life satisfaction, although these differences are not very large. While the country and gender differences noted above are significant, the most important observation is that only a minority of persons in any of the three countries regard children as necessary for a satisfying life for either men or women.

Marriage as a Precondition for Sex

In the West today, sexual intercourse before marriage is nearly universal and is increasingly regarded as normative among younger adults (Bumpass, 1998).

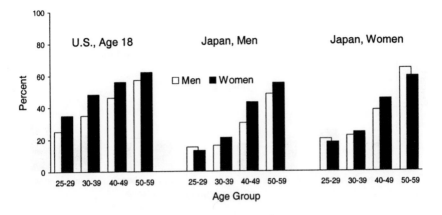

Figure 2.5. *Percent Disagreeing That It Is All Right to Have Sexual Relations While Unmarried, by Age and Sex: U.S. (1987–1988) and Japan (1994)*

Note: *The U.S. survey asked respondents whether they strongly agree, agree, neither agree nor disagree, disagree, or strongly disagree with the statement, "It is all right for unmarried 18 year olds to have sexual relations if they have strong affection for each other." Respondents who chose one of the last two categories are classified as disagreeing. The Japanese survey asked respondents whether they strongly agree, agree, are uncertain, disagree, or strongly disagree with the statement, "It is all right for an unmarried man to have sex," or "It is all right for an unmarried woman to have sex." Respondents who chose one of the last two categories are classified as disagreeing.*

This trend has markedly reduced the social cost of remaining unmarried and has likely played an important role in the delay of marriage and the declining significance of marriage for major life-course transitions in Western societies (Bumpass 1990, 1998). Evidence of a similar trend is emerging in Japan (Tsuya 1993). Therefore, for Japan as well, the erosion of normative orientations toward marriage as a precondition for sex and increases in premarital sex may have played an important role in the decline in the perceived necessity of marriage.

Figure 2.5 shows the percentages of respondents in Japan and the U.S. disagreeing that it is all right to have sexual relations while unmarried. Somewhat different questions were asked in the two countries. In the U.S., the question asked whether it was all right for an unmarried *18-year-old* to have sex. In Japan, questions were addressed separately to women and to men, and these asked only whether it was all right for unmarried women/men to have sex.[3] It is clear that the question for the U.S. is more limited in its coverage by focusing on teenagers rather than including all unmarried adults (as in Japan). Because of the late age at marriage in Japan (as noted in chapter 1), this difference in

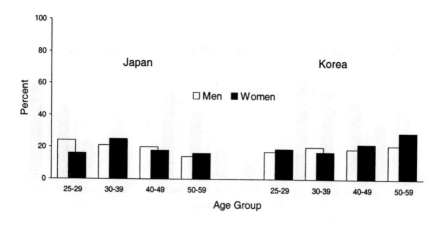

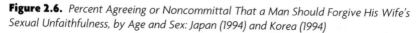

Figure 2.6. *Percent Agreeing or Noncommittal That a Man Should Forgive His Wife's Sexual Unfaithfulness, by Age and Sex: Japan (1994) and Korea (1994)*

Note: *The Japanese and Korean surveys asked respondents whether they strongly agree, agree, are uncertain, disagree, or strongly disagree with the statement, "A man should forgive his wife's sexual unfaithfulness." Respondents who chose one of the first two categories are classified as agreeing, and respondents who chose the third category are classified as noncommittal.*

questions is very likely responsible for the higher levels of disapproval in the U.S. compared to Japan.

Nonetheless, there are dramatic age differences in the acceptability of unmarried sex, suggesting a rapid change in attitudes about appropriate sexual behavior and also suggesting that such changes have been rather contemporaneous in Japan and the U.S. In both countries, the younger generation is likely to bring about a transformation of the normative climate with regard to unmarried sex as it becomes the older generation. In addition, in contrast to attitudes about the necessity of marriage and children, women tend to have more traditional views on premarital sex in both Japan and the U.S. This may reflect the greater negative impact of premarital pregnancy on women's lives.

We do not have a comparable measure on attitudes about unmarried sex from the 1994 Korean survey. However, there appears to have been relatively little change in attitudes toward sex and marriage since the 1991 Korean fertility survey found that 80 percent of young persons aged 25–29 agreed that a woman should be a virgin at marriage. Two-thirds of male respondents and three-quarters of female respondents held this opinion with respect to men before marriage (Kong et al. 1992: 271). All the same, increasing premarital sexual activity among teenagers in Korea in recent years (see chapter 1) may well lead to a change in attitudes similar to those in Japan and the U.S.

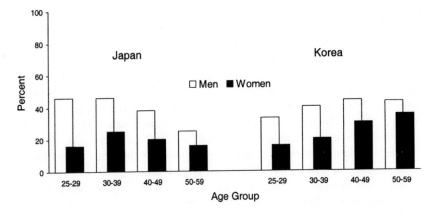

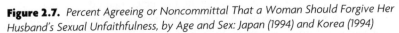

Figure 2.7. *Percent Agreeing or Noncommittal That a Woman Should Forgive Her Husband's Sexual Unfaithfulness, by Age and Sex: Japan (1994) and Korea (1994)*

Note: The Japanese and Korean surveys asked respondents whether they strongly agree, agree, are uncertain, disagree, or strongly disagree with the statement, "A woman should forgive her husband's sexual unfaithfulness." Respondents who chose one of the first two categories are classified as agreeing, and respondents who chose the third category are classified as noncommittal.

Extramarital Sex

This is a topic that requires special care when "traditional" and "nontraditional" viewpoints are considered. In East Asia, traditional normative orientations toward extramarital sex (as well as premarital sex) have been very different for men than for women. Extramarital sex on the part of a wife often resulted in her expulsion from the marital home or even criminal prosecution. On the other hand, the traditional view toward men's extramarital sex was quite lenient. For example, in prewar Japan and Korea, it was regarded as "masculine" and common for men to visit prostitutes or to have a mistress or concubine (Tsuya 1993), and this may still be so.

For the sake of clarity in this instance, rather than coding in terms of traditional expectations, we simply show the percent *agreeing* (or noncommittal) that unfaithfulness should be forgiven. Despite the increasing incidence of premarital sex, only a small minority—about one-fifth—of both women and men agree that a *wife's* extramarital sex should be forgiven (see figure 2.6). There is little systematic pattern by age, although older men in Japan are somewhat less likely than younger men to agree that a man should forgive his wife's sexual unfaithfulness: 16 compared to 24 percent.

In contrast, there are much larger differences by age and gender with respect to whether a *man's* unfaithfulness should be forgiven by his wife. Men are considerably more likely than women to agree that a woman should forgive a husband's extramarital sex (see figure 2.7). Though agreement among men is never more than one-half in either country, the gender difference is greater for the youngest, rather than the oldest, cohorts. This widening gap between men and women over cohorts arises, however, from different age patterns by gender in the two countries. The gender difference increases in Korea because cohort differences are greater among women than among men. Women seem to have been moving away from what may have been a more conventional acceptance of men's extramarital sex. In Japan, on the other hand, the higher approval among younger men accounts for the larger gender difference for the youngest cohort. Nevertheless, in both countries, this is another brush stroke in what is emerging as a clear picture in which women and men have increasingly different expectations with respect to marriage. In the youngest cohort, 46 percent of Japanese men agree compared to 16 percent of women, and in Korea the respective figures are 33 percent of men and 16 percent of women. Young women in both Korea and Japan are likely to share men's double standard with respect to extramarital sex, and this may make women further disenchanted with what marriage would bring to their lives.

The U.S. survey had only a single item pertaining to the acceptability of extramarital sex: "Couples ought to overlook isolated occasions of sexual unfaithfulness."[4] Because it does not differentiate between female and male behavior, it does not allow us to observe directly the extent to which there may be a double standard on extramarital sex. Nonetheless, men are half again as likely as women to agree with this statement: 32 percent compared to 22 percent. Thus, there is some indication of a double standard in the U.S. as well. We did not find any clear patterns by age in the U.S., but rough comparisons with the responses from Korea and Japan suggest that the opinions of women are similar across the three countries, whereas American men seem to be less approving of extramarital sex than men in Japan and Korea.

Gender Roles

Figure 2.8 shows responses to the central gender role question of whether it is better for everyone if the man earns the living and the woman takes care of the home and family. The most striking pattern is the large difference across the three countries in support for the traditional gender division of labor. As we move from the oldest cohort in Korea to the youngest cohort in the U.S., the proportion agreeing with this traditional value declines dramatically and almost linearly across countries within each age category. The youngest age group in Korea agrees slightly more than the oldest in Japan, the youngest in Japan agrees slightly more than the oldest in the U.S., and the youngest age group in the U.S. agrees least. As with many other measures of attitudes examined

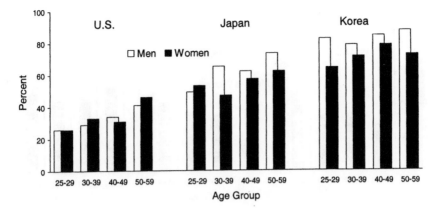

Figure 2.8. *Percent Agreeing That It Is Better for Everyone If the Man Earns the Main Living and the Woman Takes Care of the Home and Family, by Age and Sex: U.S. (1987–1988), Japan (1994), and Korea (1994)*

Note: *The U.S. survey asked respondents whether they strongly agree, agree, neither agree nor disagree, disagree, or strongly disagree with the statement, "It is much better for everyone if the man earns the main living and the woman takes care of the home and family." Respondents who chose one of the first two categories are classified as agreeing. The Japanese and Korean surveys asked respondents whether they strongly agree, agree, are uncertain, disagree, or strongly disagree with the statement, "It is better for everyone if the man earns the living for the family and the woman takes care of the home and family." Respondents who chose one of the first two categories are classified as agreeing.*

in this chapter, this result provides a visual impression of a positive relationship between changes in gender role attitudes and the recency of economic development. The percentage agreeing with the traditional position ranges from around 85 percent of men aged 50–59 in Korea to only about one-quarter of men and women aged 25–29 in the U.S. Within each country, the younger cohorts tend to be less supportive of this traditional position than the older ones, and in Korea and Japan, men are more likely to support it than are women (except for the youngest cohort in Japan).

Although opinions about the effects of married women's employment on family life are likely related to views regarding the gender division of labor, the patterns by age and gender shown in figure 2.9 do not exactly match those on gender roles discussed above. In all three countries and in all age groups, women are less likely than men to agree with the statement, "Preschool children suffer if their mother works." In the U.S., agreement with this traditional position declines sharply as we move from older to younger cohorts among

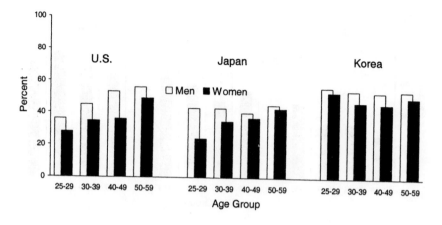

Figure 2.9. *Percent Agreeing That Preschool Children Suffer If Their Mother Is Employed, by Age and Sex: U.S. (1987–1988), Japan (1994), and Korea (1994)*

Note: *All three surveys asked respondents whether they strongly agree, agree, are uncertain (neither agree nor disagree in U.S.), disagree, or strongly disagree with the statement, "Preschool children are likely to suffer if their mother works." Respondents who chose one of the first two categories are classified as agreeing.*

both men and women, although very substantial gender differences persist across cohorts. While there is no clear age pattern in Korea or among Japanese men, the youngest generation of Japanese women is almost half as likely to agree as the oldest. The lack of age differences among men compared with the sharply lower level of agreement among women is a further dramatic contrast between men and women in the youngest age group. Young Japanese men are almost twice as likely as young Japanese women to agree that a mother's employment is harmful to small children. This is another of the cleavages between the sexes in the struggle to reconcile the rapid expansion of paid employment among Japanese married women with men's expectations concerning family roles (see also chapter 6). Similar though smaller gender differences persist in the U.S.

It is surprising that there are no clear differences across cohorts of Korean women about the effects of a mother's employment on small children, as there are in the other two countries. Perhaps the recency of rapid economic development and paid employment among married women means that grandparents help more with child care in Korea than in Japan and the U.S. Furthermore, privately arranged paid child care at home may be more readily available and affordable in Korea.

We asked an additional item in the Japanese and Korean surveys that extends the concern about the consequences of wives' employment beyond

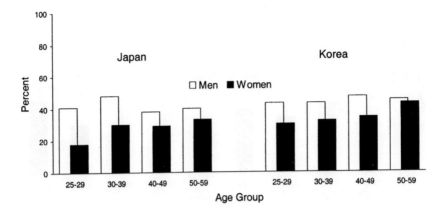

Figure 2.10. *Percent Agreeing That Family Suffers If Wife Is Employed, by Age and Sex: Japan (1994) and Korea (1994)*

Note: *The Japanese and Korean surveys asked respondents whether they strongly agree, agree, are uncertain, disagree, or strongly disagree with the statement, "All in all, family life suffers when the wife has a full-time job." Respondents who chose one of the first two categories are classified as agreeing.*

effects on young children. Figure 2.10 presents the proportions agreeing that the *family* suffers if the wife is employed full-time. The proportions endorsing this statement are somewhat lower than those believing that a mother's employment harms small children. Nonetheless, gender differences are larger among the younger cohorts, especially in Japan. Thus, here too, younger men and women have different expectations of marriage.

This gap between men and women is further illustrated by the question asked in Japan and Korea on domestic power relations between the sexes: should most of the important decisions in the family be made by men? (See figure 2.11.) In the context of the patriarchal family heritage in the two countries, it is surprising that only about one-half of the men in both countries agreed with this statement. However, this may reflect the delegation of "family" matters to wives while husbands retain the ultimate authority. Even so, women are less likely than men to agree with this assertion, especially among the younger cohorts in Korea: of those aged 25–39, only about one-quarter agreed, compared to over one-half of the men. It is also notable that there is a much greater difference between men and women on this item than there was with respect to the gender division of labor seen in figure 2.8. This may suggest that aspirations for greater equality in marriage among Korean women are increasing faster than we would infer from their responses concerning the gender division of labor in general.

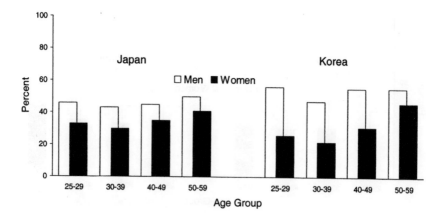

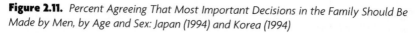

Figure 2.11. *Percent Agreeing That Most Important Decisions in the Family Should Be Made by Men, by Age and Sex: Japan (1994) and Korea (1994)*

Note: *The Japanese and Korean surveys asked respondents whether they strongly agree, agree, are uncertain, disagree, or strongly disagree with the statement, "Most of the important decisions in the family should be made by men." Respondents who chose one of the first two categories are classified as agreeing.*

Marital Stability and Intergenerational Obligations

Increasing divorce suggests that the marital well-being of adults is often given precedence over obligations of parents to children. As divorce rates increased to their current very high levels, the U.S. witnessed a rapid decline in the proportion of men and women agreeing that parents should stay together for the sake of their children (Thornton and Freedman 1983). Figure 2.12 presents levels of agreement with the statement that for the sake of the children, parents should not divorce. Three patterns stand out in this figure. First, the level of agreement is over twice as high in the two East Asian countries than in the U.S. This, of course, is consistent with differences in the cultural backgrounds and levels of divorce (see chapter 1). Less than 10 percent of U.S. women aged 25–49 agreed that parents should not divorce, and around 20 percent of U.S. men of all ages did so. Nevertheless, the relatively low levels of disagreement with divorce in Japan and Korea—about one-half of the respondents in both countries—seem remarkable. In both countries, until the early postwar years, divorce had been considered legitimate only in the case of "bad behavior" by the wife, who was usually expelled from the family of marriage (Choi 1970; Tsuya and Choe 1991).[5] It is likely that the levels of "approval" that we have measured here represent substantial changes from prior periods as both causes and consequences of the rapid increases in divorce in these countries.

Second, the percentage agreeing that parents should not divorce for the

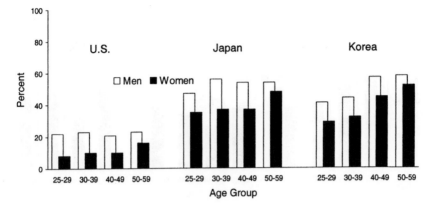

Figure 2.12. *Percent Agreeing That for the Sake of the Children, Parents Should Not Divorce, by Age and Sex: U.S. (1992–1994), Japan (1994), and Korea (1994)*

Note: *The U.S. survey asked respondents whether they strongly agree, agree, neither agree nor disagree, disagree, or strongly disagree with the statement, "When a marriage is troubled and unhappy, it is generally better for the children if the couple stays together." The Japanese and Korean surveys asked respondents whether they strongly agree, agree, are uncertain, disagree, or strongly disagree with the statement, "Parents should not divorce for the sake of the children." Respondents who chose one of the first two categories are classified as agreeing.*

sake of the children is lowest for the youngest cohort, further implying shifting attitudes toward the acceptability of divorce. Such cohort differences in the disapproval of divorce are most consistent in Korea. Finally and most important, there are very large differences between women and men in all three countries that reflect the persisting inequalities within marriage in the context of the marked gender differences in attitudes about these inequalities.

While the preceding discussion has considered the obligations of a couple to stay together for the sake of the younger generation, we now turn to attitudes concerning obligations to aging parents (see chapter 4 on intergenerational coresidence and contact). Figure 2.13 presents the percentages agreeing that children should live with parents when the parents become old. The expected pattern of cohort differences appears only in Japan, where agreement declines over cohorts, with the marked exception of the youngest women. Unexpectedly, there are no clear cohort differences in Korea. Women are less likely than men to agree with intergenerational coresidence in both East Asian countries.

The fact that younger persons in the U.S. agree more than the older cohorts that parents and children should live together is striking, even though it has been reported before (Thornton and Freedman 1983; Logan and Spitze 1996). The U.S. survey specifically asks whether respondents think that children

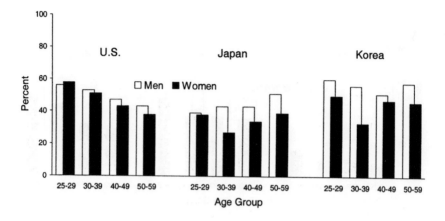

Figure 2.13. *Percent Agreeing That Children Should Live with Parents When the Parents Become Old, by Age and Sex: U.S. (1987–1988), Japan (1994), and Korea (1994)*

Note: *The U.S. survey asked respondents whether they strongly agree, agree, neither agree nor disagree, disagree, or strongly disagree with the statement, "Children ought to let aging parents live with them when the parents can no longer live by themselves." The Japanese and Korean surveys asked respondents whether they strongly agree, agree, are uncertain, disagree, or strongly disagree with the statement, "Children should live together with their parents when the parents become old." Respondents who chose one of the first two categories are classified as agreeing.*

should live with their parents "when parents can no longer live by themselves," as opposed to the more general phrasing in the Japanese and Korean surveys about "when the parents become old." The U.S. survey specifies a much more restrictive circumstance, implying the need for providing substantial care for elderly parents. Earlier evidence indicates that despite the strong preference for residential independence on the part of the elderly in the U.S., about one-quarter of persons in their fifties have had a parent live with them during a spell of illness or disability (Bumpass 1994). Hence, the decline in agreement with age in the U.S. may reflect the increasing proportion of men and women in midlife whose parents are approaching the loss of residential independence and for whom the question raises a real and pressing possibility (or even recent experience). In other words, these differences may reflect a youthful idealism about supporting parents that begins to diminish in the face of approaching reality. A similar process may be suggested by the fact that it is the youngest cohort among women in Japan and among both men and women in Korea who is most likely to agree that the generations should live together when the parents are old.

A key element of the Confucian family system is the obligation of eldest sons to take care of their elderly parents. Figure 2.14 presents the percentages

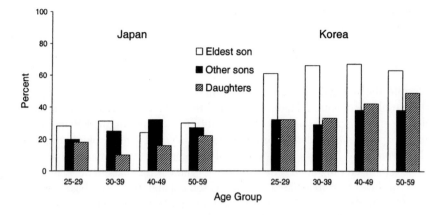

Figure 2.14. *Percent Agreeing That It Is the Eldest Son's Duty to Take Care of Parents, by Age and Sex: Japan (1994) and Korea (1994)*

Note: *The Japanese and Korean surveys asked respondents whether they strongly agree, agree, are uncertain, disagree, or strongly disagree with the statement, "It is the eldest son's duty to take care of his parents." Respondents who chose one of the first two categories are classified as agreeing.*

in Japan and Korea agreeing with the statement, "It is the eldest son's duty to take care of his parents." It is surprising, in light of changes in attitudes toward the care of elderly parents (Ogawa and Retherford 1993a) that we find no systematic age differences in these measures. There are some interesting results, nonetheless. Given that the primary obligation falls on an eldest son, we analyzed the responses of eldest (or only) sons separately from those of other sons and daughters.

As expected, in both Japan and Korea, the level of agreement with this statement is notably higher among eldest sons and lower among women. The highest level of agreement is seen among eldest sons in Korea, nearly two-thirds of whom agree that it is their duty to take care of their parents, whereas the corresponding percentage in Japan is around one-third. Indeed, the level of agreement is lower in Japan than in Korea among both men and women, again perhaps reflecting the more recent economic development in Korea. The much lower agreement among women than among men in Japan may, yet again, signal dramatic differences in gender role expectations since the weight of this obligation falls primarily on the daughter-in-law. All together, these findings reflect the commitment of eldest sons in the two East Asian societies to being the chief agents of filial obligation, a sense of tradition that is stronger in Korea than in Japan. At the same time, the findings document surprisingly low levels of support for this obligation even among eldest sons, especially in Japan.

Even in Korea, about four of ten eldest sons do not agree that it is their obligation to take care of their elderly parents.

Conclusion

Despite the marked differences in cultural backgrounds and the timing of industrialization among Japan, Korea, and the U.S., there are surprising similarities in the general patterns of cohort differences (and implied changes) in many aspects of attitudes toward marriage, family, and gender roles across the three countries. In particular, traditional orientations toward marriage appear to be rapidly eroding in all three countries. Whereas the marked delay in marriage in the U.S. is associated with increased cohabitation (Bumpass, Sweet, and Cherlin 1991), cohabitation is not yet a major factor in the two East Asian countries. This difference can be misleading, however, because sexual activity outside marriage has increased rapidly in Japan and, to a lesser extent, in Korea (as it has in the U.S.). While cohabitation is important for other reasons, whether or not sexually active unmarried couples live together should not obscure the changing relationship between marriage and sex in all three countries. Cohort differences in all three countries foreshadow continuing change in the normative climate with respect to orientations toward marriage, childbearing, and intergenerational obligations. Given its centrality to filial piety, it is a particularly important finding that only a low proportion of Japanese eldest sons agrees that eldest sons are obligated to care for their elderly parents.

The increasing delay in marriage in Japan and Korea raises the prospect that women's and, to a lesser extent, men's life orientations are moving away from marriage and childbearing. The greater time spent as an adult outside of marriage provides a "role hiatus" (Mason 1993), when one is not dependent on parents (or a woman is not dependent on a husband) and when other interests, such as occupational aspirations and self-oriented consumption, may become expected parts of adult life. Our analysis in this chapter repeatedly found age and gender differences in gender role orientations, opinions about women's employment, and intergenerational obligations. We conclude by emphasizing a point we have noted throughout the chapter: these gender differences may, in turn, have feedback effects reinforcing the delays in marriage as men and women are increasingly facing the prospect of marriage with different expectations of what marriage should be like. Such gender differences in attitudes are likely to affect the stability, as well as the timing, of marriage. In addition, they may contribute to the delay of childbearing within marriage (Ogawa and Retherford 1993b; Retherford, Ogawa, and Sakamoto 1996).

Chapter Three

Views of Marriage among Never-Married Young Adults

Noriko O. Tsuya, Karen Oppenheim Mason, and Larry L. Bumpass

In this chapter, we examine how younger, never-married adults perceive the costs and benefits of marriage and whether they want to get married. Our aim is to understand more fully what is happening to the institution of marriage from the perspective of single young people in Japan and the United States. There is a particular concern in Japan with the sharply increasing age at marriage since the mid-1970s and with the dramatic increases in the proportions never-married among persons in their late twenties and thirties (see chapter 1). Marriage age has risen more slowly in the U.S. However, concern about delayed marriage is part of a broader concern about what appears to many observers to be a weakening of the institution of marriage (e.g., Bumpass 1990, 1998; Goldscheider and Waite 1991). Is there widespread disenchantment with marriage as an institution in either or both countries, or is marriage simply being postponed in connection with education or employment? Does the higher age at marriage in Japan than in the U.S. reflect greater disaffection with marriage in that country, at least among young women, or is it simply easier for young people in Japan to remain single than is the case in the U.S.? We hope to learn more about these issues in this examination of country and gender differences in views of marriage and desires to marry, as well as about the individual correlates of these views and desires.

Data and Measures

We use data from the 1994 NSWFL in Japan and from NSFH1 in the U.S. We are unable to include Korea because the Korean data do not provide a representative sample of never-married adults. (See chapter 1 for specifics of the surveys.) We restrict our analysis to never-married individuals aged 20–27. The relevant questions were asked only of never-married persons. The youngest age in the Japanese sample is 20. In both countries, never-married individuals aged 28 and older are likely to be increasingly selected for less favorable attitudes toward marriage. As a partial check on the extent of the bias that may remain even when the sample is limited to adults under age 28, we briefly examine a parallel set of attitudinal questions asked of currently married individuals. Most of the analysis, however, is only for never-married persons.

In both surveys, the perceived costs and benefits of marriage were measured by asking how life would be different if the respondents were married now. Response categories for each dimension ranged from "much worse" to "much better." Both surveys included four dimensions that are analyzed here: freedom to do what you want, standard of living, emotional security, and overall happiness.[1] Although these dimensions obviously are only a subset of the costs and benefits of marriage, they are likely to be important components of the overall attractiveness of marriage in modern settings and should thus provide insights about the evaluation of marriage as an institution.

We also analyze the desire to marry as reported by these young adults. Somewhat different questions were used in the two surveys. In Japan, respondents were asked the following: "Supposing you had an appropriate partner of the opposite sex right now; would you: (1) Want to get married as soon as possible? (2) Want to wait a year or two, then get married? (3) Want to wait longer than this, but eventually get married? (4) Not want to get married ever? (5) Don't know."[2] In the U.S., individuals not in a cohabiting relationship (88 percent of unmarried persons ages 20–27) were asked whether they agreed or disagreed with the statement, "I would like to get married someday," with responses ranging from "strongly agree" to "strongly disagree."[3] Because the Japanese question includes a timing component that is not in the U.S. question, we have coded responses to make them as comparable as possible with respect to the desire to ever marry. For Japan, we group the first three response categories—"as soon as possible" through "eventually"—and for the U.S., "strongly agree" and "agree." In the multivariate analysis, those who respond "don't know" in Japan and those who are in the neutral category in the U.S. are grouped with those who say they never want to marry.

We begin by examining the distributions on the various dimensions of perceived costs and benefits of marriage and on the desire to marry. We then turn to a multivariate analysis of the relationship, first of the cost and benefit variables with socioeconomic background, living arrangements, and desire for children, and then of the desire to marry, in which we also include the perceived costs and benefits of marriage.[4]

Means and standard deviations for the variables used in the analyses of marriage perceptions and desires are shown in table 3.1. Socioeconomic background such as education and income may well reflect differences in attitude formation. For example, available resources may generally be negatively related to desires to marry to the extent that gains from marriage depend on the mutual dependence between spouses resulting from the gender division of labor as argued by Becker (1981). This might especially be the case for women because of the increased feasibility of independence from a husband. On the other hand, Oppenheimer (1994) suggests that with the increasing acceptance of women's paid employment, income effects may offset this independence effect so that there is little relationship overall.

Table 3.1 *Means and Standard Deviations (in Parentheses) for Variables Used in Analysis of Marriage Perceptions and Desires: Never-Married Men and Women Aged 20–27 in Japan (1994) and the U.S. (1987–1988)* [a]

Variable	Japan	U.S.
Perceptions of marriage scale [b]	10.401	10.830
	(2.259)	(2.555)
Wants to get married [c]	0.798	0.884
	(0.402)	(0.320)
Female	0.527	0.406
	(0.500)	(0.491)
Age	23.139	22.822
	(2.295)	(2.156)
Years of education	13.079	13.076
	(1.164)	(0.491)
Income last year	1.939	9.850
(millions of yen/$1,000s)	(1.398)	(9.552)
Lives with parents	0.824	0.500
	(0.381)	(0.500)
Wants to have children [d]	0.662	0.888
	(0.474)	(0.315)
Minimum number of cases [e]	286	514

[a] In the U.S. data, the means and standard deviations shown are weighted, but the number of observations is the actual number of individuals interviewed.

[b] Scale formed from the items on standard of living, emotional security, and overall happiness if married. Range is from 3 to 15.

[c] In Japan, the original question was asked as follows: "Supposing you had an appropriate partner of the opposite sex right now; would you: (1) Want to get married as soon as possible? (2) Want to wait a year or two, then get married? (3) Want to wait longer than this, but eventually get married? (4) Not want to get married ever? (5) Don't know." Wanting to get married is coded as 1 if respondents expressed any desire to marry, regardless of preferences on timing, choosing an answer from (1) to (3); 0 if otherwise. In the U.S., marriage desires were measured through a question asked only of noncohabiting respondents on whether he/she would like to get married someday. The original response categories to this question were strongly agree, agree, neither agree nor disagree, disagree, and strongly disagree. Wanting to get married is coded as 1 if respondents strongly agreed or agreed to this question.

[d] Those who definitely or probably want children are scored 1; all others (including those who are undecided) are scored 0.

[e] In the U.S., number shown is for the marriage desires question, which was asked only of non-cohabiting individuals.

Living arrangements are potentially important to the extent that they affect the "value added" by marriage. At the same time, a young person's current living arrangement may partly result from his or her views of the benefits of marriage. This may especially be the case in the U.S., where living with parents is less a norm than in Japan (50 percent of the U.S. sample currently lives with one or both parents versus 82 percent of the Japanese sample; see table 3.1). In particular, individuals who are skeptical about the value of marrying may choose to live with their parents, or enter into a cohabiting relationship in the U.S., precisely because they wish to ensure some degree of companionship and income pooling while avoiding marriage. Thus, although we treat living arrangements as exogenous to marriage perceptions and desires, some degree of endogeneity between these variables may exist (Saluter 1996). Higher housing costs, especially in large cities, may also be a reason for a much higher rate of coresidence with parents among young Japanese persons than among their U.S. counterparts. Thus, living with parents may seem a more attractive option economically even if it has little effect on the perceived desirability of marriage.

We also include desires for children in the analyses of marriage perceptions and desires because having children remains a major reason for marrying, especially in Japan, where out-of-wedlock births are socially unacceptable and extremely rare (less than 2 percent of all births; see chapter 1).

Finally, in the analysis of marriage desires, we also include three of the four perceived costs and benefits of marriage as a possible factor influencing the desire to marry.[5] Admittedly, the causal ordering between marriage perceptions and marriage desires is somewhat unclear. We do not know the extent to which the various perceived costs and benefits affect marriage desires or the extent to which these perceptions are rationalizations of a life plan determined by normative expectations or other factors or whether these two factors may be formed simultaneously. In any event, the analysis should shed some light on variations in the desire to marry in each of our two countries and on how this varies by marriage perceptions and background variables.

Descriptive Analysis

Table 3.2 shows responses to the four questions on marriage costs and benefits by gender and country. The obligations of marriage are likely to be viewed by many as limiting to their personal freedom, and this is indeed seen in the responses to the first item—especially in Japan. While American men are somewhat less likely than Japanese men to feel that marriage would entail a loss of personal freedom (53 compared to 63 percent), fewer than one-third of young women in the U.S. feel that their freedom would be worse if married, compared to over two-thirds in Japan. Thus, among women, this item shows a striking difference between countries, with a greater skepticism about marriage in Japan than in the U.S. Japanese women see marriage as more restrictive than American women, and indeed marriage is more restrictive for women in Japan than in the U.S. (Tsuya 2000; Tsuya and Choe 1991; Tsuya and Mason 1995). Yet Japanese men are only slightly less likely than Japanese women to feel this way, even though marriage is probably less restrictive for them than for Japanese women.

For men, marriage involves the obligation to support a family, and for many women it redirects earnings from their own wants and needs to those of their family. At the same time, however, marriage provides the opportunity for pooling income, and the U.S. has long had a saying that "Two can live as cheaply as one." We find that somewhat less than one-half of the young Americans believe that their standard of living would improve were they to marry. The proportion is only about one-quarter among young Japanese people, about one-third of whom say that their living standard would actually be worse. Thus, instead of expecting marriage to improve their standard of living, young Japanese women and men view marriage as materially neutral or costly. Again, American men are only somewhat less likely than Japanese men (and women) to see marriage as imposing economic constraints, and American women are substantially less likely to do so than Japanese women. On each of these first two measures, it is young American women who stand out as the most favorable to marriage. On these dimensions, too, young Japanese have a less favorable view of marriage than do young Americans, especially American women.

Table 3.2 Percentage Distribution on Whether Life Would Be Better or Worse on Various Dimensions If Respondent Were Married: Never-Married Men and Women Aged 20–27 in Japan (1994) and the U.S. (1987–1988) [a]

| | JAPAN | | | | U.S. | | | |
Dimension	Worse	Same	Better	Base (N)	Worse	Same	Better	Base (N)
Personal freedom								
Males	63	32	5	(139)	53	36	11	(368)
Females	69	23	8	(155)	29	55	16	(319)
Standard of living								
Males	35	41	24	(140)	29	27	44	(370)
Females	35	42	23	(155)	16	36	48	(319)
Emotional security								
Males	3	25	72	(140)	8	40	52	(370)
Females	6	28	66	(155)	6	30	63	(319)
Overall happiness								
Males	7	30	63	(140)	10	30	61	(368)
Females	11	38	51	(154)	8	23	69	(318)

[a] Percentages for the U.S. are weighted using sampling weights, but base numbers shown are the actual numbers of individuals interviewed.

As we might expect from popular beliefs about romantic love, a majority of these young adults feel that marriage would improve their emotional security. In contrast to the two dimensions discussed above, women's views on this issue are very similar in the two countries, and the major contrast is among men. Surprisingly, perceptions of the emotional consequences of marriage are more positive among Japanese than among American men, with 72 percent of Japanese men compared to 52 percent of men in the U.S. feeling that their emotional security would improve with marriage. While this large difference might be attributed to insecurity associated with the high divorce rate in the U.S., the lack of a difference between women in the two countries leaves the question open. With regard to gender differences, in Japan, women are less likely than men to see marriage as improving their emotional security (66 percent versus 72 percent), while the opposite is true in the U.S. (63 percent versus 52 percent). Thus, although emotional security is widely perceived as a benefit of marriage in both countries, this perception is most widespread among Japanese men and least common among American men.

Finally, a majority of young women and men in both countries think their overall happiness would be better if they were married. In Japan, however, this view is more common among men than among women (63 percent versus 51 percent), while in the U.S., it is more common among women than among men (69 percent versus 61 percent). Japanese women are more skeptical of the emotional benefits of marriage than Japanese men, whereas American men are more skeptical than American women, even though a majority of all young adults regard marriage as having emotional benefits.

Overall, the evidence is mixed about whether orientations toward marriage are more or less positive in Japan than in the U.S. Young adults in Japan clearly view marriage as more restrictive of personal freedom than do their American counterparts and as carrying fewer material benefits. But Japanese men tend to regard the emotional benefits of marriage more positively than their American counterparts do. We might well regard "overall happiness" as a key summary measure of the consequences of various expectations about marriage, including but not limited to the other dimensions considered here. On this measure, it is clear that American women have the most favorable orientation toward marriage and Japanese women the least favorable—an important finding. There is no difference between Japanese and American men.

It is tempting to interpret these results as indicating that the absolute value of marriage has declined, especially in Japan, but this is not necessarily so. Especially among young Japanese women, marriage may simply compete less well as a source of happiness and both economic and emotional security than alternative activities. In recent years, higher levels of education and paid employment have given young single Japanese women far more autonomy and resources than they had traditionally enjoyed (Tsuya 2000; Tsuya and Mason

1995). Further, it is plausible that Japanese women have long found the obligations of marriage and parenthood burdensome (Jolivet 1997).

Although we have attempted to minimize selectivity bias by excluding older never-married individuals from the analysis, even this younger never-married sample may have a less positive view of marriage than their age mates who have already married. We explore this potential selectivity bias by examining the responses of currently married individuals aged 20–27 to a similar series of questions about the costs and benefits of marriage. To be sure, the current attitudes of married individuals may differ from their attitudes before marrying. Nevertheless, a small difference between the married and never-married samples would be consistent with a small selectivity bias.

The questions asked of married persons in the U.S. emphasized whether they would be better or worse off were they *separated* from the spouse, whereas the Japanese survey asked whether they would be better or worse off if they were *unmarried*. In Japan, currently married individuals tend to have a *less* positive view of marriage than do never-married individuals (data not shown). This is the reverse of what one would expect were the married selected for positive views of marriage and suggests that many young married couples are disillusioned by the experience of being married. In the U.S., on the other hand, the view of marriage held by currently married people is more positive than the view held by never-married individuals. Hence, early marriage in the U.S. may select for people with relatively positive views of marriage, although the high rate of marital dissolution in the country may also mean that the views of marriage among those who *remain* married are somewhat more positive than among all those who have ever married by age 28.[6]

Does the rather tepid endorsement of at least some of the benefits of mar-

Table 3.3 *Percentage Who Would Like to Marry: Noncohabiting, Never-Married Men and Women Aged 20–27 in Japan (1994) and the U.S. (1987–1988)*

	JAPAN		U.S.	
Marriage Desire	*Males*	*Females*	*Males*	*Females*
Yes[a]	80	80	89	88
No[b]	1	1	5	6
Don't know/neutral	19	20	6	6
(N)	(139)	(153)	(292)	(222)

[a] For Japan, "yes" refers to respondents who would like to marry as soon as possible, in 1–2 years, or eventually; for the U.S., it refers to those who strongly agreed or agreed with the statement that they would like to marry someday.

[b] For Japan, "no" refers to respondents who answered that they would never want to marry; for the U.S., it refers to those who disagreed or strongly disagreed with the statement that they would like to marry someday.

riage seen in table 3.2 mean that sizable proportions of young Japanese and American adults would prefer to avoid marriage altogether? The data shown in table 3.3 suggest the answer to this question is "no," especially in the U.S.[7] Marriage is desired by 80 percent of the unmarried young people in Japan and by nearly 90 percent in the U.S., and there is no difference between men and women in either country. Those who say they never want to marry are extremely rare: only 1 percent in Japan and about 5 or 6 percent in the U.S. It is particularly noteworthy, however, that a very substantial minority of Japanese young people (one-fifth) is uncertain, indicating a considerable ambivalence toward marriage in Japan. In the context of the increasing postponement of marriage in the country in recent years, this implies that many young Japanese may be postponing marriage not because of financial circumstances, but because they are not highly motivated to marry. Thus, marriage appears to be a more common life goal in the U.S. than in Japan.

Overall then, marriage is seen to be more beneficial in the U.S. than in Japan, especially among women; far fewer American young adults are uncertain about whether they want to marry eventually. Thus, ironically, our findings suggest that it is in Japan—where marriages remain more stable—rather than in the U.S. that the institution of marriage is under greater siege, at least among young women.

Multivariate Analysis

We use ordered logistic regression to examine the relationship between the individual characteristics described above and each of the four measures of the perceived benefits of marriage.[8] We begin by looking at gender differences.

The results shown in table 3.4 are generally consistent with those we saw in table 3.2. In the multivariate model, Japanese women are significantly less likely to feel that marriage would improve their happiness, and the effect is quite large. Gender effects on the other variables are not statistically significant in Japan, although we do see a moderate negative coefficient with respect to emotional security that is consistent with the observed differences. We found in the observed differences for the U.S. that women were more favorable than men with respect to each of these perceived outcomes. Each of the coefficients for female in table 3.4 is consistent with the observed differences, although that for overall happiness is not statistically significant. Thus, even when other factors that differ by gender are held constant, the gender effects that are statistically significant are in opposite directions in Japan and the U.S. Japanese women are more skeptical than Japanese men about the benefits of marriage, while in the U.S., women regard marriage more favorably than do men. This difference in the views of women and men in the two countries may help to explain why marriage postponement is much greater in Japan than in the U.S.

Table 3.4 Estimated Coefficients from Ordered Logistic Regression Predicting Perceptions of Marriage: Never-Married Men and Women Aged 20–27 in Japan (1994) and the U.S. (1987–1988)[a]

Predictor	PERSONAL FREEDOM		STANDARD OF LIVING		EMOTIONAL SECURITY		OVERALL HAPPINESS	
	Japan	U.S.	Japan	U.S.	Japan	U.S.	Japan	U.S.
Female	-.032	-.974**	.144	.304*	-.264	.512**	-.558*	.244**
Age	.106#	.153**	.071	.080*	-.012	.094*	-.013	.058
Lives with parents	-.607*	.125	-1.251**	-.590**	-.932**	-.069	-.446#	-.049
Years of education	-.046	-.081#	-.090	-.075#	.108	.028	.040	-.040
Income last year (millions of yen/$1,000s)	-.170#	-.021*	-.203*	-.012	.112	-.006	.003	-.009
Wants children[b]	-.020	.687**	.224*	.086	.457**	.704**	.471**	.600*
Cut point 1	-.609	1.315	-3.893	-2.087	-5.731	-.720	-5.315	-2.644
Cut point 2	1.667	2.995	-2.059	-.587	-3.710	.597	-3.934	-1.615
Cut point 3	3.758	5.440	-.140	.851	-1.403	3.000	-1.738	-.021
Cut point 4	4.852	6.325	1.634	2.669	.543	4.719	-.018	1.612
Pseudo R-square	.013*	.036**	.037**	.016**	.050**	.017**	.036**	.007**
(N)	(278)	(629)	(279)	(630)	(279)	(630)	(279)	(627)

[a] Each dependent variable is scored from 1 ("much worse") through 5 ("much better"). The estimated coefficients for the U.S. are weighted using sample weights.
[b] In both countries, those who are uncertain about having children are coded 0, along with those who definitely or probably do not want them; only those stating that they definitely or probably want (more) children are coded 1.
* Significant at p < .01.
** Significant at p < .05.
# Significant at p < .10.

Although each of the other background variables is statistically significant only for some outcomes, the significant effects are generally consistent with our theoretical expectations. Older unmarried persons in both countries view marriage more favorably than younger persons do with respect to personal freedom. Perhaps individual goals and activities held in early young adulthood seem less essential after there has been time for them to be realized. In the U.S., we also see positive effects of age on perceptions with regard to both standard of living and emotional security.

Living with parents may provide more opportunities for young people to pursue their own goals, in contrast to the time and financial obligations of marriage and parenthood. The results in table 3.4 are strongly consistent with this expectation for Japan: young Japanese adults who live with their parents regard marriage less favorably on all four of the dimensions than do their peers who do not live with parents. These results in turn support the hypothesis that living at home provides advantages that are hard to give up in order to assume the responsibilities of marriage. In marriage, personal freedom would decline, personal income would have to be redirected to family needs, and perhaps as a result of these changes, emotional security and overall happiness would be reduced. In the U.S., we see a negative effect of living with parents only for the perceived consequences of marriage with regard to one's standard of living. Hence, it is plausible that, ironically, remaining in the parental household contributes to the erosion of traditional Japanese norms that require sacrifice for one's family. Coresidence also has a negative effect on the perceived benefits of marriage on both emotional security and overall happiness among Japanese young people (though the latter difference is significant only at the 10 percent level). In the U.S., only the benefits of marriage for the standard of living are seen more negatively among young people who live with their parents.

There is some suggestion in the multivariate results that higher socioeconomic status is associated with a less favorable view of the practical, though not the emotional, benefits of marriage. In the U.S. young persons with more years of education are more likely to think marriage reduces one's personal freedom and standard of living (significant at the 10 percent level), and income has a negative effect on these variables in Japan. Those with more resources at their command may thus see marriage as having higher opportunity costs.

Finally, in both countries, those who want to have children are most likely to see marriage as improving emotional security and overall happiness. As we would expect, having children remains an important reason for marrying among young people in both countries. Given the high prevalence of unmarried childbearing in the U.S., it is surprising that the effect is just as strong as in Japan.

We turn now to logistic regression models predicting the desire to ever marry; the results are presented in table 3.5.[9] Although the dependent variable is defined identically in the two countries—those who want to marry are con-

Table 3.5 *Estimated Coefficients from Binary Logistic Regression Predicting Desires to Marry by Perceptions of Marriage, Personal Characteristics, and Desire for Children: Noncohabiting, Never-Married Men and Women Aged 20–27 in Japan (1994) and the U.S. (1987–1988)*

Predictor	JAPAN				U.S.			
	Model 1[a]	Model 2[b]	Model 3[c]	Model 4[d]	Model 1[a]	Model 2	Model 3	Model 4
Perceptions of marriage scale[e]	.141**	—	.116#	.065	.243**	—	.233**	.272**
Female	—	.061	—	.081	—	.004	—	-.199
Age	—	-.124	—	-.124	—	.006	—	-.028
Lives with parents	—	-.419	—	-.318	—	.052	—	.333
Years of education	—	.113	—	.113	—	.084	—	.139
Income (millions of yen/$1,000s)	—	-.342**	—	.346*	—	-.009	—	-.001
Wants children	—	.676*	.464	.594#	—	2.447**	2.171**	2.421**
Constant	-.043	2.133	-.083	1.440	-.439	-.927	-1.989	-3.805
Log-likelihood	-142.99	-126.77	-126.77	-126.37	-151.96	-132.19	-151.96	-121.33
LR chi² (df)	4.70	13.57	13.57	14.37	59.81	46.55	59.81	63.65
Prob> chi²	.016	.034	.034	.045	.000	.000	.000	.000
(N)	(291)	(276)	(276)	(276)	(508)	(463)	(508)	(457)

[a] Includes only marriage perception scale (see note e for the definition of the scale).
[b] Includes other predictor variables without marriage perception scale.
[c] Includes marriage perception scale and desire for children.
[d] Includes all predictor variables.
[e] Scale formed from the items on standard of living, emotional security, and overall happiness if married. Range is from 3 to 15.
* Significant at p < .01.
** Significant at p < .05.
# Significant at p < .10.

trasted with those who are uncertain or who do not want to marry ever—differences in the underlying distributions for the omitted category suggest the need for caution when interpreting the results in the two countries. Specifically, in Japan, almost no one wants never to marry, whereas in the U.S., there are equal numbers who are uncertain about marrying and who never want to marry. This difference in the omitted category may affect the results, as we discuss below.

The first predictor variable that we consider is the scale based on the questions about the benefits of marriage for standard of living, emotional security, and overall happiness, where a higher score indicates a more favorable view of marriage. The first column (Model 1) shows the relationship between this scale and the desire to marry, with no other variables controlled. As we would expect, those who regard marriage as having greater benefits are more likely to want to get married at some time in their lives. Column 2 (Model 2) reports the effects of other control variables without the marriage perception scale. The variables included in this model are gender, age, coresidence with parents, education, income, and desire for children. Because of the close normative tie between marriage and childbearing, Model 3 includes the perception variable only in conjunction with whether children are wanted. Model 4 enters all of these variables into the equation predicting the desire to marry.

Despite the systematic effects we saw in table 3.4 with respect to the various dimensions of the perceived benefits of marriage, only two of the personal characteristics examined here are significantly related to the desire to marry: in Japan, income, and in both countries, the desire to have children (see Model 2). It appears that the cultural expectation of marriage may be overriding much of the variation in the perceived benefits and costs associated with it. Even so, differentials in the perceived attractiveness of marriage may well represent the varying strength with which the desire to marry is held and thus affect ultimate marriage behavior.

The positive effect of income in Japan is puzzling given the *negative* effect we saw in table 3.4 with respect to the perceived costs and benefits of marriage. We would expect income to increase the ability to marry, even if the opportunity costs of marriage were seen as higher among those with more income. It may be relevant that the dependent variable in Japan is primarily a contrast between those who definitely want to get married and those who are uncertain. Those with lower income may be less certain that they want to get married because of their lower resources, even though they view marriage more favorably than persons who are better off.

Wanting children is strongly related to wanting to marry, as we would expect on the basis of the cultural linkage between marriage and childbearing. In both countries, those who want children are more likely to want to marry. At first, it might seem unexpected that the relationship appears stronger in the U.S. than in Japan, especially since marriage and childbearing are much more

Tsuya, Mason, and Bumpass

tightly linked in Japan than in the U.S. The difference in the effect may reflect the difference in the omitted category between the two countries. In the U.S., not desiring children predicts wanting never to marry much more strongly than not wanting children predicts being *uncertain* about marrying in Japan.

Nonetheless, because of the link between childbearing and marriage in the two countries, we might expect the desire for children to account for some of the effect of perceptions of marriage on wanting to get married. We see this result in Japan but not in the U.S. (Model 3). When all of the variables are controlled in Model 4, the effect of the marriage perception scale disappears altogether in Japan but increases in the U.S. Further, models for Japan (not included in the table) indicate that income and desire for children play about equal roles in accounting for the perceptions effect, and adding them jointly reduces the zero-order coefficient of 0.14 to -0.09, which is no longer statistically significant.

We saw in table 3.3 that in both countries, men and women were equally likely to want to marry. This remains the case when other variables are controlled. There is, however, a suggestion of an interesting interaction of coresidence with gender in Japan. While we have not included the coefficients in the table, this interaction seems worth a tentative discussion, even though it is not significant at conventional levels. In Japan, living with parents may be negatively related to wanting to marry among men but weakly positively related among women. When we estimate values from an equation including an interaction, it appears that Japanese men who do not live with their parents stand out as wanting to marry most (92 percent), whereas women who do not live with their parents are the least likely to want to marry (78 percent). Perhaps living alone makes men more aware that the household services provided by their mothers could be enjoyed in marriage as well. At the same time, some unmarried women who live apart from their parents may find that they wish to maintain independence from exactly these family responsibilities. This interpretation is consonant with a theme found throughout this book that delayed marriage and childbearing may be a consequence, in part, of men and women bringing different expectations to marriage.

Conclusion

In this chapter, we have examined views of marriage and the desire to marry among young, never-married adults in Japan and the U.S. Age at marriage is later in Japan than in the U.S., and among women, views of the benefits of marriage are less positive as well. In particular, compared to American women, Japanese women see marriage as more restrictive of their personal freedom, more likely to reduce their economic well-being, and less likely to improve their overall happiness.

At the same time, the overwhelming majority of the never-married in both countries wants eventually to marry. It is nonetheless surprising that one-fifth of all never-married Japanese aged 20–27 are uncertain whether they want to marry. Uncertainty may be an important transition stage en route to decisions not to marry. As discussed in the introductory chapter, childbearing is closely linked with marriage in Japan, and there is similarly a high level of uncertainty about wanting to have children in Japan; this is true of approximately one-third of the respondents, compared to one-tenth in the U.S. This in turn leads us to speculate that although Japan's cohort marital fertility has been stable at around two children among women in their late forties (National Institute of Population and Social Security Research 2002: 60–63), it may decline in the future, as most of the currently unmarried intend to marry eventually, but a substantial proportion of them are ambivalent about having children.[10]

Earlier studies on marriage timing and the status of women in Japan have suggested that a combination of increased education and employment have given young unmarried women far more autonomy and resources than they traditionally enjoyed, at the same time that gender relationships in the home have remained traditional (Tsuya 2000; Tsuya and Mason 1995). This is seen, in turn, as leading many young women to avoid marriage until late in their twenties or, in some cases, permanently. The findings presented in this chapter are consistent with this argument. Although young Japanese men are just as negative as young women about the material benefits of marrying and are almost as negative about the loss of personal freedom that marriage entails, they tend to be more positive than young Japanese women about the *emotional* benefits of marriage and especially about the effect of marriage on their overall happiness. Thus, young Japanese women are not only very negative about the loss of personal freedom that marriage entails—seven-tenths say they would be worse off in this respect if they were married—but they are also lukewarm about the emotional benefits of marriage. This is consistent with the argument that women's situation when married has come to contrast starkly and unfavorably with their situation as young adults prior to marriage (Tsuya 2000).

Recently, several authors have suggested that it is only when highly developed societies offer full equality to women that birthrates may possibly return to levels at or near the long-term replacement level (e.g., Chesnais 1996; McDonald 2000). So long as women receive similar education to men, are employed in large numbers, and yet do not enjoy equality in the family or support for their family roles, they are likely to be reluctant to marry or to have children (or more than one child).

In contrast to the U.S., the postwar feminist movement in Japan has been small and largely ineffective, and in part because of this and also because of a strong Confucian cultural heritage, the institution of marriage has remained largely unchanged (Steinhoff 1994). Marriage in Japan is still characterized by a sharp division of labor between husbands, who work long hours, and wives,

Tsuya, Mason, and Bumpass

who spend long hours on household tasks and the supervision of children's education, as well as working in the marketplace (see chapters 5–7; Tsuya and Bumpass 1998). Marriage also remains characterized by an impersonal status for wives that many young women find unappealing. At the same time, the traditional character of marriage and parenthood in Japan means much greater family stability than in the U.S. Although the divorce rate in Japan has been rising rapidly in recent years (see chapter 1), it remains far below that of the U.S., and out-of-wedlock childbearing, as noted, is also very rare. The price of this family stability, however, may be the increasing reluctance of young women to enter into marriage. Thus, while the institution of marriage appears to "work" better in Japan than in the U.S. in terms of providing a stable environment for bearing and rearing children, it may be under as much or more threat as an institution in Japan as in the U.S. Certainly it is striking that young people in the U.S. retain what one sociologist has called "a touching faith" in marriage that many of their counterparts in Japan seem to lack. Thus, it is open to debate whether the path that Japan has taken is less a threat to the viability of marriage than the one taken in the U.S.

Chapter Four

Intergenerational Relations

Ronald R. Rindfuss, Minja Kim Choe, Larry L. Bumpass, and Yong-Chan Byun

The parent-child bond is among the strongest and longest lasting of all social relationships, typically beginning at birth, when the child is completely dependent on the parent for nourishment, shelter, and protection, as well as intellectual stimulation and guidance.[1] This relationship most often ends with the death of the parent, and it is not unusual for the parent to be dependent before death on his or her children and/or their spouses.[2] Just as parents and children experience their own life courses, with individual transitions—leaving school, work, marriage, childbearing, and retirement—the life courses of parents and children are intertwined, and, indeed, one can think of the life course of the parent-child relationship (e.g., parenting/grandparenting or home leaving/nest emptying).

In this chapter, we consider the parent-child relationship after the child has reached adulthood and after he or she has married. This phase of the relationship is important because there continue to be flows of information, support, and assistance in both directions. One of the premises of Caldwell's (1982) now famous theory of fertility decline is that adult children in modern societies frequently receive resources from their parents rather than the reverse. Findings from the U.S. and Japan suggest that the net flow favors children over much of the life course, and this can take the form of help with child care, financial assistance, or simply emotional support (e.g., Morgan and Hirosima 1983; Spitze and Logan 1991; Tsuya 2000; Wolf and Soldo 1994). Parents also provide a variety of support services when their children experience major life course crises, such as marital dissolution or unemployment (Cherlin and Furstenberg 1986).

However, assistance and support flow from adult children to parents as well, especially when parents are elderly (Bumpass 1994). The psychological well-being of the elderly is related to levels of intergenerational contact (e.g., Aquilino and Supple 1991; Lawton, Silverstein, and Bengston 1994; Rossi and Rossi 1990). While it is possible that this relationship appears because parental psychological problems impede relationships with their children, it is more likely that frequent contact provides emotional and social support and that it enhances self-esteem and psychological well-being more generally. The elderly are particularly likely to receive financial, nursing, and emotional support from their adult children in times of illness. Clearly, flows of support and assistance from adult children to their parents can begin well before the parents are elderly. For example, they may provide financial assistance or information on new products or services that the senior generation would not otherwise know about.

In this chapter, we examine three types of interactions—coresidence, seeing, and phoning—between married children and their parents or parents-in-law.[3] We do so from the perspective of the children, asking about their experience of living with, seeing, or having telephone contact with their parents or parents-in-law. In comparisons across societies, intergenerational interactions are a function of both normative and cultural factors, as well as of structural constraints such as the nature of the economy and age patterns of mortality. As noted in chapter 1, with only three countries, we are unable to separate these quite different sources of country-level variation in intergenerational interactions. However, we have suggestive evidence that both types of factors are operating. Below, we compare and contrast Japan, Korea, and the U.S. with respect to both cultural and structural factors likely to affect intergenerational interactions. The three data sets used are described in chapter 1.

Methodological Approach

Intergenerational relationships can be approached from either the perspective of the senior generation (looking down the generational lines) or from that of the junior generation (looking up). The Japanese and U.S. survey data allow either or both perspectives (see Rindfuss and Raley 1998). With the Korean survey data, however, we can examine only adult children's relationships with their parents. Hence, in order to extend our analysis to all three countries, we focus on the perspective of the younger generation. In the interpretation of our results, it is important to remember that the pattern of results is likely to differ if one is looking down the generations as opposed to looking up— although the two are obviously related.[4] Our approach is also ego-centered, rather than a complete social network approach (Raley and Rindfuss 1999), because this is necessary in order to include all three countries in our analysis. Thus, we will be examining the experiences of husbands' and wives' contact with their parents and parents-in-law.

We also restrict our attention to currently married couples where the respondent is aged 30–59. The upper age limit is that of the Japanese survey. The lower age limit was chosen to minimize an age-at-marriage bias for our sample (that is, we did not want a sample biased toward those who marry at very young ages). Finally, the restriction to currently married couples was based on the assumption that coresidence and contact patterns might interact, in a theoretical and statistical sense, with marital status, and we did not have a sufficient number of unmarried respondents in all three countries to test for such interactions.

In each of the three countries, a series of variables was collected about the respondent, the respondent's spouse, the respondent's parents, and the respondent's spouse's parents. Since many of our hypotheses are gender-based, we arranged the files so that the variables referred to wife, husband, wife's parents, and husband's parents. This means that the respondent is sometimes a female and sometimes a male. In order to check for potential gender bias in responses, we include a gender-of-respondent variable in our multivariate analyses.

Normative or Cultural Expectations

Even though the specifics of expectations vary across societies, it is testimony to the importance of intergenerational relations that all societies have normative and cultural expectations about them. Different societies have reached different solutions, just as over time different languages have evolved within distinct populations. Whatever the cultural prescription for intergenerational relations, further change must occur from this base, thus building in a certain amount of inertia.

Among the three countries compared here, expectations regarding intergenerational relations are most dissimilar between the U.S., on the one hand, and Japan and Korea, on the other. The normative expectation in the U.S. is that contact will occur with the parents of both the husband and wife, rather than advantaging either the maternal or paternal lines, and that both sets of parents will maintain their own households. Nevertheless, in practice women are much more involved than men in maintaining kin contact, and this leads to somewhat greater kin contact along maternal lines (Rossi and Rossi 1990). In contrast, in Japan and Korea, intergenerational interactions on the paternal side receive greater emphasis, including a preference for coresidence along paternal lines. The normatively expected pattern is for the eldest son and his wife and children to live in an extended household with his parents (Kurosu 1994; Martin 1990; Taeuber 1958: 100–104). In practice, these normative expectations must be balanced against the practical exigencies dictated by career paths, health and mortality circumstances, and the like.

Bilateral versus patrilineal relationships and coresidence versus independent living are the two important and distinct dimensions in our comparison. The emphasis on maintaining strong bilateral relations in the U.S. undoubtedly reflects the heterogeneity of the different groups migrating to the country and the gradual blending of those groups' maternal, paternal, or bilateral dispositions. Historically, the substantial Confucian influence in both Korea and Japan may partially account for similarities. In both countries, it was (and still is) important to maintain links among past, current, and future generations, and this has been accomplished primarily through the paternal lineage.

In both East Asian countries, administrative procedures maintained by civil authorities reinforce this linkage across generations. In Japan today, every individual has a *koseki,* which is essentially a register that records information such as sex, birth order, date of birth, and place of birth, as well as parents' dates and places of birth. Korea has a similar system, under which each individual has a *hojeok,* which contains information for that individual and the previous generations.[5] When a young woman marries, her *koseki/hojeok* is moved from the administrative unit responsible for her parents' household to the administrative unit responsible for her husband's household, which frequently is the administrative unit responsible for her husband's parents' household.[6]

There are differences, however, between Korea and Japan. In Korea the emphasis is on paternal biological linkages, whereas in Japan it is more on continuing the family name (Tsuya and Choe 1991). The Korean emphasis on the preservation of paternal bloodlines has led to one of the world's strongest preferences for sons (Arnold 1987; Cho, Arnold, and Kwon 1982).

Another dimension of difference between the U.S., on the one hand, and Korea and Japan, on the other, involves coresidence versus the maintenance of independent households. The emphasis on residential independence in the U.S. might reflect the country's frontier history, but in some cases the roots also go back to the origins of some of the peoples who immigrated to America. This preference for independence is so strong that a variety of programs sponsored by governments, nongovernmental organizations, and private industry have emerged to allow the elderly to live independently as long as possible. Coresidence does occur in the U.S., however, and it is an acceptable and expected mechanism for coping with various contingencies and emergencies, such as unemployment, marital dissolution, or a very serious illness. By midlife, about 25 percent of U.S. adults have had a parent live with them (Bumpass 1994).

The situation is almost the mirror image in Japan and Korea, where intergenerational coresidence is the normative expectation (see chapter 2), with rules suggesting the preferred pattern. For example, other things being equal, the first choice is for parents to coreside with their eldest son. If for some reason that is not possible, then coresidence with the next eldest son is preferred. Put differently, coresidence is the expected normal state of affairs (at least for eldest sons), not a mechanism to cope with emergencies, as in the U.S. Nonetheless, there are many situations in both Korea and Japan that might lead both generations to decide that living together is not desirable. Perhaps the most common are differences created by changes in economic opportunities for the two generations, as reflected in the extremely rapid educational and occupational shift in Korea over the past two generations. Hence, contemporary Korean parents are likely to have pursued agricultural careers in rural areas, while their children are pursuing manufacturing or service careers in urban areas. The different location of economic opportunities is also an important factor reducing coresidence.

Structural Constraints on Intergenerational Interactions

In addition to the normative and cultural forces affecting patterns of intergenerational interactions, there are structural constraints resulting from recent demographic, social, and economic transformations. Perhaps the most obvious is whether or not parents are still alive. The survival status of parents in each of the three countries is reported in table 4.1.

There are more living mothers than fathers as a consequence of both spousal age differences and the greater longevity of women. Parents are least likely to be alive in Korea.[7] This reflects a variety of factors, including the differential impacts of World War II and the Korean War, differences in the timing of mortality declines, differences in the timing of marriage and childbearing, and age differences between spouses.[8]

If the senior and junior generations are not living together, the frequency with which they see one another will be affected by travel time and costs. Of course, travel time or distance need not be exogenous to frequency of visits. Those who hold traditional values or who are emotionally close might choose to live near their parents and children. Indeed, "to be closer to one's family" is a frequent response when migrants are asked why they moved (or why non-migrants did not). For this reason, we do not include travel time or distance as an independent variable in our analysis. Nevertheless, it is important to recognize that the effort required for visiting might mean qualitatively different things in the three countries.

Though the transportation infrastructure is well developed in all three countries, the U.S. is ninety-five times larger than Korea and twenty-five times

Table 4.1 *Percentage Distribution on Survival Status of Parents: Japan (1994), Korea (1994), and the U.S. (1987–1988)*

Status of Parent(s)	Japan	Korea	U.S.
Wife's parents			
Both alive	42	38	49
Only mother alive	31	29	26
Only father alive	6	6	8
Both dead	21	27	17
Total	100	100	100
Husband's parents			
Both alive	34	30	42
Only mother alive	32	35	29
Only father alive	7	6	8
Both dead	27	29	21
Total	100	100	100
(N)	(1,658)	(1,654)	(3,294)

larger than Japan.[9] Thus, in Korea one could drive from one end of the country to the other in less than a day to see parents or adult children. In the U.S., driving across the country takes several days. Flying is generally quicker but more expensive. If we discount international migration, the potential friction of distance in intergenerational interaction is greatest in the U.S. and least in Korea, though less developed and more congested transportation routes in Korea may make the same distance take much longer to traverse.

From our data, it is difficult to compare the actual travel times or distances between adult children and their parents because the three surveys did not ask comparable questions. The U.S. survey asked about miles, whereas the two East Asian surveys asked about qualitative and political boundary units (i.e., same house, next door, same neighborhood, same municipality, different municipality in same prefecture, different prefecture). Since it is not clear how to translate miles into political units, we decided to use two cut points for the U.S.—more than 25 miles and more than 100 miles—to compare with Japan and Korea. Based on these criteria, the proportions of couples whose parents are living in a different municipality/district are shown below in table 4.2.

As we can see from this table, Korea and Japan are qualitatively different from one another, with Koreans living further from their parents than Japanese. This reflects the recentness of Korea's socioeconomic development, resulting in a high percentage of individuals who were raised in rural areas and are now living in urban areas.[10] The contrast to the U.S. depends on how the category "different municipality/district" is interpreted. A respondent could live within a mile of his/her parents and still be in a different municipality. If we accept the 25-mile cutoff as an approximation of living in the same municipality, then fewer parents and their adult children live relatively close to one another in the U.S. than in either Japan or Korea. Indeed, because of the size of the U.S., many who live more than 100 miles apart are separated by several thousand miles.

As noted above, rapid social and economic change can make relations

Table 4.2 *Percentage of Couples Whose Parents Are Living in a Different Municipality/District: Japan (1994), Korea (1994), and the U.S. (1987–1988)*

	JAPAN	KOREA	U.S.	
			More Than 25 Miles Away	*100+ Miles Away*
Wife's parents	28	45	50	35
Husband's parents	24	38	50	36

across the generations more difficult. If different generations have experienced divergent life-cycle experiences and transitions, then their background knowledge and attitudes that affect everyday conversations will be dissimilar, and each generation will be less likely to intuitively understand the issues the other is facing. One important indicator in this regard is the difference in education between generations. Table 4.3 shows the educational distribution for husbands and husbands' fathers in our sample for Korea and the U.S.[11] Parental education was not collected in the Japanese survey. In both Korea and the U.S., there have been substantial intergenerational shifts in educational attainment. As we would expect, however, the shift has been much more extreme in Korea than in the U.S. We have also looked at other possible comparisons between the generations—for example, education of wife and wife's father or husband and his father-in-law—and they all show similar patterns.

Changes between the size of place during childhood and current residence also suggest the recentness and rapidity of Korea's socioeconomic evolution. In more traditional societies, a greater percentage of the labor force is engaged in agriculture and a larger fraction lives in rural areas. The economies in all three countries have shifted new jobs into urban areas. In Korea, about one-half of the couples surveyed grew up in rural areas and now live in urban areas. The comparable figure is a little over one-third in Japan, and it is somewhat lower in the U.S. Thus, Korea again stands out for the recentness and rapidity of its shift from a predominantly agricultural society to an industrialized society, with the resulting intergenerational differences.

The shift from an agrarian to a manufacturing and service economy has also likely changed the relative power between the generations. For example, until

Table 4.3 *Percentage Distribution on Educational Attainment of Husband and Husband's Father: Korea (1994) and the U.S. (1987–1988)*

	KOREA		U.S.	
Educational Attainment	*Husband*	*Husband's Father*	*Husband*	*Husband's Father*
Less than junior high	15	73	3	25
Completed junior high	16	14	6	12
Attended/completed high school	39	9	31	35
Some college	7	1	25	11
College graduate or more	23	4	35	17
Total	100	100	100	100
(N)	(1,648)	(1,351)	(3,034)	(1,328)

Note: Those with missing data are excluded from these percentages. The weighted percent with missing data are as follows: Korea: husband—4 percent, father—22 percent; U.S.: husband—10 percent, father—11 percent.

Rindfuss, Choe, Bumpass, and Byun

recently, in Korea, the senior generation had power over the younger generation, and the mother had power over the daughter-in-law, in part because of the Confucian heritage (Tsuya and Choe 1991) and in part because the senior generation tended to own the family farm and hence the means of livelihood. Another structural aspect that might affect patterns of coresidence and contact with parents is the tradition of younger women marrying older men. This pattern is most evident in Korea, where only 4 percent of wives are older than their husbands. For Japan and the U.S. the comparable percentages are 10 and 18 respectively. For the entire distribution of the difference between spouses' ages (data not shown), Japan has the tightest clustering around the mean, and Korea has the largest proportion of couples in which the husband is substantially older.

Employment patterns may also have important consequences for intergenerational contact by structuring the amount of time available. In general, we would expect there to be less available time when both spouses are employed. On the other hand, couples living with parents in reasonably good health may find it easier to work outside the home (Morgan and Hirosima 1983). Given this potential endogeneity between intergenerational coresidence and employment, we have not included employment in our multivariate analysis. However, structural aspects of the labor market can also affect employment opportunities, especially for women (see chapter 6), and this in turn may affect interactions with parents and parents-in-law. There are marked differences across the three countries in the percentage of couples where both spouses are employed: 22 percent in Korea, 57 percent in Japan, and 66 percent in the U.S.

In summary, Korea tends to differ from the other two countries on a number of structural characteristics that are likely to affect intergenerational interactions. The transition from an agricultural to a nonagricultural society is most recent in Korea, with resulting intergenerational differences in educational attainment and rural/urban residence. Korea has the smallest proportion of living parents. It is most distinct in terms of the age differences between husband and wife. Korea is also the smallest country geographically and has the highest population density. Finally, Korea has the lowest proportion of dual-income couples.

Coresidence

Undoubtedly, the closest form of intergenerational interaction is among those who share a common residence. Coresidence is more common in Japan and Korea, reflecting historical and cultural differences from the U.S. Based on structural differences, we expect coresidence to be more common in Japan than in Korea. Residing with both sets of parents is extremely rare (0.5 percent or less in all threes countries); thus, for ease of presentation, we exclude such cases from this analysis. The percentages coresiding with wife's or husband's parents in the three countries are shown in table 4.4.

As expected, almost no American couples live with parents at any specific time, whereas a substantial proportion of Korean and Japanese couples live with parents, and they are much more likely to be living with the husband's parents. The lower level of coresidence in Korea than in Japan very likely reflects the structural factors described above—in particular the large number of Korean urban residents whose parents live in rural areas. In addition, Korean husbands are less likely than Japanese husbands to be the eldest sons —that is, they have more siblings because of the more recent fertility decline in Korea. In 1994, 46 percent of the Korean husbands were the oldest sons, compared to 56 percent in Japan. Since the expectation is for only one son to live with his parents, the more sons there are in the younger generation who are not the eldest, the lower the proportion of this generation who will be living with the parents.

Despite the normative orientation to live with the husband's parents, a substantial proportion of couples live with the wife's parents in both East Asian countries, though more so in Japan. It also should be noted that this practice is more common in Japan today—higher than it has been historically. This trend can be seen in a series of national opinion surveys on family planning conducted by Mainichi Newspapers (Tsuya 1990). In 1977, 4 percent of married women of childbearing age lived with the wife's parents; by 1990 this had increased to 7 percent, with a monotonically increasing trend line. It may well be that because of small families and despite traditional preferences, we are seeing the consequences of the increased proportion of families without sons.[12] If this is the case, the continued fertility decline to below-replacement levels since the mid-1970s may lead to additional increases in the proportion of Japanese couples who live with the wife's parents, unless the preference for shared households also declines. Future fertility decline may also raise the important question of what the living arrangements may be when both spouses have no siblings.

In order to examine whether coresidence is related to the sociodemographic and structural variables discussed above and to see if patterns are similar across countries, we turn now to a multivariate analysis of living arrangements. The dependent variable consists of three unordered residence categories—with wife's parents, with husband's parents, and with neither—

Table 4.4 Percentage of Couples Coresiding with Their Parents: Korea (1994), Japan (1994), and the U.S. (1987–1988)

	Korea	Japan	U.S.
Wife's parents	4	9	1
Husband's parents	24	37	1

and hence multinomial logistic regression is used (see Retherford and Choe 1993: 151–165).

The independent variables represent life-course, structural, and cultural factors. Age of husband is included to index ages of the parties involved—husband, wife, husband's parents, and wife's parents—since all members of this generational network are progressing through the various phases of their lives. Members of the senior generation are more likely to become widows and widowers, and they are more likely to experience physical ailments that require care. At the same time, the junior generation is moving into its prime earning years, with its children entering young adulthood. We also include in our multivariate model an age-squared term to capture nonlinearity in the effects of respondent's age.

We control for two other aspects of age: the extent to which the husband is older than the wife and whether he is the eldest son. Other things being equal, we expect that the older the husband is relative to the wife, the more traditional the couple will be, and, as discussed above, it is the eldest son in particular who has intergenerational responsibilities.

Gender is included for both substantive and methodological reasons. As mentioned, women tend to maintain more of the kin contact than men (Rossi and Rossi 1990). In addition, wives and husbands might give different responses when reporting on the same phenomena.

Given the differences in the tempo and timing of urbanization across the three countries, it is important to control for urban/rural upbringing and whether it is the same for both spouses. We have three dummy variables with the reference category being couples in which both spouses grew up in a rural area: wife grew up in a rural area and husband in an urban area, wife grew up in an urban area and husband in a rural area, and both grew up in urban areas.

Finally, we control for both absolute and relative levels of spouses' education. We start with the husband's education, using high school graduate as the reference category, and contrast three dummy variables: husband did not complete high school, husband graduated from college, and husband attended college but did not graduate.[13] We also include a variable indicating whether the husband's education is greater than the wife's, with the expectation that such couples are more traditional. A third education variable indicates whether the husband's education is lower than his father's.[14] We expect that this downward mobility reduces intergenerational interaction.

Table 4.5 reports the results from a logistic regression model predicting the likelihood of intergenerational coresidence. Given that intergenerational households are almost nonexistent in the cross-section in the U.S., we have restricted this analysis to Korea and Japan. The first thing to notice is how few of the coefficients are statistically significant, especially in Korea. Because the predictor variables are life-cycle or demographic variables, these results suggest that demographic and life-course characteristics do not play a powerful role in determining whether a couple coresides with either parents or parents-in-law. This in turn suggests that the forces involved are more cultural or normative. It is unfortunate that our data sets are not longitudinal. It would be most desirable to have prior measures on traditional Korean and Japanese norms and values and on whether coresidence may have been intermittent over the life course.

Not surprisingly, whether a husband is the eldest son is the most consistently significant variable in both Korea and Japan. Eldest sons are more likely to live with husband's parents, as we expect from the norms, and this pattern is stronger in Japan. Eldest sons in Japan clearly avoid living with the wife's parents. That this is the case in Japan but not in Korea is likely to be related to the traditional Japanese practice of families without sons adopting a son-in-law at the marriage of a daughter in order to carry on the family name (Taeuber 1958: 100–104; Tsuya and Choe 1991).[15]

In both countries, females are more likely than males to report that they are living with the wife's parents; in Korea, they are also more likely to say that they are living in a nuclear household than with the husband's parents. This result suggests that either husbands or wives, and perhaps both, are giving biased answers about who else lives in the household and that the bias goes in the direction we would expect on the basis of norms. If circumstances sometimes lead husbands and wives not to live with one another (e.g., in Thailand, see Chamratrithirong, Morgan, and Rindfuss 1988; in the U.S., see Rindfuss and Stephen 1990), then the wife might be more likely to live with her parents and the husband more likely to live with his. Work or family reasons may also require some couples in Japan and Korea to live apart.

Contact

Interaction is undoubtedly most frequent when the generations live together, except when there is little overlap in schedules or when there is severe conflict. Nonetheless, parents and children who maintain separate households share many forms of assistance and support through visiting and telephoning.

In all three countries, in addition to the question on living arrangements, respondents were asked about the frequency with which they saw their own and their spouse's parents. Most often this would involve visits in the household of one or the other generation, though interactions at other locations would also be included. The responses were recorded in categories; the following three categories are comparable across the countries: less than once a month, 1–3 times a month, and more than three times a month. Those who live with their parents are included in the most frequent category.

Before we examine the results, it is important to note that we can infer less about contact from the measure of visiting than we can from coresidence. In contrast to the assumed frequent contact among all who are sharing a house-

Table 4.5 *Estimated Coefficients from Multinomial Logistic Regression Predicting Coresidence: Japan (1994) and Korea (1994)*

	JAPAN			KOREA		
Predictor	Husband's Parents vs. Nuclear Family	Husband's Parents vs. Wife's Parents	Nuclear Family vs. Wife's Parents	Husband's Parents vs. Nuclear Family	Husband's Parents vs. Wife's Parents	Nuclear Family vs. Wife's Parents
Husband's age	0.237*	-0.250	-0.487*	-0.108	-0.580	-0.472
Husband's age squared	-0.002*	0.004	0.006*	0.002	0.007	0.006
Respondent is female[a]	-0.162	-0.603*	-0.441	-0.395*	-1.328*	-0.933
Husband-wife age difference	0.031	0.028	-0.003	-0.032	0.155	0.187*
Husband is eldest son[b]	1.878**	2.543**	0.665*	0.996**	0.685	-0.311
Rural-urban origins[c]						
Wife only rural	-0.313	-0.192	0.121	0.364	-0.652	-1.016
Husband only rural	-0.425	-0.718	-0.294	-0.129	0.267	0.396
Both urban	-0.368*	-0.496	-0.128	-0.110	-0.047	0.063
Husband's education[d]						
Less than high school graduate	0.316	-0.041	-0.357	0.353	-0.449	-0.802
Some college	-0.250	0.209	0.459	0.440	-0.776	-1.215
College graduate or more	-0.860**	-0.214	0.646	-0.076	-0.484	-0.408
Husband's education greater than wife's education	0.548	-0.081	-0.629	-0.410	-0.768	-0.359
Constant	-7.360	4.079	11.439	0.229	13.839	13.610
Model chi^2	210.83				83.61	
(d.f.)	(24)				(24)	
(N)	(991)				(799)	

Reference categories:
[a] Respondent is male.
[b] Husband not eldest son.
[c] Both wife and husband rural.
[d] High school graduate.

* Significant at p < .01.
** Significant at p < .05.

hold, we know less about who is interacting with whom in the measure of how often parents are seen. For example, if we have a report from a wife that she sees her parents 1–3 times a month, we do not know whether the contact is just between the wife and her mother, involves her and her husband and both of her parents, or indicates some other combination.[16] This point is even more obvious when we turn to telephone contact. The issue of who is involved in the contact will be discussed at several places in the interpretation of our results.

Levels of personal contact with parents differ across countries and depend on whether we are discussing the husband's or the wife's parents (see table 4.6). Both sides are seen with about the same frequency in the U.S., with a slightly higher frequency of contact with the wife's parents. In Korea and Japan, on the other hand, the wife's parents are seen substantially less often than the husband's. These patterns are what we would expect in the contrast between the bilateral orientation in the U.S. and the East Asian emphasis on patrilineal relationships.

Differences across countries are in opposite directions, depending upon which side is being considered. The husband's parents are seen most often in Japan and least often in the U.S., with Korea intermediate. At the same time, personal contact with the wife's parents is most frequent in the U.S. and least so in Japan. These differences are very consistent with our expectations from theory and large enough to be important, but the commonalities should also not be missed. For example, substantial proportions of Japanese and Korean

Table 4.6 Percentage Distribution on Frequency of Seeing Wife's and Husband's Parents: Japan (1994), Korea (1994), and the U.S. (1987–1988)

Frequency	Japan	Korea	U.S.
Wife's parents			
Less than once a month	45	53	45
1–3 times a month	28	30	22
More than 3 times a month	27	18	33
Total	100	100	100
(N)	(1,313)	(1,120)	(2,786)
Husband's parents			
Less than once a month	35	37	48
1–3 times a month	15	26	22
More than 3 times a month	50	37	30
Total	100	100	100
(N)	(1,211)	(1,147)	(2,599)

Note: Respondents who are coresiding with parents are included and coded as seeing their parents frequently.

Rindfuss, Choe, Bumpass, and Byun

couples with living parents do not see those parents very often: over one-third see the husband's parents less than once a month, and about one-half see the wife's parents as infrequently.

Not surprisingly, the higher frequency of coresidence with husband's parents is a major factor in the differences across countries. When we look at the frequency of visiting among those who are not sharing a residence with their parents (data not shown), the U.S. has the highest frequency of personal contact and Japan the lowest. This does not necessarily imply that it is only the obligation for eldest sons to live with their parents that leads to lower levels of personal contact between noncoresident children and their parents in Japan and Korea. Even in the absence of living with their parents, eldest sons might well visit their parents with higher than average frequency. It does suggest, however, that given the obligation of their oldest male sibling, other siblings likely feel much less obligation to visit with their parents, and they do so less than sons and daughters in the U.S. (Bumpass 1994).

We next use ordered logistic regression models (see McCullagh and Nelder 1989) to examine the effects of demographic and life-cycle variables on personal contact with wife's and husband's parents respectively. The results are shown in table 4.7 and summarized in table 4.8.

The most striking feature of these analyses is that the life-cycle and demographic variables in the model are important in structuring intergenerational patterns of contact in the U.S. but essentially have no (or little) effect in either Japan or Korea. Before we interpret this disparity in patterns, it is worth asking whether it is somehow an artifact of how we are doing the analysis. One potentially relevant factor is the much larger geographic size of the U.S. While the difference in geographic size is exogenous to the processes being examined here, distance between the domiciles of the two generations is not exogenous. This makes the effects of distance difficult to investigate, and an instrumental variables approach is not suitable because we lack theoretically appropriate instrumental variables. Consequently, as a way to gain some insight, we have rerun the U.S. models, eliminating those who lived more than 250 miles from their parents (data not shown). Given the endogeneity of distance to the process being examined, this is not an entirely statistically or theoretically satisfactory solution. Nonetheless, it does provide some insight. When we performed this exercise in the model for wife's parents, three of the eight variables that had been statistically significant were no longer so. For the model for husband's parents, five of the seven previously significant variables lost statistical significance; however, all but one remained significant at the 10 percent level. While somewhat inconclusive, this suggests that the clear differences across the countries in our models are not totally a function of the countries' different sizes.

Another potential explanation is that the U.S. sample is approximately

Table 4.7 *Estimated Coefficients from Ordered Logistic Regression Predicting Personal Contact with Wife's Parents and Husband's Parents: Japan (1994), Korea (1994), and the U.S. (1988–1989)*

Predictor	WIFE'S PARENTS			HUSBAND'S PARENTS		
	Japan	*Korea*	*U.S.*	*Japan*	*Korea*	*U.S.*
Husband's age	-0.010	0.006	-0.135**	-0.091	-0.119	-0.175**
Husband's age squared	0.000	0.000	0.001*	0.001	0.001	0.002**
Respondent is female[a]	0.107	0.218	0.480**	-0.192	-0.477**	-0.334**
Husband-wife age difference	0.030	-0.037	0.016	0.034	-0.010	0.034**
Husband's education[b]						
Less than high school graduate	0.001	-0.097	-0.338*	-0.068	0.264	-0.200
Some college	0.094	-0.097	-0.468**	-0.263	0.237	-0.376**
College graduate or more	-0.038	0.118	-0.983**	-0.533**	-0.267	-0.835**
Missing data	-0.099	-0.127	-0.970*	0.061	1.288*	-0.708
Husband's education greater than wife's education	-0.021	-0.363**	0.209*	0.106	-0.152	0.200*
Cut point 1	-0.864	-0.017	-3.753	-2.586	-3.245	-4.652
Cut point 2	0.337	1.373	-2.787	-1.936	-2.174	-3.629
Model chi²	17.75	17.62	165.35	25.46	43.40	126.21
(d.f.)	(9)	(9)	(9)	(9)	(9)	(9)
(N)	(1,292)	(1,054)	(2,434)	(1,190)	(1,076)	(2,305)

Note: Respondents who are coresiding with parents are included and coded as seeing their parents frequently.

Reference categories:
[a] Respondent is male.
[b] High school graduate.

*Significant at p < .01.
**Significant at p < .05.

twice as large as those for Korea and Japan. To explore whether there are more statistically significant effects in the U.S. simply because of the larger sample size, we drew a 50 percent sample for the U.S. and reran the models. In each model (husband's and wife's parents), only one variable (husband's education greater than wife's education) changed from being significant to insignificant. Hence, the different pattern we find for the U.S. does not result from the larger size of the U.S. sample.

Accepting that the pattern of results across the three countries is generally reasonable, we also note that the pattern of effects in the U.S. is primarily as would be expected. The age effect is curvilinear, with the frequency of contact decreasing until about age 50 and then increasing afterward.[17] A turning point of around age 50 makes sense from a life-course perspective. By age 50, for many people, time commitments for raising children have diminished, and parents (or in-laws) are likely to be at an age and health status where they need some assistance.

In the results for the U.S., both husbands and wives see their own parents more often than their spouses do. A wife may often visit her parents without her husband being along. That there is an equally large effect for the reverse —husbands see their parents more often than their wives do—seems surpris-

Table 4.8 *Summary of Results from Ordered Logistic Regression Analysis of Factors Affecting Personal Contact with Parents*

Factor	WIFE'S PARENTS			HUSBAND'S PARENTS		
	Japan	*Korea*	*U.S.*	*Japan*	*Korea*	*U.S.*
Husband's age			— c			—
Husband's age squared			+ d			++
Respondent is female a			++ e		—	—
Husband-wife age difference						++
Husband's education b					++	++
Less than high school graduate			++			++
High school graduate			++	++	+	++
Some college			++		+	
Missing data						+
Husband's education greater than wife's education		—	+			

Reference categories:
a Respondent is male.
b College graduate or more.
c "—" indicates statistically significant negative coefficient with p < 0.01.
d "+" indicates statistically significant positive coefficient with p < 0.05.
e "++" indicates statistically significant positive coefficient with p < 0.01.

ing. Husbands who are five or more years older than their wives also see their own parents more often than their wives do.

College education in the U.S., especially graduation from college, is associated with lower personal contact with parents on both sides. This would be expected to the extent that training for a national job market results in greater distances from parents. Very likely for the same reason, we see in Japan a similar negative effect of education on the frequency of contact with husband's parents. In contrast, when we look at the discrepancy between the education of husbands and wives, the effects on contact are in opposite directions in Korea and the U.S. In Korea, contact with the wife's parents is lower when her husband has more education than she does, and this is probably a consequence of both greater traditionalism and greater male power in such couples. In the U.S., on the other hand, contact with both spouses' parents is more frequent when the wife has less education than her husband. One possible explanation of this pattern would be that a couple may stay closer to their parents when a wife is not in a national job market even though her husband is.

Table 4.9 adds to the model whether the husband is the eldest son and whether husbands and wives grew up in a rural area. The former is relevant only to Japan and Korea, and the latter is available only for these two countries. As we saw in table 4.5 on coresidence, the major factor affecting personal contact in Japan and Korea is whether or not the husband has older brothers. When the husband is the eldest son, personal contact with his parents is more frequent in both East Asian countries (but more so in Japan). In contrast, personal contact with the wife's parents is reduced among Japanese couples if he is the eldest son.

There are several significant effects of rural background on personal contact. These effects, however, are very scattered in direction and are different in the two countries, so we will not attempt to interpret them.

In addition to the generations seeing one another face-to-face, contact can be maintained by phone or correspondence. The Korean and U.S. surveys combined these two activities, whereas the Japanese survey asked only about contact by phone. It is much easier to phone than to write; we expect that phoning is the major component of this measure in Korea and the U.S., so we will refer only to contact by phone. Telephones are widely available in all three countries and affordable for all but the very poor.[18]

The frequency of phone contact with parents is shown in table 4.10, which is limited to respondents who are not living with their parents. Phone contact with the wife's parents is greatest in the U.S. and lowest in Japan. The pattern is somewhat similar for husband's parents, except that the U.S. and Korea are almost identical. Approximately one-half of the respondents in Japan who are not living with their parents talk on the telephone with the husband's parents less than once a month, compared to about one-fifth in Korea and the U.S.

Table 4.9 *Estimated Coefficients from Ordered Logistic Regression Predicting Personal Contact with Parents, Including Whether Husband Is Eldest Son and Size of Place of Residence during Childhood: Japan (1994) and Korea (1994)*

Predictor	WIFE'S PARENTS		HUSBAND'S PARENTS	
	Japan	Korea	Japan	Korea
Husband's age	-0.031	-0.009	0.006	-0.124
Husband's age squared	0.000	0.000	0.000	0.001
Respondent is female[a]	0.151	0.209	-0.246*	-0.468**
Husband-wife age difference	0.025	-0.003	0.032	-0.007
Husband is eldest son[b]	-0.214*	0.220	1.206**	0.643**
Rural-urban origins[c]				
Wife only rural	-0.946**	0.151	0.154	0.339
Husband only rural	0.092	0.717**	-0.591**	-0.259
Both urban	0.107	0.815**	-0.029	0.385*
Husband's education[d]				
Less than high school graduate	-0.018	0.084	-0.040	0.287
Some college	0.073	-0.039	-0.407	0.092
College graduate or more	-0.200	-0.075	-0.723**	-0.296
Missing data				
Husband's education greater than wife's education	-0.007	-0.243	0.152	-0.202
Cut point 1	-1.544	-0.021	0.084	-3.017
Cut point 2	-0.321	1.410	0.789	-1.910
Model chi²	56.03	51.33	148.65	85.28
(d.f.)	(13)	(13)	(13)	(13)
(N)	(1,282)	(1,037)	(1,182)	(1,061)

Note: Respondents who are coresiding with parents are included and coded as seeing their parents frequently.

Reference categories:
[a] Respondent is male.
[b] Husband not eldest son.
[c] Both wife and husband rural.
[d] High school graduate.

*Significant at $p < .01$.
**Significant at $p < .05$.

Given the emphasis on paternal linkages, it is surprising that a relatively high percentage of Japanese have such infrequent phone contact with their parents. It is, however, important to remember that almost two-fifths of Japanese couples live with the husband's parents. On the other hand, the other three-fifths do not. When couples are not living with the husband's parents, the husband is less likely to be the eldest son and hence may well have a brother who is living with his parents. This, in turn, may reduce the perceived need for frequent contact by phone.

Unlike the analysis of personal contact, the models predicting phone contact show more similarity across the three countries (see table 4.11). With the exception of a few scattered coefficients, education seems not to have a major effect in any of the countries. Age, on the other hand, is important in all the countries. The frequency of telephone contact decreases with the husband's age until about age 53 and then begins increasing again, reflecting the life-course stages of both parents and adult children.[19] There is a large difference between males and females in the U.S. in terms of which side of the family is contacted on the phone. Both husbands and wives are likely to talk to their own parents more often than their spouses do. For both Korea and Japan, we were able to look at more detailed models (not shown), like those in table 4.9 for personal contact. As might be expected in both countries, there is a statistically significant increase in the amount of telephone contact with the husband's parents when the husband is the eldest son. Somewhat surprisingly, we see that telephone contact with the wife's parents in Korea is more likely if both the husband and wife grew up in urban areas. We expected that if both

Table 4.10 *Percentage Distribution on Frequency of Telephone Contact with Wife's and Husband's Parents: Japan (1994), Korea (1994), and the U.S. (1987–1988)*

Frequency	Japan	Korea	U.S.
Wife's parents			
Less than once a month	30	22	28
1–3 times a month	38	41	24
More than 3 times a month	31	37	48
Total	100	100	100
(N)	(1,189)	(1,065)	(2,756)
Husband's parents			
Less than once a month	50	20	24
1–3 times a month	33	39	33
More than 3 times a month	17	42	44
Total	100	100	100
(N)	(764)	(838)	(2,573)

Table 4.11 Estimated Coefficients from Ordered Logistic Regression Predicting Telephone Contact with Wife's and Husband's Parents: Japan (1994), Korea (1994), and the U.S. (1987–1988)

Predictor	WIFE'S PARENTS			HUSBAND'S PARENTS		
	Japan	Korea	U.S.	Japan	Korea	U.S.
Husband's age	-0.230**	-0.160*	-0.110*	-0.240**	-0.169	-0.182**
Husband's age squared	0.002**	0.002	0.001	0.002*	0.002	0.002**
Respondent is female[a]	0.212	0.513	1.909*	0.124	-0.372**	-0.406**
Husband-wife age difference	0.046	-0.019	0.019	-0.003	-0.005	0.029**
Husband's education[b]						
Less than high school graduate	-0.232	-0.152	-0.317	-0.160	-0.191	-0.403*
Some college	0.446	0.196	-0.219	0.297	0.618*	-0.066
College graduate or more	0.496**	0.088	-0.099	0.348	-0.058	0.218
Missing data	-0.016	-0.574	-0.047	0.072	0.182	0.265
Husband's education greater than wife's education	-0.289	-0.411**	-0.186	-0.254	-0.142	-0.017
Cut point 1	-6.466	-5.274	-3.257	-5.950	-6.040	-5.538
Cut point 2	-4.785	-3.399	-1.999	-4.298	-4.214	-4.098
Model chi²	60.82	51.17	545.90	32.60	42.83	74.68
(d.f.)	(9)	(9)	(9)	(9)	(9)	(9)
(N)	(1,179)	(1,005)	(2,409)	(755)	(785)	(2,284)

Reference categories:
[a] Respondent is male.
[b] High school graduate.

*Significant at p < .01.
**Significant at p < .05.

spouses grew up in urban areas, there might be less pressure to adhere to traditional family values, especially when family change is in the earlier stages of transition, as it is in Korea.

Conclusion

The three countries examined here provide provocative material for a long-standing topic in our sociological and demographic understanding of the family, especially coresidence, personal contact (including both coresidence and visiting), and phoning—important behavioral aspects of relations between parents and their adult children. Throughout the twentieth century, sociologists, and more recently demographers, have debated the relative influence of cultural and structural factors. In terms of cultural, normative, and historical factors, Japan and Korea share a number of common characteristics likely to affect parent-adult child relationships; these characteristics, in turn, are quite different in many respects from characteristics in the U.S. This is not to say that the cultural factors are identical in Korea and Japan—they clearly are not. Rather, the point is that there are some important similarities when viewed in contrast to the U.S. The most prominent examples are a preference for coresidence and an emphasis on patrilineal relations.

Yet from a number of socioeconomic and demographic perspectives, Japan and the U.S. are more like one another, and Korea is more distinctive. Korea's mortality and fertility declines are more recent than either Japan's or those of the U.S. In Korea, the generation of middle-aged adults examined here has experienced all the dislocations and opportunities that go with a recent and rapid shift from an agricultural to a manufacturing and service economy, from a rural to an urban settlement pattern, and from a low level to a higher level of educational attainment. In the U.S. and Japan, these transitions occurred somewhat earlier, and it is expected that the timing and nature of these transitions would affect patterns of intergenerational relations.

Sorting out cultural and structural explanations is always difficult for a number of reasons. First, sociologists and demographers do a much better job measuring structural variables than cultural variables. Further, although cultural variation often exists across countries, there is frequently variation within a country as well, such as Quebec within Canada. Also, cultural boundaries often cross national borders, as with the similarities between the Germanic parts of Switzerland and Germany. Rarely do we have comparable surveys in a large enough number of countries to have a firm statistical grasp on cultural factors. In the present case, we have three countries, a number clearly insufficient to statistically analyze the effects of cultural factors. Nevertheless, our results provide insight into the roles of cultural and structural factors.

With respect to coresidence, Japan and Korea are clearly more like one another than either is like the U.S. The long-standing American preference for independence in old age is evident empirically. While other evidence suggests that there have been declines in coresidence in Japan and Korea (Atoh 1988; Byun 1996; Ogawa and Retherford 1997), both countries still have moderately high levels of paternal coresidence, especially compared to the U.S. There is also evidence that Japan is experiencing an increase in maternal coresidence. This is a trend that bears watching. It may or may not be linked to the prewar *ie* system, but it does suggest that the society is pushing for additional solutions in the face of constraints deriving from low fertility and the exigencies of the modern economy/job market.

Our examination of patterns of personal and telephone contact has suggested that both structural and cultural explanations are likely to be important, as would be expected. On the one hand, factors like age and education have little, if any, effect on the frequency with which parents are seen in Korea and Japan, but they have substantial effects in the expected direction in the U.S. Similarly, the husband's being the eldest son has the culturally prescribed effects in Japan and Korea. On the other hand, Korea and Japan are very dissimilar in patterns of telephone contact with the husband's parents.

Chapter Five

Investments in Children's Education, Desired Fertility, and Women's Employment

Noriko O. Tsuya and Minja Kim Choe

The belief that parents should invest heavily in after-school programs may be an important factor in the very low fertility in Japan and Korea. As noted in chapter 1, Japan's fertility has declined to below-replacement levels, with a particularly sharp decline since the mid-1980s. With some fluctuation in the early 1990s, fertility in Korea is also very low. The TFR in 1999 was 1.3 in Japan and 1.4 in Korea (National Institute of Population and Social Security Research 2002: 51; National Statistical Office 2000: 106). Why is fertility so low in Japan and Korea? Declines in Japan's fertility after the mid-1970s can statistically be attributed almost entirely to delayed marriage (Tsuya 2000; Tsuya and Mason 1995), as can around 40 percent of Korea's decline from 1980 to 1990 (Choe et al. 1995). However, it is possible that marriage is being delayed in order to postpone the costs and obligations of childbearing. Further, the costs of child rearing, particularly the demands of children's education, are likely reducing fertility within marriage.

In Japan and Korea, there are strong social and psychological pressures to provide children with a "good" education through admission to "good" schools, and this can be very costly. When asked why they work, Japanese wives most frequently have said "to pay for children's education" (Mainichi Shimbun Jinko Mondai Chosakai 1992: 288, 300, 315; Population Problems Research Council 1996: 49; Atoh 1992; Institute of Population Problems 1993: 24). The need to be employed to help pay for children's education can further increase the difficulty and stress of reconciling labor market and domestic roles (see chapter 7), producing yet another disincentive to additional childbearing. These costs and pressures are also argued to be chiefly responsible for very low levels of actual and desired fertility among Korean wives (Kwon 1993). Admittedly, the causal ordering between children's enrollment in after-school programs and wives' employment is unclear, as some employed mothers may enroll their children in after-school programs to obtain child care while they are working. Although causation undoubtedly runs in both directions, we believe that the need to invest in children's education is an important factor of wives' employment.

In this chapter, we examine how investments in children's after-school programs are related to both employment and desired fertility in Japan and Korea. We focus on these two East Asian countries because there is not a comparable concern in the U.S., and hence relevant data are not available. We begin with a brief overview of formal education and academic after-school programs, especially cram schools (*juku* in Japan and *kwa-oe* in Korea) and private tutoring (*katei-kyoshi* in Japan and *ka-jeong kyosa* in Korea). Although there is a great deal of public concern in Japan and Korea about the high costs of the excessive competition to enter good high schools and universities, there are few systematic evaluations of the sociodemographic implications of after-school programs.[1]

Formal Education and After-School Programs

Although parents in the U.S. regard education as important for their children's future, there is not the same obsession with children's academic success as in Japan and Korea.[2] Japanese and Korean parents are, in general, greater "stakeholders" in their children's life-course decisions than American parents (Brinton 1992) and play a much more active role in shaping major life-course transitions such as entry to higher education. This greater parental involvement in children's education is due in large part to the highly competitive, age-graded nature of the educational system in these two countries.

In contrast to the U.S. System, the educational systems in Japan and Korea are characterized by high levels of tracking, agreement on the hierarchy of universities (and even high schools), and rigidity in student admissions.[3] Ultimate importance is attached to getting into a university as high as possible up the hierarchy and, toward that goal, to successful entry into and completion of each stage on the educational ladder (Brinton 1990, 1992). Such success is seen as critical because educational failures cannot be made up at later ages. Thus, parents often feel compelled to invest heavily in children's after-school programs designed to prepare their children for entrance examinations.

Reflecting their Confucian backgrounds, education has traditionally been a source of high esteem in both Japan and Korea (Brinton 2001). Rapid industrialization and rising educational expectations in Japan after World War II have transformed this traditional emphasis into educational credentialism (Abelmann 1997; Hanley and Yamamura 1975; Rohlen 1980; Yamazaki et al. 1983). Thus, educational attainment (rather than learning per se) is strongly linked (or widely believed to be linked) to children's future careers, earning power, and overall social mobility. Educational credentialism became increasingly prevalent in Korea after the late 1970s (Brinton, Lee, and Parish 1995) and currently appears to be even stronger and more deeply entrenched than in Japan. For example, according to a study based on a small-scale survey in the Taegu area, a majority (58 percent) of the households with secondary school students had their children enrolled in some form of academic after-school programs, and household expenditures on such programs were significantly higher among couples who viewed education as a means for their children's social mobility (Y. S. Chung 1996).

Another important factor is that the system of compulsory education (to ninth grade) is often seen by parents as failing to provide the training necessary for competitive success. In Japan, because they are compulsory and mostly public, elementary and middle schools are based on a democratic ideal of egalitarianism and hence lack formal mechanisms for differentiating students.[4] There are no special programs for either the gifted or for those falling behind (Fukuzawa 1994; Rohlen 1980). Upon graduation from middle schools, however, children must take entrance examinations leading to hierarchically ranked high schools and then to even more extensively ranked universities. Thus, in the face of intense competition for entry to good universities, there is a substantial gap between the practices of formal educational institutions and the kind of education needed to prepare students for entrance examinations. After-school programs are used in the attempt to fill this gap.

In Korea, until the mid-1970s, secondary education had been a differentiated system with a small number of elite middle schools leading to an equally small number of elite high schools and ultimately to a few top universities. However, because of the increasing competition to enter elite middle schools, the Korean government abolished entrance exams for secondary schools in 1973–1975 and replaced them with a lottery within each local district.[5] While the new policy was aimed at equalizing secondary education across the country, this policy change resulted in the proliferation of enrollment in after-school programs, especially among high school students. As in Japan, many parents felt it necessary for their children to obtain additional training in order to pass university entrance exams. The government then banned after-school programs in 1980 because of concerns about the high costs that parents were bearing and because of a fear that the proliferation of such programs posed a threat to formal education. Despite the ban, however, the need for such programs remained, or even intensified, as increases in income made it possible for more parents to afford supplementary education. As a consequence, the government began to slowly relax the ban on after-school programs in the late 1980s. Secondary education in Korea remains largely egalitarian, as in Japan's middle schools, and this provides a clear niche for after-school programs.

Academic after-school programs are not unique to Japan and Korea, but their prevalence and the pragmatism of their approaches are notable. The primary purpose of these programs is to raise the likelihood of passing entrance examinations by giving children both intensive academic training and skills to "beat the system." Hence, there is intense competition to get into "good" after-school programs, which are assessed solely in terms of how well their students do in entrance exams, and good programs tend to be expensive. To our knowledge, there are no such well-developed after-school programs in the U.S. The closest example may be the programs that coach for college qualification examinations, such as the SATs, and these are designed primarily to teach skills for answering multiple choice questions.

Japanese and Korean parents feel a strong obligation to spend money and energy on children's after-school programs in order to help their children succeed—a burden that may well be contributing to reductions in desired (and actual) family size. As noted above with respect to reasons for mothers' employment, children's educational expenses were the reasons most frequently cited by Japanese women for having fewer children than they considered ideal (Institute of Population Problems 1993: 24).[6] We do not know of a nationally representative survey in Korea that directly inquired about reasons for wanting few children. Nonetheless, the deterring effect of educational expenses on desired fertility may be as serious in Korea as in Japan, if not more so. For example, Korea's largest national daily reported that the average proportion of educational expenses in household budgets was almost twice that in Japan and that the rate of increase was much more rapid than in Japan (*Digital Chosunilbo* 1997).

Data and Measures

Data

This chapter uses data from the 1994 Japanese survey and, in the analysis of desired fertility, the 1994 Korean survey. Because the 1994 Korean survey did not collect information on children's enrollment in after-school programs, however, our analyses of investments in children's after-school programs and mother's employment draw on data from the 1989 Survey on Family Life Cycle. Conducted by the KIHASA, the 1989 survey included information on enrollment of school-aged children in after-school programs, as well as on marriage, fertility, employment, family roles, and attitudes toward family life (for specifics, see Kong et al. 1990).[7]

Our comparative analysis does not include the U.S. because the NSFH did not ask about children's academic after-school programs. As noted in the previous section, academic after-school programs exist in the U.S. but are either limited to specific time periods (such as before the SATs) or are remedial for children who are not doing well in school.

The analysis of desired fertility is limited to wives under age 45, whereas that of children's enrollment in after-school programs is based on school-aged children (ages 6–18) of currently married female respondents aged 20–59.[8] There are 1,504 school-aged children in the 1994 Japanese survey, and there are 3,277 school-aged children in the 1989 Korean survey. Although some children under age 6 or those over age 18 are enrolled in cram schools or after-school private tutoring, such cases are rare—only about 6 percent of those enrolled in after-school programs in Japan. The Korean survey asked about cram school enrollment only for children attending primary and secondary schools.

Dependent Variables

We examine three dependent variables: desired fertility, parental investments in children's after-school programs, and women's employment. The 1994 Japanese and 1994 Korean surveys both asked whether the respondent wanted to have a(nother) child, with five precoded responses—definitely yes, probably yes, uncertain, probably not, and definitely not. We use two alternative measures of desired fertility, which differ in how the "uncertain" responses are coded. In Japan, 19 percent of wives under age 45 and 24 percent of husbands in the same age group gave an indefinite response; the corresponding proportion was 9 percent for both women and men in Korea. In our first measure—the "high" estimate—those who were undecided are categorized as *wanting* a child, as is often done in developing countries (Bongaarts 1990). Our second measure, the "low" estimate, treats all of those who were "uncertain" as *not wanting* any more children. Being "uncertain" is often an intermediate stage between wanting an additional birth and deciding not to have any more children (Morgan 1982), and it is likely that the best estimate of desired fertility lies somewhere between these two extremes.

Using these alternative assumptions about "uncertain" responses, we constructed the Wanted Total Marital Fertility Rate (WTMFR) and the wanted family size distribution. The WTMFR measures a hypothetical level of marital fertility that would be achieved if all wives who wanted to have more children were to do so and those who did not want to have any more children stopped at their current parity (number of children born already).[9] The wanted family size distribution, on which the WTMFR is based, is estimated by adjusting for differences between the observed proportions wanting another child at each parity, and the actual period parity progression ratios.

Investment in children's education is measured by a dichotomous variable based on whether or not each school-aged child is enrolled in an academic after-school program. The 1994 Japanese survey asked respondents for the age and sex of all children and for the ages of children who were enrolled in cram schools or private tutoring. Thus, matching the responses to these two questions, we can measure the number, age, and sex of children enrolled in these academic after-school programs. In the 1989 Korean survey, children's enrollment in after-school programs was measured by a set of questions asking respondents to list only children who were enrolled in primary or secondary school and then to identify whether or not each child was in a cram school or private tutoring after school. Thus, for Korea, we have information on enrollments in after-school programs only for primary or secondary school students, but there is no information on their exact age and sex or on children who are not enrolled in primary or secondary schools.

Women's employment is measured in Japan as follows: not employed, employed part-time (1–34 hours per week), or employed full-time (35 or more hours). The 1989 Korean survey asked only whether a woman was "employed" or a "full-time homemaker." As discussed in chapter 6, only a small proportion of wives is employed in Korea, and most of the employment is full-time because opportunities for part-time employment are very limited.

Independent and Control Variables for Multivariate Analysis

The likelihood of enrollment of school-aged children in cram schools or private tutoring is examined with binary logistic regression models using three groups of predictor variables: children's own characteristics, characteristics of their siblings, and their parents' socioeconomic status. Children's own characteristics include schooling level, place of residence, and, for Japan, sex and birth order. Prior studies of cram school enrollments have found differences by these characteristics (Monbusho 1985; Rohlen 1980). The categories of schooling used are elementary school, middle school, and high school. Residence consists of three categories: large metropolitan cities of 1 million or more in Japan and Seoul in Korea, smaller cities, and rural areas. Eldest sons are distinguished from other sons and daughters. Sibling characteristics include the number of school-aged siblings (ages 6–18), whether the index child has at least one sibling of preschool age (under age 6), and whether the child has at least one sibling over age 18.

Mother's education is included as a proxy for the educational aspirations of the children, and father's income represents the financial resources available. Mother's education is measured in Japan by a categorical variable: middle school or less; high school; junior college or post–high school professional training school; and four-year college or higher. Father's 1993 income is included as a continuous variable. For Korea, mother's education is measured by the number of years of education, and father's education is included as a proxy for his income since the 1989 Korean survey did not ask a question on income. As would be expected, the 1994 Korean survey reveals a strong correlation between the two.

Desired Fertility

Table 5.1 shows the proportion of women under age 45 at each parity who want to have another birth. We look first at the proportions saying that they are uncertain whether or not they wish to have another child. Compared to Korea, the proportion uncertain is much higher in Japan, and this is true for both women and men at every family size. Moreover, uncertainty is notably high among those with two children—the most sizable group—suggesting that the degree of ambivalence about future family formation is clearly higher in Japan than in Korea.

Nonetheless, the proportion uncertain is substantial in both countries, and the conclusions to be reached about desired fertility depend heavily on how we interpret this response. If we assume that those who say that they are uncertain are inclined to have another child, many mothers with two children would like to have a third (38 percent in Japan and 25 percent in Korea). This proportion is even higher among mothers under age 40 with two children—46 percent in Japan and 27 percent in Korea. It would indeed be remarkable if, in these two countries with very low fertility, such high proportions want to have more than two children. These estimates, however, are based on an extreme assumption about the meaning of "uncertain" responses.

If, on the other hand, being uncertain is a transitional stage in the process

Table 5.1 *Percentage Distribution on Whether Another Child Is Wanted, by Parity: Currently Married Women and Men under Age 45, Japan (1994) and Korea (1994)*

Desire for Children	TOTAL	DISTRIBUTION BY PARITY			
		0	1	2	3+
Japanese women					
Want more	30.1	70.0	67.3	14.5	8.0
Uncertain	19.3	16.7	16.2	23.1	17.0
No more	50.6	13.3	16.5	62.4	75.0
(N)	(508)	(60)	(101)	(234)	(113)
Japanese men					
Want more	36.9	80.4	72.1	23.0	12.5
Uncertain	23.7	13.5	17.9	31.8	17.9
No more	39.4	6.1	10.0	45.2	69.6
(N)	(426)	(46)	(86)	(204)	(90)
Korean women					
Want more	30.0	83.0	53.3	18.2	4.7
Uncertain	9.0	10.5	13.0	6.3	7.7
No more	61.0	6.5	33.7	75.5	87.6
(N)	(630)	(53)	(148)	(324)	(105)
Korean men					
Want more	39.7	82.0	67.2	24.3	9.5
Uncertain	9.0	11.0	9.2	10.1	8.8
No more	51.4	7.0	23.6	65.6	81.7
(N)	(531)	(49)	(136)	(284)	(63)

Note: Percentages for Korea are weighted; the numbers of cases are unweighted.

of deciding not to have another child (Morgan 1982), then it is more appropriate to regard "uncertain" responses as indicating that no more children are desired. Under this assumption, the level of desired fertility is much lower and more similar between the two countries—less than 20 percent of women with two children would like to have another child. Comparing desired levels of fertility between Japan and Korea obviously depends heavily on which of the two assumptions seems most plausible. Both Korean men and women are more likely than the Japanese to say that they want no more children. Further, it is noteworthy that Koreans are considerably more certain than Japanese about how many children they want.

Table 5.2 presents the two alternative estimates of the WTMFR based on these "high" and "low" estimates of desired fertility, together with the wanted family size distribution. As we can see from the table, even based on the "high" estimate, the level of desired fertility for Japanese wives is low (WTMFR = 1.96 per woman), and it is even lower in Korea (WTMFR = 1.73). The "low" estimate is very low and essentially identical in the two countries—1.42 in Japan and 1.49 in Korea.

In order to put the WTMFR estimates of desired fertility in the context of actual fertility, we look at the parity progression based Total Marital Fertility Rates (TMFR$_{ppr}$).[10] Based on period parity progression ratios of married women in 1990, the TMFR$_{ppr}$ is 1.93 per woman in Japan and 1.90 per woman in Korea. Comparing these with the estimates of WTMFR, we can see that the "high" estimate of desired fertility is about the same as marital fertility in Japan and somewhat lower than marital fertility in Korea. As we have noted, these estimates undoubtedly bracket the true level of desired fertility. The implication of this is that desired fertility is very likely lower than the levels currently experienced among married women, especially in Korea. To the extent that desired fertility is closer to the "low" estimate, these numbers suggest the possibility of very low marital fertility in the future for both countries. If only women who are certain that they want another child were to have it (and they were to follow the parity-specific pattern of wanted fertility in 1994), roughly one-half of married women would have fewer than two children (see the "low" estimates columns of table 5.2).

We can also see that the level of fertility wanted by men is somewhat higher than that for women in both countries (see tables 5.1 and 5.2). This result is as expected. Though the financial costs and time pressures associated with children's education are no doubt felt by both parents, it is overwhelmingly the mother who has the chief obligation for raising children on a day-to-day basis and who is primarily responsible for children's academic success (Brinton 1990; Kwon 1993; Moon 1990). The costs and stress associated with educating children may be among the key factors contributing to the low level of desired fertility in Japan and Korea.

Table 5.2 *Estimated Mean and Distribution on WTMFR under Two Different Assumptions about Responses of "Uncertain":
Currently Married Women and Men under Age 45, Japan (1994) and Korea (1994)*

| | HIGH ESTIMATE[a] | | | | | LOW ESTIMATE[b] | | | | |
| | WTMFR[c] | Percentage Distribution of Wanted Family Size | | | | WTMFR[c] | Percentage Distribution of Wanted Family Size | | | |
Respondents		0	1	2	3+		0	1	2	3+
Japan										
Women	1.96	13	13	46	28	1.42	30	11	49	11
Men	2.23	6	15	39	40	1.65	20	17	47	17
Korea										
Women	1.73	6	30	45	20	1.49	17	32	37	14
Men	1.94	7	18	49	26	1.67	18	17	46	19

[a] Assumes that all persons who are "uncertain" want another child.

[b] Assumes that all persons who are "uncertain" want no more children.

[c] Based on the proportions of men and women of given parity who want more children, adjusted for the differences between these proportions and actual period progression ratios. Estimates are based on the 1994 Japanese and Korean surveys. For specifics of the measure, see Kulkarni and Choe (1998).

After-School Programs and Investments in Children's Education

Patterns of Enrollment in After-School Programs

The percentages of children aged 6–18 enrolled in a cram school or private tutoring is reported in table 5.3 for Japan in 1994 and for Korea in 1989. The proportion enrolled increases notably in Japan from elementary school (28 percent) to middle school (53 percent) and then drops at high school (17 percent). When examined by single years of age, the enrollment rate in Japan increases rapidly and steadily from fourth grade, peaking at 59 percent at

Table 5.3 *Percentage of School-Aged Children of Currently Married Women under Age 60 Who Are Enrolled in After-School Programs, by Children's Education Level and Residence: Japan (1994) and Korea (1989)*

Characteristic	Japan	Korea
Total	33.5	19.8
Child's education level [a]		
Elementary school	28.0	23.0
Middle school	53.3	17.0
High school	16.6	16.9
Residence		
Large metropolitan city [b]	40.6	25.8
Smaller city	33.8	20.2
Rural area	28.0	15.4
Child's residence and education		
Large metropolitan city		
Elementary school	30.2	30.4
Middle school	68.9	24.9
High school	27.3	17.6
Smaller city		
Elementary school	28.9	20.9
Middle school	53.0	20.6
High school	16.9	18.2
Rural area		
Elementary school	23.6	19.3
Middle school	45.8	9.1
High school	8.9	15.4
(N)	(1,583)	(3,277)

[a] For Japan, ages 6–12, 13–15, and 16–18 are considered as ages at elementary school, middle school, and high school respectively. For Korea, information on exact ages is unavailable, but the level of schooling is available and used for computation.

[b] For Japan this category includes cities with a population of one million or more; for Korea it includes only Seoul.

ninth grade, at about age 15 (data not shown). This age pattern of enrollment in Japan is as expected. As the time for entrance examinations for high schools approaches, the perceived necessity of academic after-school programs probably becomes more intense for both parents and children. While an admission to one of the nation's top universities remains the ultimate goal, entry to an elite high school is a crucial prerequisite for that objective.

Contrary to our expectation, the percentage of Korean children enrolled in after-school programs drops from elementary to middle school and stays at around the same level for high school. The reported rate of enrollment in after-school programs is conspicuously low among children in middle school. The surprisingly low enrollment of middle school students in Korea may be due to the abolition of entrance examinations for high school (in effect since the mid-1970s). It is also likely that enrollment was underreported in the context of rules banning such programs. After-school programs were still illegal when the 1989 survey was conducted. Given this situation, mothers of secondary school students may have felt hesitant to report their children's enrollment in such programs.

The rate of enrollment in after-school programs is considerably higher in cities than in rural areas in both Japan and Korea, and it is especially high in large metropolitan cities in Japan, where roughly 70 percent of middle school children are enrolled.[11] We cannot tell whether preferences for after-school programs are greater in large cities or whether such preferences simply reflect their greater availability in these areas. In any event, after-school programs are widespread in Japan's urban population.

Factors Associated with Enrollment in After-School Programs

Table 5.4 presents the adjusted probabilities of enrollment in after-school programs for a number of relevant variables. These adjusted probabilities were estimated from a logistic regression in which the values of the other covariates were set at their means. Descriptive statistics and estimated coefficients are presented in the appendix tables of this chapter.

The multivariate results are similar to the bivariate patterns. Specifically, we see in table 5.4 a sharp contrast between the two countries in that all but one of these variables have statistically significant effects on enrollment in Japan but only one (mother's education) does so in Korea. Consequently, the following discussion of effects will focus on Japan except in the case of mother's education, which is also significant in Korea. The probability of enrollment doubles among Japanese children between elementary and middle school and then declines sharply among high school students. As expected, urban residence, especially residence in a large metropolitan area, is positively associated with enrollment in after-school programs.

Most important, contrary to our expectations, there are only very small (and nonsignificant) differences between eldest sons and other sons or daughters

Table 5.4 *Adjusted Probabilities of Children's Enrollment in After-School Programs: Japan (1994) and Korea (1989)*

	PROBABILITY OF ENROLLMENT	
Characteristic	Japan	Korea
Child's education level		
Elementary school†	0.26	0.20
Middle school	0.53**	0.17#
High school	0.16**	0.17#
Residence		
Large metropolitan city	0.38**	0.20
Smaller city	0.31#	0.19
Rural area†	0.26	0.18
Sex and birth order		
Eldest son	0.33	—
Younger son	0.30	—
Daughter†	0.29	—
Number of school-aged siblings		
Zero	0.36*	0.20
One	0.31*	0.19
Two	0.27*	0.18
At least one sibling of preschool age		
No†	0.32	—
Yes	0.26#	—
At least one sibling aged 18+		
No†	0.33	—
Yes	0.26#	—
Mother's education		
Elementary school	—	0.16**
Middle school	0.19†	0.21**
High school	0.29*	0.27**
Junior college or equivalent[a]	0.40**	—
Four-year college or more	0.38**	0.37**[b]
Father's income in 1993		
2 million yen	0.25**	—
4 million yen	0.28**	—
6 million yen	0.31**	—
8 million yen	0.35**	—
10 million yen	0.39**	—
12 million yen	0.43**	—

(continued on next page)

Table 5.4 (continued) *Adjusted Probabilities of Children's Enrollment in After-School Programs: Japan (1994) and Korea (1989)*

	PROBABILITY OF ENROLLMENT	
Characteristic	Japan	Korea
Father's education		
Elementary school	—	0.18
Middle school	—	0.19
High school	—	0.19
Four-year college or more	—	0.20
(N)	(1,583)	(3,277)

Note: Adjusted probability is predicted by logistic regression, with the values of the other variables in the model set at their mean values. The model for Japan includes, as the covariates, age category of school-aged children, mother's education, father's income, and number of children. The model for Korea includes the age category of school-aged children, mother's education, father's education, urban/rural residence, and number of children. A dagger (†) indicates a reference category.

[a] Includes advanced technical school and post–high school professional training school.
[b] Includes only women with four-year college education.

*Significant at p < .01.
**Significant at p < .05.
#Significant at p < .10.

in Japan. Given the traditions of strong son preference and high values placed on eldest sons in Korea (Kwon 1993), we expect that these differences may well be larger in Korea. Unfortunately, however, we do not have these variables for Korea. The number and ages of siblings do affect enrollment in after-school programs in Japan. The probability of enrollment of the index child decreases significantly with the number of preschool-aged siblings and with the presence of a sibling over age 18, probably reflecting increasing competition for family resources.

Mother's education has a very large effect on enrollment in after-school programs in Japan. Moreover, mother's education is the only variable that is significant in Korea, and the effect is similar in Japan and Korea. In both countries, the adjusted probability of enrollment of children of college-educated mothers is twice that of mothers with only a middle school education. As in the U.S. (Kuo and Hauser 1996), a more highly educated woman's own experience is likely to increase her appreciation of the benefits of education for her children's future in the two East Asian countries and hence have a major effect on her aspirations for, and determination to invest heavily in, her children's education.

Father's income is available only for Japan, and it is significantly and positively associated with the probability of children's enrollment in after-school programs, suggesting the importance of financial resources for enrollment in such programs.[12] It is an important contrast that father's education has no statistically significant effect in Korea. We would have expected some effects because of its high correlation with income and because of effects on fathers' aspirations for their children.[13]

Women's Employment and Family Responsibilities

The strong pressure and high costs that many Japanese and Korean parents have to bear in order to educate their children may also compel married women to seek employment outside the home. As noted above, given the absence of longitudinal data, the causal ordering between children's enrollment in after-school programs and mother's employment is uncertain, as employed mothers may enroll their children in such programs as a way to obtain child care. Despite this potential endogeneity, however, we do believe that the cost of after-school education is likely to have an important effect on wives' employment. As noted, concern with paying for children's education has been the reason most frequently cited by Japanese women for why they are employed. After-school programs are usually expensive, and families often need the second source of income to pay for them.

We have not found national studies for Korea on the relationship between investments in children's education and mother's employment. However, a recent study based on a small-scale survey in the Taegu area found that about 35 percent of the mothers of secondary school students were employed. Further, it was the wife's income, rather than the husband's, that was positively associated with the likelihood of their children's enrollment in after-school programs, especially expensive ones (Chung and Choe 2001). Thus, whereas only a minority of Korean mothers of school-aged children works in the labor market (see chapter 6), if they do so, it may often be to pay for their children's after-school programs.

Given that Japanese and Korean wives are responsible for maintaining the home, employment can add further stress to the balancing of economic and domestic responsibilities and often result in a "double shift" (Tsuya and Bumpass 1998; also chapter 7). This is another path through which children's enrollment in after-school programs may reduce both desired and actual fertility. Because the rate of employment among Japanese wives is much higher than among Korean wives (57 versus 26 percent), the potential fertility impact of the cost of children's extracurricular education is likely to be greater in Japan. On the other hand, the extremely limited opportunities for part-time employment for Korean mothers could accentuate the effect on fertility, as many must remain at home and not have extra income that might be applied to their children's education.

Table 5.5 shows the distribution on women's employment by the number of school-aged children and whether they are enrolled in an after-school program. The results differ markedly between Korea and Japan. While we find the expected patterns in Japan, we do not do so in Korea. Japanese women

Table 5.5 *Percentage Distribution of Women's Employment Status by Number of School-Aged Children and Their Cram School Enrollment Status: Currently Married Women under Age 60 Who Have at Least One Child, Japan (1994) and Korea (1989)*

| Characteristic | WOMEN'S EMPLOYMENT STATUS | | | |
	No Work	Part-Time	Full-Time	(N)
Japan				
No school-aged child	44.4	19.4	36.2	(423)
One school-aged child	41.3	28.7	29.9	(167)
Not enrolled in cram school	43.4	27.4	29.3	(106)
Enrolled in cram school	37.7	31.2	31.2	(61)
Two school-aged children	35.3	31.3	33.3	(198)
Neither enrolled	38.4	32.3	29.3	(99)
At least one enrolled	32.3	30.3	37.4	(99)
Three or more school-aged children	34.4	23.0	42.6	(61)
None enrolled	37.0	22.2	40.7	(27)
At least one enrolled	32.4	23.5	44.1	(34)
All women with at least one school-aged child	37.6	29.1	33.3	(426)
None enrolled	40.5	28.9	30.6	(232)
At least one enrolled	34.0	29.4	36.6	(194)
Korea[a]				
No school-aged child	89.6		10.4	(996)
One school-aged child	84.6		15.4	(493)
Not enrolled in cram school	84.5		15.5	(394)
Enrolled in cram school	84.1		15.2	(99)
Two school-aged children	82.3		17.7	(547)
Neither enrolled	81.7		18.3	(387)
At least one enrolled	83.7		16.3	(160)
Three or more school-aged children	82.7		17.3	(527)
None enrolled	78.8		21.9	(354)
At least one enrolled	90.8		9.2	(173)
All women with at least one school-aged child	83.2		16.8	(1,567)
None enrolled	81.8		18.2	(1,135)
At least one enrolled	86.8		13.2	(432)

Note: Cram school enrollment includes children who have a private tutor coming to the home after school.

[a] Figures for Korea indicate whether women are employed or not. The 1989 Korean survey did not collect information on women's employment hours/types to distinguish part-time and full-time employment.

with a child enrolled in a cram school are about 6 percentage points more likely to be employed than those who do not, and there is a similar difference between those who have two or more children and those with only one child. Full-time employment accounts for virtually all of these differences. (The one exception is that the proportion working part-time appears to drop off sharply among those with three or more children compared to those with fewer, but this estimate is based on a rather small number of cases.) We do not see, however, an interaction between these two variables—that is, the effects of each are approximately the same within categories of the other. These findings suggest that the costs associated with having two or more school-aged children or having one child enrolled in a cram school do increase women's employment.

By contrast, enrollment in after-school programs does not appear to be associated with women's employment in Korea, with the exception of those with three or more school-aged children. Further, among these women with a relatively large family, children's enrollment in after-school programs is *negatively* associated with their employment. These women tend to be older and less educated than women with smaller families. Once we control for women's age, education, residence, and husband's education, the negative association between women's employment and children's enrollment disappears (data not shown). All together, these results suggest that in Korea, unlike in Japan, mother's employment is unrelated to children's enrollment in after-school programs.

Conclusion

Desired fertility among married women is low in Japan and even lower in Korea. Further, women want fewer children than men in both countries. Even though a substantial proportion of women with two children said that they wanted to have more children, the conclusion to be reached about desired fertility depends on how we interpret the substantial proportion of "uncertain" responses. The level of desired marital fertility based on the "high" estimate is roughly consistent with the level of actual marital fertility in Japan and below the level of marital fertility in Korea. Even based on this "high" estimate, Japanese and Korean wives desire small families. However, this estimate is indeed likely to be high, so current levels of marital fertility are higher than desired in both countries.

We have also argued that a potentially important factor for the low levels of desired fertility in both countries is the heavy costs and pressures felt by parents, especially mothers, to successfully educate their children. For many, this perceived obligation results in large investments in education, especially in after-school programs, because the compulsory education system in both countries has so far failed to provide children with the kind of training seen as necessary for competitive success.

The proportion of Japanese children enrolled in after-school programs is highest at age 15 (ninth grade). Compared to Japan, the rate of enrollment of Korean middle school students is unexpectedly low, either as a result of the elimination of entrance exams for high schools or because of underreporting. Further, enrollment varies little in Korea with the variables considered with the exception of mother's education. We do find the expected patterns, however, in Japan. There the level of after-school program enrollment is especially high in large metropolitan areas, either as a result of greater pressure for educational achievement in cities or the greater accessibility of such programs in big cities compared to rural areas.

Mother's education has a pronounced effect on children's enrollment in after-school programs in both countries: children whose mothers have completed college are twice as likely to be enrolled, compared to those whose mothers had only a middle school education. Because educational attainment, especially that of women, has been rapidly and steadily increasing in both Japan and Korea (see chapter 1), parental investments in after-school programs may increase further.

The high costs that Japanese and Korean parents face in order to educate their children may have compelled many mothers to seek employment outside the home. Consistent with this expectation, we find that Japanese mothers are indeed more likely to be employed if they have a child enrolled in an after-school program and also if they have two or more school-aged children. In Korea, however, children's enrollment was not generally associated with mother's employment, due probably to the lack of suitable employment opportunities for married women that would allow them to combine work and family responsibilities, as documented in chapter 6.

All together, our findings suggest that the systems of education and after-school programs in Japan and Korea may provide a dampening effect on women's desired fertility and, by implication, on actual marital fertility. Given the declines in the college-age population (which started in Japan in the early 1990s and at the end of the 1990s in Korea), one might speculate that the problems associated with excessive competition to pass entrance exams, and therefore the need for high parental investments in after-school programs, might be reduced.[14] Despite the these declines, however, the competition for prestigious schools may even intensify. As argued by Becker (1981), the trade-off between the quantity and quality of children could increase aspirations for "higher quality" children as the number of children declines. Existing evidence seems to suggest that this may be the case, at least in Japan.

The normative expectation that mothers are responsible for children's educational success through proper care and supervision is deeply rooted in the Confucian cultural heritage (Brinton 2001). Motherhood has been held in high esteem in the face of a strict gender division of labor and the low status of women in society at large (Tsuya and Choe 1991). This makes family relations in Japan and Korea less responsive to rapid socioeconomic changes than is the case in the West. As the employment of wives increases, they are increasingly faced with the burden of balancing economic roles and family responsibilities. The stress and financial costs of having children might be reduced if the formal education system were to become more flexible and if the home were to become more egalitarian, with children less the mother's sole responsibility. In the absence of such changes, however, an increase in fertility seems most unlikely. Indeed, it is possible that current desired fertility presages further declines in marital fertility.

Appendix

Table 5.A1 *Descriptive Statistics for Variables Used in Logistic Regression Analysis of Children's Enrollment in After-School Programs: Japan (1994) and Korea (1989)*

| | JAPAN | | KOREA | |
Variable	*Mean*	*S.D.*	*Mean*	*S.D.*
Level of schooling				
Middle school (ages 13–15)	0.32	0.47	0.26	0.44
High school (ages 16–18)	0.24	0.43	0.26	0.44
(Ref.: elementary school, ages 6–12)				
Residence				
Large metropolitan city	0.16	0.37	0.25	0.44
Smaller city	0.59	0.49	0.38	0.48
(Ref.: rural area)				
Sex and birth order				
Eldest son	0.35	0.48	—	—
Younger son	0.17	0.38	—	—
(Ref.: daughter)				
Sibling characteristics				
Number of school-aged siblings	1.07	0.76	1.53	0.98
Has a preschool-aged sibling	0.15	0.36	—	—
Has a sibling over age 18	0.25	0.43	—	—
Mother's education				
High school	0.53	0.50	—	—
Junior college or equivalent[a]	0.29	0.45	—	—
Four-year college or more	0.06	0.24	—	—
(Ref.: middle school or less)				
Years of education	—	—	7.85	3.86
Father's economic status				
Income in 1993 (in million yen)	5.77	2.75	—	—
Years of education	—	—	9.92	5.67

[a] Includes advanced technical school and post–high school professional training school.

Table 5.A2 *Estimated Coefficients from Logistic Regression Predicting Children's Enrollment in After-School Programs: Japan (1994) and Korea (1989)*

Predictor	Japan	Korea
Constant	-1.91**	-2.34**
Level of schooling		
Middle school (ages 13–15)	1.19**	-0.22#
High school (ages 16–18)	-0.58**	-0.21#
Residence		
Large metropolitan city	0.52**	0.16
Smaller city	0.24#	0.07
Sex and birth order		
Eldest son	0.18	—
Younger son	0.03	—
Sibling characteristics		
Number of school-aged siblings	-0.21*	-0.04
Has a preschool-aged sibling	-0.31#	—
Has a sibling over age 18	-0.34#	—
Mother's education		
High school	0.56*	—
Junior college or equivalent	1.08**	—
Four-year college or more	1.01**	—
Years of education	—	0.11**
Father's economic status		
Income in 1993	0.08**	—
Years of education	—	0.01
Log likelihood	-891.56	-1,569.61
Chi^2 (d.f.)	235.30 (13)	125.39 (7)
Prob > chi^2	0.000	0.000
(N)	(1,583)	(3,277)

* Significant at $p < .01$.
** Significant at $p < .05$.
\# Significant at $p < .10$.

Chapter Six

Employment

Minja Kim Choe, Larry L. Bumpass, and Noriko O. Tsuya

The increasing employment of married women outside the home has been one of the most dramatic changes in the industrialized world after World War II. Both Japan and the U.S. have witnessed the influx of married women into paid employment in the postwar decades (Bianchi and Casper 2000; Shimada and Higuchi 1985; Tsuya 1992). Although employment among Korean women remains low, it has increased in recent years among both married and unmarried young women but has changed little among older women (Cho et al. 1997; Hong et al. 1994; Yi et al. 1996). Thus, it seems likely that Korea may be on a similar upward trajectory in the employment of married women, though some evidence in this chapter suggests that the labor market conditions may be more limiting than in the U.S. or Japan.

In this chapter, we compare the patterns of employment among married women and men across Japan, Korea, and the U.S. Specifically, we examine employment status and working hours of wives, as well as working hours of husbands and related differences in commuting time and the time of day when wives and husbands return home from work. Because some of the major changes are those in gender roles associated with wives' employment (Bianchi and Spain 1986, 1996; Goldscheider and Waite 1991; Waite 1981), we focus much of our discussion on wives, including the preferences of both husbands and wives concerning whether wives should work. Because the employment of married women is closely related to their husbands' employment and their own family responsibilities, it must be examined in the context of these factors. Throughout, we examine the comparative effects of a range of family and socioeconomic factors thought important to the employment of married women. While we have examined multivariate models, we present mostly observed percentages and numbers to simplify presentation.[1] The multivariate results are noted only when they reveal substantially different results from those seen in the observed differences.

Measures

Dependent Variables

Three sets of dependent variables are examined: (1) wives' employment and the employment hours of both husbands and wives; (2) commuting time and the time of day when husbands and wives come home from work; and (3) the preferences of both husbands and wives about wives' employment. Wives' employment status is coded simply in terms of whether a wife is employed or not; we do not examine this for husbands because the vast majority of husbands in all three countries is employed. The usual hours of employment per week are examined as a continuous variable.

For the U.S., NSFH1 was used because its questions on employment hours were most comparable to those in Japan and Korea. The exception is the analysis of preferences for wives' employment, for which the NSFH2 was used, owing to the lack of comparable data in NSFH1. Because the 1994 Japanese survey (NSWFL) measured employment hours as a categorical variable, employment hours for Japanese wives and husbands were estimated by imputing the midpoint of each category. Exceptions were the category of 35–41 hours and that of 60 hours and more per week, for which the values of 39 and 66 hours were assigned respectively, based on data from the 1993 Japanese national wage structure survey.[2] The 1994 Korean survey (NSQFL) asked about hours worked on a workday. Hence, we computed the weekly employment hours for Korea by multiplying the hours spent per day on employment by 5.5 (estimating that the regular workdays in the country total 5.5 days per week).[3]

Commuting time is a critical component that is often ignored in considerations of the potential effects of employment on family life. All three surveys collected information on the number of minutes needed to commute one way. The Japanese and Korean surveys also asked about the usual time of day when the respondent returned home for work, although this was not asked in the U.S. survey.

Preferred employment hours for self and spouse were asked in both the U.S. and Japan.[4] Although a similar question was included in Korea, it was addressed only to employed persons. Hence, we compare only Japan and the U.S. on this item because only about one-quarter of Korean wives were employed and we therefore do not have data on preferred employment hours for a large majority of female respondents. Given the importance of wives' employment for family life and gender roles, we focus simply on preferences that wives *not* be employed as reported by husbands and wives themselves.

Independent and Control Variables

Given the persistence of traditional gender role expectations, the presence and ages of children have major effects on women's employment (e.g., Bianchi and Spain 1986; Brinton 1988; Sweet 1970; Tsuya 1992; Waite 1981). We have coded the age of the youngest child into three categories: preschool age (0–6 for Japan and Korea, 0–4 for the U.S.); school age (7–17 for Japan and Korea, 5–17 for the U.S.); and no child under age 18.

The role conflict between motherhood and employment may be reduced when mothers share a household with parents or have parents nearby since the grandmother is a potential source of child care and other household assistance (Casper, Hawkins, and O'Connell 1991; Martin and Tsuya 1992; Morgan and Hirosima 1983; Tsuya 1992). We have coded proximity to parents into three categories: (1) coresidence with at least one parent or parent-in-law; (2) not living with parents/parents-in-law but at least one parent/parent-in-law living nearby (in same neighborhood for Japan and Korea, within three miles of respondent's residence for the U.S.); and (3) all others, including those with no surviving parents/parents-in-law. Given that an extremely small percentage of married couples in the U.S. live with their parents at any time, the first two categories are grouped together for the U.S.

We use four categories for place of residence in the U.S. and Japan: large metropolitan cities (with population of 1 million and above), medium-sized cities (with population of 100,000 or more), small cities (with population less than 100,000), and rural areas. Since Seoul is the only large metropolitan city in Korea, we used three categories for Korea: Seoul, other cities (classified as medium-sized cities), and rural areas.

Education is classified the same for Japan and the U.S.: less than high school, high school, some college (including junior college), and four-year college or more. However, given the recency of its educational improvements (see chapter 1), this variable is classified differently for Korea: less than junior high school, junior high school, high school, and more than high school. Because the education of spouses is highly correlated, we use either husband's or wife's education, depending on whether we are examining the husband's or wife's employment.

The ages of spouses were included in the multivariate analysis using the following categories: younger than age 30, 30–39, 40–49, and 50 and over. Because of the correlation between spouses' characteristics, we use husband's age or wife's age, depending on whether husband's or wife's employment is examined. Whether the husband is five or more years older than the wife is also included in the multivariate analysis because couples may be more traditional, with a larger gender difference in power, when a husband is considerably older than his wife. In addition, in order to control for the effect of proxy reporting in Japan and Korea and for the "mode" effect of responses in the NSFH1 (Sweet 1989), we also include the gender of respondents in the multivariate analysis.

Employment Patterns

Husbands' Employment Hours

Consistent with gender role expectations, in all three countries, virtually all husbands are employed, ranging from 96 percent in Japan to 91 percent in the U.S. (see table 6.1). Among the employed, however, there are quite substantial differences in the average number of hours worked and especially in the proportion of those working long hours. Korean husbands work the most hours per week (fifty-two), whereas American husbands spend the least amount of time on employment (forty-four hours), with Japanese husbands intermediate at forty-nine hours. The difference between the U.S. and Korea mounts to almost one full day of work per week.

We are uncertain as to what extent the differences in husbands' employment hours should be attributed to cultural factors affecting labor supply, on the one hand, or to the structure of opportunities in terms of available options in the marketplace, on the other. It is likely that these two issues are not separable and that the closer a rural past is in the history of a society, the more long hours are regarded as normal both in individual expectations and in the norms or regulations affecting employment. In any event, it is clear that differences this large are likely to have an impact on husbands' involvement in family life, especially participation in various household tasks (Tsuya and Bumpass 1998; see also chapter 7). This is especially so when these employment hour differences are compounded by differences in commuting time, as described below.

Wives' Employment Status and Hours

Married women's employment has increased greatly in recent decades in Japan and the U.S., and it has begun to increase in Korea. Decisions to work and the number of work hours among the employed can be simultaneous labor supply decisions, especially when there are limited options with respect to the number of employment hours that can be chosen. For the present, we simply

Table 6.1 *Percentage Distribution of Usual Employment Hours for Husbands and Wives Aged 20–59: Korea (1994), Japan (1994), and the U.S. (1987–1988)*

	HUSBANDS			WIVES		
Hours Worked per Week	*Korea*	*Japan*	*U.S.*	*Korea*	*Japan*	*U.S.*
Not employed	5.1	3.9	9.5	73.7	42.7	33.8
Employed						
15 or less	0.2	2.9	1.0	0.1	7.0	5.6
16–34	3.2	2.0	2.8	2.5	15.2	16.3
35–41	1.7	16.1	41.5	0.9	12.4	33.0
42–48	27.7	29.7	15.5	8.1	12.9	6.0
49–59	38.7	26.1	17.4	7.7	5.8	4.0
60+	23.4	19.4	12.3	7.0	4.0	1.3
Mean hours of work among employed	52.3	49.2	44.5	49.7	36.2	35.9
(N)	(1,744)	(1,825)	(3,577)	(1,795)	(1,821)	(3,553)

examine whether wives are employed and the number of hours worked among employed wives.

Having undergone industrialization most recently, Korea remains the most traditional with respect to attitudes toward appropriate gender roles, as we saw in chapter 2. Consistent with this, table 6.1 indicates that while the proportion of employed wives is similar in Japan and the U.S., it is much lower in Korea. Only about one-quarter (26 percent) of Korean wives are employed, compared to 57 and 66 percent of Japanese and U.S. wives respectively. However, among those who are employed, Korean wives work much longer hours than either Japanese or American wives. Employed Korean wives spend on average almost fifty hours per week on employment, whereas the Japanese and U.S. counterparts spend on average about thirty-six hours. This large difference results primarily from the virtual absence of part-time employment in Korea, precluding flexible employment opportunities for married women. Employed wives in all three countries shoulder heavy responsibilities in both the home and the workplace (Tsuya and Bumpass 1998; see also chapter 7). With employed Korean wives working an average fifty hours per week—a higher average than that for Japanese and American *husbands*—it must be especially difficult to combine work and family responsibilities for married women in Korea. This may, in turn, be a major reason why only a small percentage of Korean wives is employed.

Factors Affecting Wives' Employment

Because of the rapid increases in wives' employment in Japan and the U.S. and the emerging increase in Korea, and also the potential importance of their employment for family life, we next consider an array of variables that are likely to affect women's employment in the three settings. Our findings reveal both similarities and differences in the effects of family and socioeconomic variables on wives' employment. Because our focus is primarily on work and family life, we begin with the effects of husbands' employment hours and of family factors on wives' employment, rather than with the human capital emphasis on education, which might seem the logical starting point from other perspectives.

Husband's Employment Hours

The first part of table 6.2 presents the proportions of wives employed by husbands' employment hours. Whereas there is no clearly discernable relationship between wives' employment and husbands' employment hours in Japan and Korea, these variables are negatively and almost linearly associated in the U.S. This inverse relationship holds even after the effects of other family, socioeconomic, and demographic factors are controlled (data not shown). That is, American wives are less likely to be employed when their husbands work more. We see no ready explanation for why this would be true in the U.S. and not in Japan. For example, if this pattern in the U.S. reflects a greater need for a wife to attend to home and family when her husband works long hours, this should be even more the case in Japan.

When we look at hours of work among employed wives, we see a very different picture—and one consistent with a "joint economic response hypothesis," whereby the perceived economic need of the household may affect the employment patterns of both husband and wife. Wives' employment hours have a strong *positive* relationship with husbands' employment hours in all three countries. In Korea, mean employment hours of wives increase from thirty-four for women whose husbands work less than thirty-five hours per week to fifty-eight for those whose husbands work sixty hours or more per week. The corresponding numbers are from twenty-three to forty-five hours per week for Japan and from thirty-one to thirty-eight hours per week for the U.S. This positive relationship remains even after we control for the effects of the other independent and control variables (data not shown). Therefore, the positive association implies that the economic needs of the household, such as mortgage payments or saving for children's educational expenses, are propelling both wives and husbands to work more. However, this pattern may also reflect the conditions of local labor markets, which affect married men and women in similar ways.

All together, our findings suggest that husbands' employment hours do not affect whether wives are employed or not (except in the U.S., in which they have a significant negative relationship). Once wives are employed, however, they tend to work longer when their husbands work longer in all three countries. This relationship underscores the difficulty that employed couples (especially women) experience in accommodating their family roles to their heavy labor-market responsibilities. When both husbands and wives work long hours, the time available for home life must be severely constrained.

Presence and Ages of Children

Family characteristics such as the presence and ages of children are probably the most important factors influencing married women's employment patterns. Although women's obligations with respect to children (especially small children) have historically played a major role in limiting mothers' employment in the U.S. (Bumpass 1990; Sweet 1970), one of the most dramatic changes in recent years has been the rapid increase in employment of mothers of infants and small children (U.S. Bureau of the Census 1998: 409). At the same time, the M-shaped age pattern of women's labor force participation that was once common in the U.S. is still persistent in both Japan and Korea (see chapter 1). This is related in particular to women's traditional gender roles as wife and mother, as they withdraw from the labor force upon marriage or birth of the first child (Brinton 1988; Tsuya and Choe 1991). As noted in chapter 2, the view that a mother's employment is harmful to small children is also still widespread in all three countries.

Table 6.2 *Percentage of Wives Employed and Mean Number of Employment Hours per Week of Employed Wives, by Selected Characteristics: Korea (1994), Japan (1994), and the U.S. (1987–1988)*

Characteristic	PERCENTAGE OF WIVES EMPLOYED			MEAN EMPLOYMENT HOURS OF WIVES		
	Korea	*Japan*	*U.S.*	*Korea*	*Japan*	*U.S.*
Husband's employment hours per week						
Less than 35	31.1	52.8	76.2	34.1	23.3	30.9
35–41	30.7	57.9	67.6	45.6	32.3	35.4
42–48	22.9	58.9	71.6	44.5	34.9	37.7
49–59	19.1	56.6	64.8	50.5	37.3	38.1
60+	26.0	55.1	63.6	57.5	45.4	37.9
Age of youngest child						
Preschool age[a]	20.3	33.6	57.5	48.7	37.2	33.5
School age[b]	23.8	66.2	71.1	50.5	35.4	35.8
No child under age 18	24.5	60.8	68.3	49.3	36.8	37.5
Lives with or near parents/in-laws						
Coresides	28.3	63.5	(na)	48.9	39.4	(na)
Parents/in-laws live nearby	24.3	56.8	69.3[c]	49.6	36.2	34.5[c]
Neither	22.4	53.4	65.7	49.9	33.9	36.2
Wife's education						
Less than junior high school	28.1	—	—	51.1	—	—
Junior high school	22.3	65.4	40.2	51.4	37.0	38.6
High school	19.0	58.3	62.9	48.8	35.8	36.0
Some college	(na)	51.6	70.6	(na)	36.4	35.9
Four-year college or more	30.6[d]	42.9	73.5	48.5	36.1	35.6
Place of residence						
Large metropolitan city[e]	23.6	47.1	67.3	49.9	33.2	35.7
Medium-sized city[f]	20.3	51.1	67.4	49.6	33.5	36.1
Small city[g]	(na)	62.7	66.4	(na)	37.4	36.6
Rural area	30.2	70.5	64.3	50.0	40.3	35.8
(N)	(1,795)	(1,821)	(3,553)	(472)	(1,043)	(2,352)

Note: (na)—not applicable.
[a] For Korea and Japan, 0–6 years; for the U.S., 0–4 years.
[b] For Korea and Japan, 7–17 years; for the U.S., 5–17 years.
[c] Includes five cases who coreside with parents.
[d] Includes some college in Korea.
[e] For Korea, Seoul; for Japan and the U.S., cities with population of 1 million or more.
[f] For Korea, all cities other than Seoul; for Japan and the U.S., cities with population less than 1 million but at least 100,000.
[g] For Japan and the U.S., cities with population under 100,000.

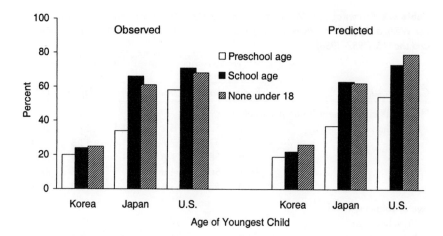

Figure 6.1. *Observed and Predicted Percentages of Wives Employed, by Age of Youngest Child: Korea (1994), Japan (1994), and the U.S. (1987–1988)*

From table 6.2, we see that the proportion employed is lower among mothers of preschool children in all three countries but particularly in Japan, where it is about half that of mothers with older children. This general pattern remains even after the effects of the other factors are controlled. While the observed effects of having a preschooler appear considerably larger in Japan than in the U.S., other factors such as women's age and education account for part of this difference (see figure 6.1). The ratio of employment among mothers of preschool children to those of older children is about the same in Korea and the U.S., despite the much lower level of employment in Korea. Nonetheless, it should not be missed in table 6.2 that employment among mothers of preschool children is not trivial even in Korea and Japan, constituting one-fifth and one-third of such mothers respectively. Although it is often taken for granted in these two countries that mothers of small children simply do not work (Jolivet 1997), a considerable proportion of them clearly do.

When we turn to work hours among employed wives, we see a different pattern in the comparison between Japan and the U.S. (see the right side of table 6.2). The results become even more distinct after the effects of the other factors are controlled in the multivariate model (see figure 6.2). The expected effect persists in the U.S., with mothers of preschool children working the fewest hours (about six hours less than those of mothers with no children under age 18). In Japan, on the other hand, it is mothers with school-age children who are likely to work the fewest hours, though the difference is smaller. This may reflect the mother's heavy responsibility for children's education, as discussed in chapter 5, or the lack of child-care centers for school-aged chil-

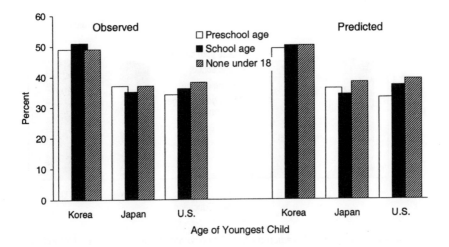

Figure 6.2. *Observed and Predicted Mean Employment Hours of Employed Wives, by Age of Youngest Child: Korea (1994), Japan (1994), and the U.S. (1987–1988)*

dren (Maeda 1997). The employment hours of Korean wives vary little with the presence and ages of children, again suggesting the dominant impact of available jobs over labor supply preferences in the country.

Proximity to Parents

Living with or near parents may influence wives' employment by providing a source for child care and other household tasks. Other studies have shown that in Japan coresidence with parents facilitates married women's employment, especially full-time employment (Martin and Tsuya 1992; Morgan and Hirosima 1983; Tsuya 1992). While few married couples share a household with their parents in the U.S.—except during brief spells of parents' or children's dependence (Bumpass 1994)—grandparents still provide a major source of child care (Casper, Hawkins, and O'Connell 1991).

As shown in table 6.2, the effects on wives' employment of living with or near parents are not large, although there are consistent differences in the expected direction in all three countries. That is, the highest proportion of wives is employed when married couples are living with a parent, and the second highest proportion is employed when parents live nearby. These patterns remain even after we control for the effects of other variables (data not shown).

When we turn to the relationship between intergenerational living arrangements and wives' employment hours, however, we find the expected positive relationship only in Japan. The seeming inflexibility of work-hour options in Korea may explain the lack of such a relationship there. It is less clear why this relationship should appear in Japan and not in the U.S., but part of this

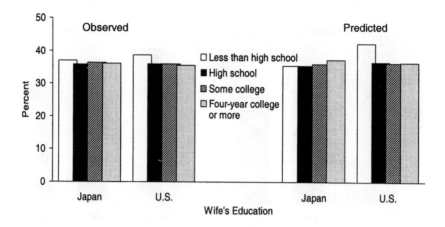

Figure 6.3. *Observed and Predicted Mean Employment Hours of Employed Wives by Wife's Education: Japan (1994) and the U.S. (1987–1988)*

difference is clearly a product of the absence of coresidence in the U.S., given that Japanese wives who are living with parents work the longest hours.

Wife's Education

From a human capital perspective and also from the expected effect of education on gender roles, the predicted effect of a wife's education on her employment status is straightforward: the rate of female employment should increase with education. Nevertheless, we find this expected positive relationship only in the U.S. (see table 6.2), and we get exactly the opposite result in Japan.[5] The negative relationship among Japanese wives remains unchanged when the effects of other family, socioeconomic, and demographic factors are controlled.[6] With the exception of a small number of wives who have attended college, we also see the negative relationship in Korea. It may well be that female education still serves to improve women's life prospects primarily through marriage in these two East Asian societies. To be sure, increasing educational attainment is a major factor in delayed first marriage among young Japanese and Korean women in recent years (Choe 1998; Tsuya and Mason 1995). However, it may also be the case in Japan and Korea that for married women, education has less impact on their employment opportunities than on mate selection. Women's education once held a similar symbolic function in many Western countries, including the U.S.

Turning to the relationship between wives' education and their employment hours, we see a quite different picture. In the U.S., wives with less than a high school education are employed slightly more hours than those with more education (thirty-nine versus thirty-six hours per week). This result persists net of the effects of other factors. On the other hand, there is no clear pattern in the observed number of work hours by women's education in Japan. Once the effects of other factors are controlled, however, it is college graduates in Japan who work somewhat longer than less-educated wives (see figure 6.3). This difference in the patterns between Japan and the U.S. is not readily explained. It seems plausible that labor market opportunities for college-educated women are more highly structured in Japan, offering more of an "all or nothing" option in terms of potential hours of work. If they wish to hold a professional job, they may have to make a full-time commitment associated with such a job.

Place of Residence

We expected metropolitan residence to be positively associated with wives' employment as a consequence of more plentiful job opportunities in large cities. Surprisingly, however, the opposite pattern is seen in both Korea and Japan. In Japan, the proportion of wives employed increases systematically from 47 percent in the largest metropolitan areas to 71 percent in the most rural areas (see the last set of figures in table 6.2). In Korea, the proportion of wives employed is 24 percent in Seoul, 20 percent in other cities, and 30 percent in rural areas. After the fact, it seems plausible that the added hardship of commuting may make it more difficult for wives in large cities to combine their family and labor market roles. This difficulty would likely increase with the size and metropolitan character of the place of residence. It may also be that the migration of many young women to larger cities improves the employment opportunities of those who remain in the more rural areas. It is also likely that there may be more jobs relative to the female population wanting jobs in rural areas.

Factors Affecting Husbands' Employment Hours

Given prevailing gender role expectations (see chapter 2), the competition between family responsibilities and employment led us to expect, and find, family effects on the employment patterns of wives. These same gender role expectations make employment the primary role obligation of husbands, and this expectation is shared by both employers and employees. Consequently, we would expect to find relatively little family-related variation in employment hours among husbands, and that is the result shown in table 6.3.

The largest difference we find in this table is by wife's employment hours: husbands work the fewest hours if their wives are employed part-time. We have already noted that part-time employment is very rare for women in Korea. The employment hours of spouses are likely responses to common stimuli, whether longer hours are a consequence of economic necessity or reflect the constraints of local employment markets. The latter explanation seems the more likely since there is little difference between families in which the wife is not employed and those in which she is employed full-time. It is when the wife is employed part-time that her husband is also likely to work fewer hours.

Consistent with the expectations of little relationship between family factors and husbands' employment hours, almost all categories differ by no more than one or two hours in all of the remainder of table 6.3 across all three coun-

Table 6.3 *Mean Number of Employment Hours per Week of Employed Husbands, by Selected Characteristics: Korea (1994), Japan (1994), and the U.S. (1987–1988)*

Characteristic	Korea	Japan	U.S.
Wife's employment hours per week			
Zero	52.4	49.0	45.4
1–34	42.2	45.9	41.6
35+	53.1	51.4	45.0
Age of youngest child			
Preschool age [a]	52.4	51.4	45.2
School age [b]	52.6	50.1	44.7
No child under age 18	51.5	46.8	43.7
Lives with or near parents/in-laws			
Coresides	51.7	50.0	(na)
Parents/in-laws live nearby	53.2	49.0	44.6 [c]
Neither	51.9	48.7	44.5
Husband's education			
Less than junior high school	52.5	(na)	(na)
Junior high school	53.3	48.2	44.6
High school	52.7	48.5	44.4
Some college	(na)	51.2	44.4
Four-year college or more	50.8 [d]	49.9	44.7
Place of residence			
Large metropolitan city [e]	53.3	49.4	44.3
Medium-sized city [f]	52.4	49.4	43.8
Small city [g]	(na)	48.8	45.0
Rural area	51.0	48.9	45.1
(N)	(1,655)	(1,754)	(3,237)

Note: (na)—Not applicable.

[a] For Korea and Japan, 0–6 years; for the U.S., 0–4 years.

[b] For Korea and Japan, 7–17 years; for the U.S., 5–17 years.

[c] Includes five cases who coreside with parents.

[d] Includes some college in Korea.

[e] For Korea, Seoul; for Japan and the U.S., cities with population of 1 million or more.

[f] For Korea, all cities other than Seoul; for Japan and the U.S., cities with population less than 1 million but at least 100,000.

[g] For Japan and the U.S., cities with population under 100,000.

tries. The one exception is the fewer hours of employment among Japanese men with no children under age 18. This may well be due to the relative concentration of these men at younger and older ages.

While we find no responsiveness of husbands' work hours to family factors, it is important to remember that the employment hours of men obviously have important implications for their families. The increased income resulting from longer employment hours helps the family by providing more financial resources. At the same time, however, long employment hours often constrain the time available for husbands to contribute to household tasks (see chapter 7) or to share in the day-to-day experiences of their families' lives. There is more reason to expect to find differences in men's work hours by their education and place of residence, but there are only very small differences by these variables as well.

Commuting Time

As we saw in the previous sections, in all three countries husbands work more than an average of forty hours a week, with Korean and Japanese husbands working especially long hours. Employed wives also work a substantial number of hours in all three countries. Though time spent commuting is usually ignored, it clearly adds to the constraints that employment places on family life.

Tokyo and Seoul have reputations as places with very long commuting times, but we find a somewhat different and more complicated story for the complete populations of Japan and Korea. The story depends, in part, on how we interpret the substantial proportion of cases for which we do not have a value on this variable (one-quarter among husbands and one-third among wives—see table 6.4). If we treat these cases as missing data, the estimated mean commuting time (one way) is seventy-seven minutes in Korea, thirty-seven minutes in Japan, and twenty-one minutes in the U.S. This construction assumes that "missing" cases spend the average time commuting.

We think, however, that these are not simply missing data: a sizable majority of the "missing" respondents were self-employed, family workers, or farmers. Many shopkeepers and small business proprietors in the two East Asian countries had no commuting time to report since they lived above or next to their place of employment.[7] Based on this alternative assumption, the mean commuting time is estimated to be fifty-seven minutes in Korea and twenty-eight minutes in Japan, compared to twenty-one minutes in the U.S. Hence, the *averages* are not all that different between Japan and the U.S., though the distribution is more bimodal in Japan. True to the widely held presumptions, the much longer average commuting time in Korea persists, even when the substantial share of those "unknown" cases is taken into account. The substantive implications of these commuting times should not be missed since

Table 6.4 *Percentage Distribution of Time Required to Commute to Work (One Way) for Employed Husbands and Wives: Korea (1994), Japan (1994), and the U.S. (1987–1988)*

Commuting Time in Minutes	HUSBANDS			WIVES		
	Korea	*Japan*	*U.S.*	*Korea*	*Japan*	*U.S.*
15 or less	9.1	19.2	46.9	14.9	37.8	61.8
16–30	9.3	25.5	29.9	11.1	20.1	24.6
31–45	4.1	8.2	9.2	5.8	4.7	5.7
46–60	11.7	13.6	4.3	11.4	2.7	2.2
61–90	16.2	7.5	1.1	14.9	1.2	0.3
91 or more	23.3	2.2	0.6	9.7	0.2	0.2
Mean commuting time in minutes	77.1	37.2	20.8	57.2	19.7	13.6
Unknown	26.3	23.8	8.0	32.3	33.3	5.2
(N)	(1,655)	(1,754)	(1,741)	(472)	(1,043)	(1,558)

they have the greatest impact in the countries with the most hours spent in employment. Commuting adds about twelve hours a week to the average fifty-two hours of employment estimated for Korean husbands (assuming six round trips for a 5.5-day work week).

Similar differences by country exist with respect to the time employed wives spend on commuting, but the time tends to be much shorter. If we treat "unknown" cases as missing, the average commuting time for wives is fifty-seven minutes in Korea, twenty minutes in Japan, and fourteen minutes in the U.S. If we treat "unknown" cases as those who have zero commuting time, the corresponding means are estimated to be thirty-nine minutes for Korea and thirteen minutes in both Japan and the U.S. This is a point where combining family and labor market obligations has a clear impact on women's employment; in order to meet these obligations, it appears that wives select from a narrower range of opportunities in order to remain closer to home. Employed Korean wives nonetheless spend almost an hour and a half a day getting to and from work.

These are average times, of course. Many of the respondents have shorter or longer commuting times. The impact on family life will be most important for those for whom commuting takes the longest. As an index of longer commuting times, from table 6.4 we can calculate the proportion spending forty-five minutes or more commuting one way (an hour and a half each work day). For husbands this proportion is 51 percent in Korea, 24 percent in Japan, and 6 percent in the U.S. For wives, the proportion is much lower: 36 percent in Korea, 4 percent in Japan, and 3 percent in the U.S.

The time spent in work and commuting has clear implications for family

Table 6.5 *Cumulative Percentages of Husbands and Wives Having Returned Home from Work, by Successive Evening Hours: Korea (1994) and Japan (1994)*

Time Returning Home	HUSBANDS		WIVES	
	Korea	*Japan*	*Korea*	*Japan*
Not working	5.1	3.9	73.7	42.7
Unknown	19.5	22.5	13.4	18.8
Among known, returned by (cumulative percent):				
5 P.M.	8.5	25.2	19.1	56.7
6 P.M.	18.6	58.7	33.8	86.8
7 P.M.	39.2	69.5	57.5	93.8
8 P.M.	64.7	87.4	75.1	97.8
9 P.M.	82.3	97.1	82.6	99.7
After 9 P.M.	100.0	100.0	100.0	100.0
(N)	(1,655)	(1,754)	(472)	(1,043)

interactions by affecting when workers return home. As shown in table 6.5, about 35 percent of Korean husbands and 25 percent of Korean wives do not return home from work until after 8:00 P.M., leaving relatively little time for household tasks and family matters. The levels returning this late are very small among Japanese wives (around 2 percent), but about one-quarter of Japanese husbands do not come home until after this hour.

Preferences for Wife's Employment

We asked comparable questions in the U.S. and Japan about the number of hours the respondent would prefer to be employed, as well as about the number of hours he/she would prefer for a spouse to work. Given the increasing importance of the wife's employment for family life and gender roles, we focus here on preferences that a wife *not* be employed as reported by both husbands and wives.

The responses are reported in table 6.6 for selected family, socioeconomic, and demographic characteristics. Three patterns are of particular interest. First, in both Japan and the U.S. the vast majority of wives prefer to work at least *some* hours. Surprisingly, this proportion is higher in Japan than in the U.S.—89 compared to 81 percent. Even among full-time homemakers, 83 percent of Japanese wives and 67 percent of American wives express a preference to be employed. These numbers are particularly impressive in light of the fact that most of the employment opportunities for women in Japan are limited to *"pa-ato"* jobs (part-time with no fringe benefits), and this is true as well of a substantial proportion of the jobs that women have in the U.S. Hence, this is strong evidence that the gender role orientation of Japanese women includes a preference for at least some time in the labor force. However, this does not necessarily mean that employed wives want to work as much as they actually do. In both countries, wives prefer to (and their husbands prefer them to) work considerably fewer hours than they actually do: the mean preferred hours of employment is thirty hours per week for Japanese wives and twenty-one hours per week for American wives.

Second, the differences by age of youngest child mirror the patterns we saw in wives' employment. Mothers of school-aged children in Japan are more likely than mothers of preschoolers to prefer not to be employed, whereas in the U.S. it is the mothers of preschoolers who most prefer to stay at home (table 6.6). It is especially noteworthy in light of the expectation that a Japanese mother should stay home with young children (Jolivet 1997) that Japanese mothers of preschoolers are less likely to want to remain at home than are their American counterparts (7 versus 23 percent). This is yet another indicator of what may be an increasing disaffection with the mother and housewife role on the part of Japanese women.

Third, education is not systematically related to employment preferences for wives in Japan. We expected that the most educated women would be the most likely to prefer to be employed (Choe, Kong, and Mason 1994; Kong and Choe 1989). Yet we saw above that the rate of employment among Japanese wives with four years of college or more was notably lower than for less-educated wives (see table 6.2). When combined with this earlier finding, these results suggest that the gap between reality and preference regarding wives' employment is indeed large among highly educated Japanese. In contrast, we do find the expected pattern in the U.S. Both husbands and wives with a college degree are more likely to want the wife to be employed, compared to less-educated women and men.

Not surprisingly, wives' actual employment hours are related most strongly with husbands' preferences for wives' employment. This association very likely reflects causality in both directions. It is possible that some husbands have learned to appreciate the additional income and other financial benefits brought about by wives' employment (and have adjusted their preferences accordingly), but it is also likely that this association reflects the influence of husbands' preferences on wives' employment patterns. As shown in table 6.6, in both Japan and the U.S., the proportion of husbands who prefer for their wives not to work is distinctly higher among husbands whose wives are a full-time homemakers than among husbands with an employed wife: 32 compared to 10 percent in Japan, and 47 compared to 27 percent in the U.S. However, there is a different perspective on this as well. The complement to these numbers indicates that one-half of U.S. husbands whose wives are not employed wish that they were; the corresponding proportion is two-thirds in Japan. Therefore, quite surprisingly, men do not appear to be the major conservative

Table 6.6 *Percentage of Wives Who Prefer Not to Be Employed and of Husbands Who Prefer for Their Wives Not to Be Employed, by Selected Characteristics: Japan (1994) and the U.S. (1992–1994)*

| | PREFERRING THAT WIFE NOT BE EMPLOYED | | | |
| | WIVES | | HUSBANDS | |
Characteristic	Japan	U.S.	Japan	U.S.
Total	11.0	18.7	19.3	34.8
Husband's employment hours per week				
Less than 35	12.8	15.8	13.5	29.5
35–41	7.5	18.7	17.7	37.0
42–48	11.8	18.0	20.8	30.8
49–59	11.3	16.8	21.5	30.0
60+	11.6	18.6	16.5	31.6
Wife's employment hours per week				
Zero	17.1	32.9	32.0	46.7
1–34	7.0	12.5	13.4	30.9
35+	6.7	12.4	10.1	27.2
Age of youngest child				
Preschool age[a]	7.0	23.3	23.2	37.5
School age[b]	11.0	16.1	15.5	33.1
No child under age 18	12.9	17.8	21.1	34.5
Lives with or near parents/in-laws				
Coresides	8.1	(na)	18.0	(na)
Parents/in-laws live nearby	12.3	16.4[c]	17.9	28.9
Neither	12.2	19.2	20.5	36.0
Own education				
Less than high school	10.9	25.8	15.6	44.4
High school	9.0	20.0	21.9	35.0
Some college	14.3	21.2	12.3	37.7
Four-year college or more	9.5	11.5	21.1	31.4
Place of residence				
Large metropolitan city[d]	12.4	18.0	19.1	31.1
Medium-sized city[e]	14.0	21.2	23.3	38.8
Small city[f]	10.2	22.9	16.3	35.8
Rural area	5.6	18.6	15.4	35.6
(N)	(872)	(1,772)	(897)	(1,639)

Note: (na)—Not applicable.

[a] For Japan, 0–6 years; for the U.S., 0–4 years.

[b] For Japan, 7–17 years; for the U.S., 5–17 years.

[c] Includes five cases who coreside with parents.

[d] Cities with population of 1 million or more.

[e] Cities with population less than 1 million but at least 100,000.

[f] Cities with population under 100,000.

force in the process of wives' increasing economic activities that they are often thought to be (especially in Japan), even though employed wives still shoulder a heavy double burden of household tasks and employment in both countries.

One final perspective on preferences for wife's employment is to contrast the mean hours preferred for an employed wife by couples in Japan and the U.S. As shown in table 6.1, employed wives work an average of thirty-six hours per week in both Japan and the U.S. On the other hand, in both countries, both husbands and wives would prefer that wives work fewer hours in the marketplace than they actually do. Both Japanese men and women prefer thirty hours for wives' employment; in the U.S. husbands prefer twenty-four hours and wives twenty-one hours. Hence, the preferred number of employment hours for wives among couples with employed wives is substantially lower in the U.S. than in Japan, despite the similarity in actual work hours. Again, this suggests the attitudinal influences of differences in the availability of labor market opportunities for married women in the two countries, with Japanese women having (and expecting) to work the longer hours structured by the labor market if they are going to work at all.

Conclusion

We began this chapter by noting the marked increase in female employment across all three of our countries. Aggregate levels of employment both reflect and contribute to the societal differences in the allocation of gender roles. Men work much longer hours in Korea than in Japan and longer in Japan than in the U.S. These differences are compounded by differences in the commuting time required to get to and from work, especially in congested cities and especially in Korea. Hence, men's time away from home for employment-related reasons is much greater in the East Asian societies than it is in the U.S. Some of these differences may reflect preferences for employment over home, but it is likely that they are also heavily structured by expectations in the workplace (including a corporate culture in which long hours are seen as a sign of loyalty to the company).

The employment of wives is rather similar in Japan and the U.S., though somewhat higher in the U.S. In contrast, Korean wives are less than half as likely to be employed as those in the other two countries, but those who are employed work much longer hours. These results imply that Korean wives in particular face very limited labor market options, with very few part-time employment opportunities. If Korean wives have only two options—to work for long hours or not at all—then Korea is an extreme example of the difficulty in reconciling employment and domestic responsibilities.

Consistent with persisting gender role expectations, family factors—such as the presence and ages of children and proximity to parents—strongly influence wives' employment status and hours but have little effect on husbands' employment patterns in all three countries. The rate of wives' employment is lower among mothers of preschool and school-aged children in all three countries. This was especially true in Japan and the U.S., where wives' employment is more prevalent. Nonetheless, levels of employment are nontrivial even among the mothers of preschool children in all three countries. When these factors converge in the context of the double burden experienced by employed women (Tsuya and Bumpass 1998; see also chapter 7), it is little wonder that young unmarried women may be reluctant to undertake the roles of wife and mother (chapter 3).

Somewhat surprising for the East Asian countries, both married men and women overwhelmingly prefer for wives to work, and this is so even for mothers with small children. The contrast between these expectations and actual patterns of wives' employment may foreshadow dramatic increases in the employment of mothers, especially in Japan.

Finally, wives' educational level was found to have a negative effect on their employment rate but had no relationship with their own and their husbands' preferences for their employment in Japan. Do these findings suggest that it is particularly wives with higher education who are likely to experience an inconsistency between actual work and their preference for work in the two East Asian countries? Can the working conditions for highly educated wives (many of whom are young) be improved so that they can fulfill their career aspirations while balancing their family roles and so that the countries can also better utilize human resources? Changes in wives' and husbands' employment are part of a much broader pattern of social change that will have to be accommodated and ameliorated by making employment opportunities and structures more compatible with family life.

Chapter Seven

Gender and Housework

Noriko O. Tsuya and Larry L. Bumpass

The interface between the worlds of work and family has long been seen as a critical fault line along which pressures toward family change accumulate (Goode 1963); at the same time, families provide resources for adapting to economic pressures (Cogner and Elder 1994; Harevan 1982). As the growth of the market economy creates increasingly similar economic opportunities and constraints across countries, there is much to be learned from comparative analyses of the work-family interface—especially between Japan and the U.S., modernized economies with dramatically different cultural heritages. The patriarchal Confucian heritage of Japan provides a strong cultural contrast to the more egalitarian U.S. for examining relationships between employment and family.

Both Japan and the U.S. have undergone profound changes in work and family in the postwar decades, the most important of which has been the increasing employment of married women (Bianchi and Casper 2000; Shimada and Higuchi 1985; Tsuya 1992). However, these changes in wives' economic roles have not brought about similar changes in husbands' domestic roles, leaving the home predominantly the responsibility of wives (Goldscheider and Waite 1991; Pleck 1985; Tsuya and Bumpass 1998). So far, women have made the major accommodations, either by adding paid employment to their existing domestic responsibilities, or by reducing the time spent in housework and/or employment (Ferree 1991; Kamo 1994). Whereas the time Japanese husbands spend on housework has remained extremely low and virtually unchanged during the last three decades (Tsuya 1992), husbands' contributions appear to have increased in the U.S. (Gershuny and Robinson 1988). In both countries, however, the time husbands spend on housework responds to the employment hours of their wives (Presser 1994; Tsuya 1992; Tsuya and Bumpass 1998), though less so in Japan.

In this chapter, we compare Japan and the U.S. with respect to employment hours and the allocation of household tasks among married couples. We exclude Korea from the analysis because we do not have comparable data on household tasks.[1] We begin with the recognition that *household production* includes time spent in the labor market as well as in household tasks; hence, we examine an estimate of "combined workload" that is a sum of these components. We believe that a focus solely on the allocation of household tasks miscasts gender equity issues by ignoring differences in employment hours (Ferree 1991; also see chapter 6). We do not intend to gloss over important gender issues affecting the trade-off between employment and home tasks (or of child-care demands, which are not measured here). However, when housework and employment are jointly considered, gender inequality in the combined workload is clearly lower on the average than one would conclude from household tasks alone; at the same time, the "double shift" is highlighted in both countries for wives who are employed full-time.

We also consider both actual and relative investments in household tasks, a point often confused in the literature. Although the relative share of each spouse reflects the gender division of labor (Goldscheider and Waite 1991), variations in relative shares may derive from differences in the housework time of *either* spouse. Increases in husbands' shares can result from either greater household contributions from husbands or reduced efforts by wives; an important adaptation by wives to their increased employment has been a reduction in the time they spend on household tasks. The total time spent on housework also depends on standards for household maintenance, the efficiency with which tasks are performed, and the availability of domestic help provided by others. We have no data on these aspects of the process, however.

We begin with a summary overview of the combined workload measure and its components by country and gender, then proceed to a comparison of distributions on combined workload by spouses' hours of employment, and then examine the relationship of household task hours of household members to employment hours and other related factors. We conclude with multivariate analyses of time spent on housework by wives and by husbands and of the proportion of couples' housework time that is performed by husbands.

Theoretical Perspectives

Four types of factors are frequently noted in the literature as relevant to the allocation of household tasks: time availability (especially as conditioned by employment hours); the amount of housework to be done (as conditioned by factors such as number and ages of children and availability of time-saving appliances); the relative resources of the spouses; and the gender role attitudes of each spouse (e.g., Coverman 1985; England and Farkas 1986; Goldscheider and Waite 1991; Presser 1994). A number of studies have viewed these four perspectives as competing hypotheses, but we, like Ferree (1991) and Presser (1994), see these as complementary components of the joint household production process.

Time Availability

Time spent in employment clearly constrains the amount of time that can be allocated to housework and hence affects the gender division of labor at home. However, findings vary depending on the measures used. For example, earlier evidence on the U.S. shows that husbands' *share* in housework increases when wives are employed, but primarily because employed wives spend *less* time on these tasks (Pleck 1977). On the other hand, husbands who work relatively few hours do contribute more to housework (Coverman and Sheley 1986; Gershuny and Robinson 1988). Husbands' contribution to household work is therefore affected by both husbands' employment hours and wives' employment status and hours (Coverman 1985). In addition, Goldscheider and Waite (1991) report that among dual-earner couples in the U.S., husbands' share in housework is influenced more by wives' employment hours than by their own. This topic has been studied much less for Japan. Nonetheless, our earlier work (of which this chapter is an expansion) shows that Japanese husbands' housework increases significantly only when wives are employed full-time (Tsuya 1992; Tsuya and Bumpass 1998).[2] This suggests that Japanese husbands respond to the hours (and probably the rigidity of the schedule) of wives' employment rather than to wives' employment per se.

Amount of Housework

The amount of housework to be done (even exclusive of child care) is influenced strongly by the number, age, and sex of children. Evidence from the U.S. shows that when the employment hours of both spouses are taken into account, the presence of small children increases wives' housework time dramatically while only slightly increasing that of husbands (Kamo 1988; Rexroat and Shehan 1987).[3] Analyzing dual-earner couples in the U.S., Presser (1994) also found that the number of nonadult children reduces husbands' share of housework, not because husbands do less housework, but because wives' housework increases more than husbands'. Even though the contribution of Japanese husbands to housework is lower than that of their U.S. counterparts, we expect that similar effects of the presence of preschool children will be found in both countries.

Whereas the presence of small children increases the amount of housework to be done, older children can both create more housework and contribute to household tasks. Older children, especially teenage or adult daughters, are found to contribute substantially to household tasks in the U.S. (Blair 1992; Goldscheider and Waite 1991; Spitze and Ward 1995) and thus reduce fathers' share in housework by substituting for their contribution to domestic tasks. Bergen (1990), on the other hand, found that the presence of school-aged children had no effect. We expect that in Japan as well help from coresident adult children, primarily daughters (and daughters-in-law) may reduce parents' domestic responsibilities. Thus, although the direction of the effect of the presence of school-aged children is unclear, we hypothesize that the presence of adult daughters (and in Japan daughters-in-law) may decrease even further the fathers' share in housework.

The amount of housework that needs to be done can also be influenced by the presence of an older generation in the household. As noted in chapter 4, living with parents is extremely rare in the U.S. (at any time) but much more common in Japan. At the same time, it is not as high in Japan as is frequently presumed; about two-thirds of Japanese couples in 1994 were not living with parents. For this majority, we can compare the two countries without the confounding effect of parental presence in the household. Coresidence with parents in Japan may affect the gender division of household labor as well as the combined workload. Help provided by parents (in particular mothers and mothers-in-law) may replace some of the small contributions that husbands might otherwise make, as well as facilitate wives' employment (Morgan and Hirosima 1983; Tsuya 1992; Martin and Tsuya 1992). This chapter examines how multigenerational coresidence—both upward and downward—influences the gender division of labor in the two societies.

Relative Resources of Spouses

Classic resource theories (e.g., Blood and Wolfe 1960) see the key factor determining the gender division of labor at home as relative power, defined as a function of the external resources of each spouse, such as income and education. Though the gender gap is narrowing, women traditionally have less earning power and lower social status than men, and this gender disadvantage in the wider society is transmitted into the domestic power relations between spouses (Ferree 1991).

The "new home economics" predicts a similar allocation of home tasks, but because of the relative efficiency of "trading" in a gender-based division of labor rather than as a result of power differences. Because of differences in human capital investments in the two spheres, men derive greater marginal productivity (wage rates) in the marketplace and women's investments in household skills make them more efficient at those tasks (Becker 1981).

Whereas little empirical support has been found for women's higher efficiency in household tasks and/or men's higher labor force productivity (Coverman 1985; Farkas 1976; Huber and Spitze 1983; Spitze 1986), some studies have demonstrated the relevance of resources for explaining the gender division of labor (Ferree 1991; Maret and Finlay 1984; Presser 1994; Ross 1987). Kamo (1994) also suggests that the relative resource perspective is more relevant to the U.S. because the allocation of tasks in Japanese households is affected more strongly by traditional gender relations based on the patriarchal family system than by economic rationality, thus shifting the ground from "rational economic efficiency" back to power. We therefore hypothesize that while the relative resources of spouses will influence the gender division of household labor, such effects should be stronger among U.S. couples than among Japanese couples.

Gender Role Attitudes

To the extent that attitudes affect behavior, we would expect men with non-traditional gender role attitudes to do more housework and women with such attitudes to try harder to enlist their husbands' assistance. Evidence on the effect of gender role attitudes on the division of household labor is mixed. Many U.S. studies have found that egalitarian attitudes of husbands increase their contribution to housework but that wives' attitudes have little or no effect (e.g., Huber and Spitze 1983; Kamo 1988; Ross 1987; Stafford, Beckman, and Dibona 1977). In contrast, Coverman (1985) found that participation in housework was actually lower among husbands with nontraditional gender role attitudes, whereas other studies on the U.S. showed that gender role attitudes of *both* spouses influence the gender division of household labor (Ferree 1991; Presser 1994). Given these mixed findings from prior research, the gender role attitudes of both spouses are hypothesized to affect the gender division of household labor, although the nature of these relationships is uncertain.

Patterns of Couples' Housework Time and Combined Workload

This chapter examines time and share of household tasks as well as combined workload. Excluding child care, our analysis of housework focus on a common set of tasks traditionally gender-typed as female: cleaning house, doing laundry (for the U.S., laundry and ironing), cooking, cleaning after meals, and grocery shopping.[4] Time spent on housework was computed as the sum of hours spent per week on these tasks by each spouse (then top-coded at the 98th percentile to reduce the effect of extreme values on the analysis), and the relative share was determined by dividing husbands' task hours by the combined hours of both spouses.

The combined workload was computed by adding the hours spent per week on household tasks and the usual hours spent per week on employment. The Japanese recorded employment time in categories, so we imputed the mid-point of each category. Exceptions were for those who reported to have worked 35–41 hours or 60 hours or more per week; the values of 39 and 66 hours were assigned respectively to the two categories, based on the results of the 1993 national wage structure survey in Japan.[5]

Table 7.1 presents the mean hours per week of each spouse and husbands' average share on household tasks, employment, and combined workload. The data indicate a surprising similarity in our measures of average housework hours of wives (33.5 hours in Japan and 32.4 hours in the U.S.). On the other hand, as expected, there are considerable differences in the time husbands spend on housework: Japanese husbands spend an average of 2.5 hours per week on domestic tasks, whereas American husbands report almost 8 hours per week on those tasks. Consequently, the estimated share of housework contributed by husbands is about 7 percent in Japan, compared to 21 percent in the U.S. Nonetheless, clear gender inequality persists in the division of these female household tasks in both societies.

We should point out, however, that Japanese husbands spend considerably more time at work than their U.S. counterparts: around forty-eight hours per week, compared to forty-one hours among American men. Like their time on housework, women in the two countries spend very similar hours employed—twenty-one hours per week in Japan, compared to twenty-three hours in the U.S.

Given the longer hours of men's employment, it is not surprising that when household and labor market hours are considered jointly, gender inequality is much less than implied by a focus solely on household tasks. Furthermore, we see no country differences in men's contribution to household production.

Table 7.1 *Mean Hours per Week Spent on Household Tasks, Employment, and Combined Workload: Japan (1994) and the U.S. (1987–1988)*

	JAPAN			U.S.		
	Mean			*Mean*		
Characteristic	*Hours*	*S.D.*	*(N)*	*Hours*	*S.D.*	*(N)*
Housework[a]						
Wife's hours per week	33.5	14.2	(1,799)	32.4	19.6	(3,435)
Husband's hours per week	2.5	3.8	(1,786)	7.8	8.0	(3,143)
Husband's share (percent)	7.4	12.3	(1,769)	20.9	19.7	(2,991)
Employment[b]						
Wife's hours per week	21.5	21.4	(1,821)	23.1	20.7	(3,553)
Husband's hours per week	47.5	14.8	(1,825)	41.4	18.0	(3,557)
Combined workload[c]						
Wife's hours per week	54.7	21.8	(1,784)	55.2	22.4	(3,352)
Husband's hours per week	50.0	14.8	(1,778)	49.6	17.4	(3,097)
Husband's share (percent)	48.1	13.9	(1,748)	47.7	15.9	(2,839)

Note: Means for the U.S. are weighted; the numbers of cases are unweighted. Figures for Japan are based on currently married men and women aged 20–59 and their spouses; figures for the U.S. are based on non-Hispanic white respondents aged 20–59 and their spouses.

[a] Number of hours spent on housework is computed by adding the time spent on such traditionally female household tasks as cleaning house, doing laundry (in the case of the U.S., laundry and ironing), cooking, cleaning after meals, and grocery shopping, and then top-coding at the 98th percentile.

[b] For Japan, the number of employment hours is estimated by imputing the original categorical data, with two exceptions: for those who worked 35–41 and 60+ hours, the values of 39 and 66 hours were assigned respectively.

[c] The combined workload is computed by adding the number of hours spent on housework and the number of hours spent on employment.

Men's average share of the combined workload measure is approximately 48 percent in both Japan and the U.S. (bottom, table 7.1).

We must again note, however, that while we believe this measure moves us conceptually in the right direction in thinking about gender inequality, it underrepresents women's contributions by excluding child care and men's contributions by excluding such male household tasks as home and auto repair. Men are more likely to engage in such "do it yourself" activities in the U.S. than in Japan, and U.S. men report almost as many hours for these tasks as for the tasks examined here. Nonetheless, this combined measure clearly reveals the large differences in workload that wives carry depending upon their employment hours.

Table 7.2 presents the mean combined workload by employment hours for husbands and wives in the two countries. We can see that as wives' employment hours increase, their combined workload increases, clearly revealing the "second shift" of unpaid housework among wives who are employed full-time (Hochschild 1991). The "double shift" of housework and employment is espe-

Table 7.2 *Mean Hours per Week Spent on Combined Workload, by Employment Hours: Japan (1994) and the U.S. (1987–1988)*

	COMBINED WORKLOAD							
	JAPAN				U.S.			
	HUSBANDS		WIVES		HUSBANDS		WIVES	
Weekly Employment Hours	*Mean Hours*	*(N)*	*Mean Hours*	*(N)*	*Mean Hours*	*(N)*	*Mean Hours*	*(N)*
Total	50.0	(1,778)	54.7	(1,784)	49.6	(3,097)	55.2	(3,352)
Wife's employment hours								
Zero	49.1	(707)	37.6	(720)	47.6	(949)	40.1	(1,110)
1–15	40.8	(137)	42.0	(138)	51.8	(171)	45.2	(185)
16–34	49.3	(291)	60.2	(294)	48.7	(480)	57.0	(517)
35–41	49.7	(223)	67.7	(227)	50.1	(1,035)	65.3	(1,139)
42–48	51.4	(230)	73.1	(230)	52.4	(199)	69.0	(209)
49 or more	59.9	(176)	84.9	(175)	54.0	(165)	76.9	(178)
Husband's employment hours								
Less than 35	12.9	(148)	43.6	(149)	17.4	(364)	52.2	(409)
35–41	42.0	(285)	53.4	(289)	47.4	(1,278)	56.3	(1,347)
42–48	47.6	(533)	53.5	(529)	52.9	(508)	56.5	(535)
49–59	56.3	(465)	56.9	(458)	58.7	(557)	54.1	(570)
60 or more	67.7	(347)	60.0	(342)	69.0	(388)	55.0	(388)

Note: Means for the U.S. are weighted; the numbers of cases are unweighted. For the definitions of measures, see the notes to table 7.1.

cially notable in Japan. Not only does a higher proportion of Japanese wives work long employment hours, but also those with long employment hours spend more time on household tasks—resulting in an estimated eighty-five hour week of combined workload for the highest employment category, compared to seventy-seven hours among American wives.[6]

Contrary to usual expectations, the gender division represented by this measure of combined workload is clearly favorable to wives who are full-time homemakers or who are employed for only a few hours. Given that many wives who work few or no hours are mothers of small children and that child-care time is not considered here, differences between men and women are understated, and those between wives employed full-time and those not employed are also understated. Even when we limit our analysis to couples without preschool children, however, this main point still holds (data not shown).

Differentials in Housework Time among Household Members

Tables 7.3 and 7.4 present the mean number of hours spent per week on household tasks by different household members for an array of relevant characteristics for Japan and the U.S. respectively. These tables show the observed relationships as a context for the multivariate analysis that follows; we will therefore limit our discussion to a few key points.

As we expected, there is a sharp reduction in wives' housework hours as their employment hours increase, and the patterns are very similar in the two countries. Husbands' household hours increase in response to their wives' employment hours, though the absolute levels remain very low in Japan. These increases in husbands' housework time are, however, not nearly enough to compensate for the reduction in wives' hours in response to their own employment.

While husbands' employment hours reduce the time husbands spend on household tasks, they do not affect the time that wives and other household members spend on housework. The exception is a small group of husbands employed less than thirty-five hours per week.[7] In Japan, wives and parents of these men spend considerably less time on housework; in the U.S., children of men who are not employed full-time spend more time on such tasks.

The presence of preschool and school-aged children is positively associated with wives' housework time (and this is especially true for the presence of preschool children) in both countries, even when child-care time has been excluded. But the presence of nonadult children shows no clear association with husbands' housework time in Japan. Instead, when preschool children are present in the household, the time that grandparents spend on housework becomes notably higher, implying that grandmothers, rather than husbands, help wives with the extra housework created by small children (Morgan and Hirosima 1983). In contrast, U.S. husbands do help more around the house

Table 7.3 *Mean Hours per Week Spent on Household Tasks by Household Members, by Selected Characteristics: Japan (1994)*

Characteristic	HUSBAND Mean Hours	(N)	WIFE Mean Hours	(N)	PARENTS Mean Hours	(N)	CHILDREN Mean Hours	(N)
Total	2.5	(1,786)	33.5	(1,799)	10.9	(560)	2.6	(1,393)
Wife's employment hours per week								
Zero	2.2	(709)	37.6	(720)	8.4	(189)	2.1	(564)
1–15	1.6	(138)	34.0	(138)	6.2	(32)	2.3	(105)
16–34	2.1	(292)	35.2	(294)	9.4	(82)	2.4	(236)
35–41	3.4	(224)	28.7	(227)	12.1	(77)	3.1	(165)
42–48	3.2	(232)	28.1	(230)	14.8	(109)	3.0	(176)
49 or more	3.1	(176)	26.6	(175)	13.7	(67)	3.8	(135)
Husband's employment hours per week								
Less than 35	3.1	(148)	31.2	(149)	5.3	(26)	3.8	(97)
35–41	3.0	(285)	33.5	(291)	11.3	(86)	2.3	(219)
42–48	2.6	(533)	33.0	(535)	11.5	(185)	2.4	(400)
49–59	2.3	(465)	34.3	(464)	10.7	(149)	2.5	(388)
60 or more	2.1	(347)	34.0	(349)	11.0	(112)	2.7	(283)
Age of Youngest Child								
0–6	2.5	(457)	35.1	(463)	15.0	(167)	1.0	(432)
7–17	2.1	(590)	33.6	(590)	10.6	(214)	2.6	(571)
No child under age 18	2.9	(738)	32.3	(746)	7.4	(179)	4.3	(390)
Coresidence with adult daughters and/or daughters-in-law								
No	2.5	(1,444)	33.4	(1,454)	11.9	(474)	1.6	(1,067)
Yes	2.4	(342)	33.8	(345)	5.3	(86)	5.7	(326)
Coresidence with parents								
No	2.8	(1,211)	33.9	(1,216)	—	(0)	2.9	(911)
Yes—total	1.9	(575)	32.5	(583)	10.9	(560)	2.0	(482)
With male parent only	2.4	(61)	37.8	(62)	1.8	(59)	3.7	(50)
With at least one female parent	1.9	(514)	31.9	(521)	11.9	(501)	1.8	(432)

Note: For the measurement of time spent on housework, see the notes to table 7.1.

Table 7.4 *Mean Hours per Week Spent on Household Tasks by Household Members, by Selected Characteristics: U.S. (1987–1988)*

Characteristic	HUSBAND Mean Hours	(N)	WIFE Mean Hours	(N)	ALL OTHERS Mean Hours	(N)
Total	7.8	(3,143)	32.4	(3,435)	7.0	(1,437)
Wife's employment hours per week						
Zero	6.1	(961)	40.1	(1,110)	7.4	(465)
1–15	6.7	(172)	35.5	(185)	5.5	(99)
16–34	7.8	(489)	32.3	(517)	6.4	(244)
35–41	8.8	(1,053)	26.4	(1,139)	7.2	(438)
42–48	9.8	(203)	24.5	(209)	6.8	(84)
49 or more	11.0	(167)	24.5	(178)	9.6	(62)
Husband's employment hours per week						
Less than 35	10.8	(364)	31.8	(415)	9.4	(149)
35–41	7.7	(1,278)	32.7	(1,379)	6.4	(603)
42–48	7.8	(508)	32.0	(548)	8.1	(218)
49–59	7.1	(557)	31.2	(586)	6.5	(245)
60 or more	5.9	(376)	34.2	(403)	6.6	(187)
Age of youngest child						
0–4	8.7	(1,035)	37.1	(1,113)	5.6	(425)
5–17	7.2	(1,000)	32.4	(1,100)	7.7	(830)
No child under age 18	7.6	(1,108)	28.7	(1,222)	6.9	(182)
Coresidence with adult daughters						
No	7.9	(2,961)	32.1	(3,233)	5.9	(1,274)
Yes	6.7	(182)	34.5	(202)	12.7	(163)
Coresidence with parents						
No	7.8	(3,102)	32.4	(3,386)	6.7	(1,397)
Yes	6.9	(41)	30.5	(49)	16.1	(40)

Note: Means are weighted; the numbers of cases are unweighted. For the measurement of time spent on housework, see the notes to table 7.1.

when there are preschool children. Having adult daughters (and/or daughters-in-law) in the household is associated negatively with husbands' housework hours but positively with wives' housework hours in both countries, although the associations are weak in Japan.

Coresidence with parents reduces the housework time of all other household members by similar degrees, especially in Japan. Not surprisingly, it is particularly female parents who help with housework (see table 7.3); when couples are living only with male parents, though this is rare, the time wives spend on housework *increases* substantially. This is as expected, given the low contri-

Table 7.5 *Descriptive Statistics for the Variables Used in Regression Analyses of Gender Division of Household Labor: Japan (1994) and the U.S. (1987–1988)*

Variable	JAPAN		U.S.	
	Mean	*S.D.*	*Mean*	*S.D.*
Wife's employment hours per week and income				
1–34 (part-time)	0.24	0.43	0.22	0.44
35 or more				
Lower income[a]	0.18	0.39	0.09	0.31
Higher income[b]	0.17	0.38	0.35	0.51
(Reference category is no work.)				
Husband's employment hours per week				
Less than 35	0.08	0.28	0.13	0.36
42–48	0.30	0.46	0.16	0.39
49–59	0.26	0.44	0.18	0.41
60 or more	0.19	0.39	0.12	0.35
(Reference category is 35–41 hours.)				
Age of youngest child				
Preschool age[c]	0.26	0.44	0.30	0.49
School age[d]	0.33	0.47	0.34	0.51
(Reference is no child under age 18.)				
Lives with adult daughters and/or daughters-in-law	0.19	0.39	0.09	0.31
Lives with parents	0.32	0.47	0.02	0.16
Husband's yearly income				
Level 2[e]	0.33	0.47	0.25	0.46
Level 3[f]	0.20	0.40	0.24	0.45
Level 4[g]	0.18	0.39	0.23	0.45
(Reference is the lowest category.)				
Husband's income data missing	0.02	0.14	0.04	0.22
Husband's education				
High school	0.46	0.50	0.35	0.51
Some college[h]	0.12	0.33	0.23	0.45
Four-year college or more	0.26	0.44	0.30	0.49
(Reference is less than high school.)				
Wife's education				
High school	0.50	0.50	0.43	0.53
Some college[h]	0.27	0.44	0.24	0.46
Four-year college or higher	0.06	0.24	0.22	0.44
(Reference is less than high school.)				

(continued on next page)

Table 7.5 (continued) *Descriptive Statistics for the Variables Used in Regression Analyses of Gender Division of Household Labor: Japan (1994) and the U.S. (1987–1988)*

Variable	JAPAN		U.S.	
	Mean	*S.D.*	*Mean*	*S.D.*
Husband's age	45.03	9.79	39.88	11.20
Wife's age	42.18	9.53	37.54	10.68
Respondent = female	0.49	0.50	0.50	0.54

  [a] For Japan, less than 2 million yen per year; for the U.S., less than $9,000.
  [b] For Japan, 2 million yen or more per year; for the U.S., $9,000 or more.
  [c] For Japan, 0–6 years; for the U.S., 0–4 years.
  [d] For Japan, 7–17 years; for the U.S., 5–17 years.
  [e] For Japan, 4–5.99 million yen per year; for the U.S., $17,000–27,999.
  [f] For Japan, 6–7.99 million yen per year; for the U.S., $28,000–39,999.
  [g] For Japan, 8 million yen or more per year; for the U.S., $40,000 or more.
  [h] For Japan, graduates of junior college, advanced professional school, or professional training school.

bution of Japanese men (especially those from the older generation) to household tasks and also the additional housework that they are likely to create.

Multivariate Analysis of the Gender Division of Household Labor

Independent and Control Variables

Table 7.5 describes the independent and control variables used in the multivariate analysis of the gender division of household labor.[8] These variables are introduced in order to measure time availability, the amount of housework, resources, and gender role attitudes.

Time availability is indexed by the usual weekly employment hours of both spouses. Wives' employment hours were grouped into three categories: zero (does not work), 1–34 hours (part-time), and 35 hours or more (full-time). Husbands' employment hours were grouped into five categories: less than 35 hours, 35–41 hours, 42–48 hours, 49–59 hours, and 60 hours or more.

We employ three variables to represent factors affecting the amount of housework to be done (and people available to work) in the household: coresidence with parents of one or both spouses; coresidence with daughters (and daughters-in-law, in the case of Japan) aged 18 or older; and age of the youngest child. Age of youngest child is coded into three categories: preschool (0–6 years for Japan and 0–4 years for the U.S.); school age (7–17 years for Japan and 5–17 years for the U.S.); and no child under age 18.

Resources are represented by categorical variables measuring husbands' and wives' income.[9] Because employment hours of both spouses are also included in the model, these measures index wage rates. Husband's yearly income was divided approximately into quartiles in each country. Since there are a considerable number of missing cases on income in the U.S., we have included a dummy variable for missing data.[10]

Many wives are not employed or employed only part-time, and their income is largely a function of their employment hours (and this is especially true in Japan). Hence, we further dichotomized wives employed full-time into those with higher incomes and those with lower incomes.[11] Based on bivariate analyses, the cut-off point was chosen to be 2 million yen for Japan and $9,000 for the U.S.

Education and age are used as indirect sociodemographic indicators of gender role attitudes. There are large attitudinal differences by these variables in both countries (see chapter 2), and education is often found to be a major variable affecting gender-related behavior (Goldscheider and Waite 1991: 127–129). Presser (1994) also suggests that the effects of husband's education on both husband's and wife's housework hours may reflect egalitarian gender role ideology more than resource issues. We classify education into four categories: less than high school; high school; some college (including junior college, and for Japan also advanced professional school or post–high school professional training school); and four-year college or more. Husband's or wife's age, each measured by a continuous variable, is also included as a proxy for the gender-related normative environment in which he/she grew up.

In addition, we examine a direct measure of gender role attitudes that has long been used as a key indicator of preferences for the gender division of labor. Both the Japanese and U.S. surveys had the following proposition: "It is much better for everyone if the man earns the main living and the woman takes care of the home."[12] We put responses into three categories: (1) "traditional," combining "strongly agree" and "agree"; (2) "neutral," for those indicating that they were uncertain; and (3) "egalitarian," combining "disagree" or "strongly disagree." However, whereas the NSFH1 collected information from both respondents and their spouses, the Japanese survey did so only from respondents because proxy reports of attitudes are highly unlikely to be reliable. Thus, we restrict the analysis to respondents themselves when we analyze the effect of the direct measure of gender role attitudes. We first examine our full set of variables in a model without this direct attitude measure and then add the variable and report its results in the subsequent table.

We have also included the respondent's sex to control for the potential effect of proxy reporting in Japan and of different modes of data collection for the U.S. In the case of Japan, proxy reports for spouses could differ systematically from what those spouses would report for themselves. For the U.S. we used self-reports for both spouses. However, primary respondents were interviewed in person, whereas their spouses filled out a self-administered questionnaire that was returned by mail. A "mode effect" is therefore possible if different hours are likely to be reported directly to an interviewer than in private or if there was confusion about how the questionnaire was to be filled out (Sweet 1989). Including respondent's sex also controls for any potential gender bias in the reporting of household task hours for self (and for spouse in Japan) —for example, against any tendency to exaggerate one's own contributions.

Results

Table 7.6 presents the results of three sets of multivariate analysis: ordinary least squares (OLS) multiple regression analysis of wives' household task hours; tobit regression analysis of husbands' household task hours; and tobit regression analysis of husbands' share in housework.[13] In both Japan and the U.S., husbands' share of housework is affected significantly by the wives' employment hours, but the patterns differ somewhat. In both countries, wives reduce their own time on housework with increasing hours of their employment. This, of course, will tend to increase husbands' share even if men do not pick up more of the work at home. In both countries, however, the increase in men's share also reflects an increase in their own household hours. The major difference is that in Japan, this occurs only among couples in which the wife is working full-time. Nonetheless, these results demonstrate the effects of time availability of both husbands and wives on the gender division of labor at home. Among wives working full-time in the two countries, there is also evidence in support of resource theories, in that it is among wives earning the highest incomes that wives' household time is lowest and both men's household time and share are highest.

Although the effects of husbands' employment hours are less systematic, two patterns are significant in both countries. Among the low proportion of couples in which the husband works less than full-time, wives' task hours are significantly shorter and husbands' shares are higher. The effect on husbands' household efforts is statistically significant in the U.S. but not in Japan. The second significant effect of husbands' employment hours is that in both countries, husbands' household efforts and share are markedly reduced among those working sixty or more hours a week. Hence, effects of the differential time availability of husbands on the gender division of labor at home are restricted to the two extremes of the distribution of husbands' employment hours.

Coresidence with parents significantly reduces husbands' share of housework in Japan. While living with parents reduces the housework hours of both husbands and wives in the country, the degree of reduction in husbands' hours is much greater (and significantly so) than in wives' hours. This suggests that while coresiding parents may contribute to household tasks by shouldering part of the housework, husbands are likely to benefit more from such contributions than are their wives. Coresidence also reduces American husbands' housework time. With such a small fractions of U.S. couples living with parents, however, coresidence has no effect on the overall picture. Coresidence with

Table 7.6 *Estimated Coefficients from Regression Analyses Predicting the Gender Division of Household Labor: Japan (1994) and the U.S. (1987–1988)*

Predictor	WIVES' TASK HOURS[a]		HUSBANDS' TASK HOURS[b]		HUSBANDS' SHARE[b]	
	Japan	U.S.	Japan	U.S.	Japan	U.S.
Intercept	29.0**	37.9**	3.6**	5.8**	11.8**	20.7**
Wife's employment hours per week and income						
1–34 (part-time)	-2.6**	-6.1**	-0.7	1.4**	-0.01	4.3**
35 or more						
Lower income	-8.7**	-8.8**	0.8#	2.8**	4.6**	8.4**
Higher income	-11.4**	-13.1**	2.4**	3.5**	8.0**	12.3**
Husband's employment hours per week						
Less than 35	-4.4**	-2.6*	0.1	3.8**	2.3#	9.1**
42–48	-0.3	-0.7	-0.7	-0.1	-0.4	0.1
49–59	1.0	-1.1	-1.3**	-0.7	-2.0*	-1.9*
60 or more	1.0	0.9	-1.7**	-1.8**	-2.1*	-4.1**
Age of youngest child						
Preschool age	3.2**	8.3**	-0.4	1.7**	-1.6	-2.3*
School age	2.1*	3.7**	-0.8*	-0.1	-2.2**	-3.2**
Lives with adult daughters and/or daughters-in-law	0.5	2.1#	-0.8#	-0.02	-1.1	0.1
Coresides with parents	-0.6	-2.2	-1.8**	-2.9**	-2.6**	-3.2
Husband's income						
Level 2	1.5	1.4	-0.5	-0.1	-1.1	0.04
Level 3	0.7	2.1*	0.04	-0.8	-0.4	-1.5
Level 4	1.4	-0.6	-0.8	-1.8	-1.6	-2.4*
Husband's income data missing	1.1	-2.0	-1.0	-0.6	-2.7	0.7
Husband's education						
High school	-3.0**	-2.1*	0.1	0.9	1.7	0.6
Some college or equivalent	-4.5**	-2.3*	0.04	2.3**	1.8	4.4**
Four-year college or more	-3.6*	-4.6**	0.3	2.5**	2.1#	5.4**
Wife's education						
High school	2.4*	-1.3	-0.1	-0.7	-0.5	-0.9
Some college or equivalent	3.2*	-3.8**	-0.2	0.4	-0.8	1.7
Four-year college or more	1.8	-7.4**	1.4	0.5	2.3	4.9**
Wife's/husband's age[c]	0.2**	0.1#	-0.01	-0.03*	-0.1	-0.2**

(continued on next page)

Table 7.6 (continued) *Estimated Coefficients from Regression Analyses Predicting the Gender Division of Household Labor: Japan (1994) and the U.S. (1987–1988)*

Predictor	WIVES' TASK HOURS[a]		HUSBANDS' TASK HOURS[b]		HUSBANDS' SHARE[b]	
	Japan	*U.S.*	*Japan*	*U.S.*	*Japan*	*U.S.*
Respondent = female	-0.5	0.7	-1.4**	-0.9**	-2.2**	-1.6*
Adjusted R-square	0.11	0.19	—	—	—	—
F-value	9.69**	30.87**	—	—	—	—
(N)	(1,669)	(3,010)	(1,667)	(2,784)	(1,651)	(2,655)

  [a] Coefficients are estimated by OLS multiple regression.

  [b] Coefficients are estimated by tobit regression.

  [c] Wife's age is used in the analysis of wife's task hours, and husband's age is used in the analyses of husband's task hours and share.

  * Significant at $p < .01$.

  ** Significant at $p < .05$.

  # Significant at $p < .10$.

adult daughters (and daughters-in-law) does not significantly affect the gender division of household labor, although there is a small and marginally significant reduction in husbands' hours in Japan.

Having preschool children reduces husbands' share of housework in the U.S., despite the fact that both husbands and wives do significantly more housework. This is a consequence of the greater effect of small children on wives' workload than on husbands'. In Japan, however, preschool children do not affect husbands' share in housework, primarily because Japanese husbands, unlike their U.S. counterparts, do not respond to the presence of small children by spending more time on housework. As expected, Japanese wives, like their U.S. counterparts, spend significantly more time on housework when they have small children. The presence of school-age children also reduces husbands' share in housework in both countries by disproportionately increasing wives' workload.

We discussed above wives' income in terms of income differences among wives employed full-time. An additional analysis showed that women's employment hours are very similar for the higher and lower income groups, whereas the occupational composition is quite different: a much higher proportion of higher income women hold a professional or managerial job. Hence, these findings for women employed full-time support the relative resource hypothesis. In contrast, husbands' income does not generally affect husbands' share in housework, except for husbands in the highest income category in the U.S. (their share is significantly smaller than that of husbands in the lowest income category).

In both countries, wives of the least educated husbands do the most housework, perhaps reflecting the more traditional expectations of their husbands.

Further, college-educated husbands in the U.S. do more housework than those with less education, and hence they do a greater share of the total as a consequence of the patterns for both husbands and wives. In Japan, however, a man's education is unrelated to the time he spends on household tasks.

Contrary to what we might expect, wives' education has no effect on husbands' household efforts in either country. As expected, women with higher education in the U.S. do considerably less housework than those with less education, even if their husbands are not picking up any of the slack. It is somewhat surprising that in Japan it is the middle educational categories in which wives contribute the most hours to household tasks.

Older husbands in the U.S. shoulder a smaller share of housework than younger husbands because they spend less time on housework. In Japan, although age does not affect husbands' share in housework, it is associated significantly and positively with wives' housework time. When we control for the other variables in the model, we see that older Japanese wives are likely to spend more time on household tasks than younger ones. Perhaps older Japanese wives hold a higher standard for household maintenance.

Husbands' housework time was significantly lower in both countries when the primary respondent was the wife. This leads to the straightforward interpretation for Japan that husbands report more household hours for themselves than their wives report for them. In the U.S., this could reflect the same gender bias, but it may also be a mode effect since the husband always filled out the self-report form when the wife was the primary respondent. There appear to be neither mode nor proxy effects on the reports of wives' time spent on household tasks.

Finally, we turn to the direct measure of gender role attitudes (see table 7.7). We did not include this measure in table 7.6 because we wanted to examine theoretically relevant variables without "controlling away" the potentially mediating role of gender role orientations. As noted above, we can consider only the respondent's own attitude because the Japanese survey collected attitudinal data only from the respondents. In order to provide a sense of scale for these results, table 7.7 presents predicted mean values based on the coefficients from the OLS and tobit regression analyses.

The results for Japan provide only limited support for our expectations. In terms of the household task hours contributed by husbands and wives, only the higher contribution of husbands whose *wives* hold egalitarian values is statistically significant. As a result, the share of housework done by Japanese husbands is higher (and marginally significant) when the wife holds egalitarian values, although the absolute level of husbands' contributions remains very low.

In contrast to Japan, all but one of the comparisons are significant for the U.S. These differences for the U.S. are consistent with our expectations concerning the gender division of labor at home: the less traditional the gender

Table 7.7 *Predicted Mean Hours per Week Spent on Household Tasks and Predicted Husbands' Share of Total Household Task Hours, by Gender Role Attitudes and Gender: Japan (1994) and the U.S. (1987–1988)*

ATTITUDE[a]	WIVES' HOURS		HUSBANDS' HOURS		HUSBANDS' SHARE (PERCENT)	
	Japan	U.S.	Japan	U.S.	Japan	U.S.
Male						
Traditional	34.1	33.1	2.9	7.6	9.6	20.2
Neutral	33.2	32.7	3.0	8.4	9.8	21.6
Egalitarian	32.2	27.7**	2.7	9.0*	8.8	26.0**
Female						
Traditional	33.6	34.0	2.4	6.8	6.6	18.6
Neutral	32.7	33.3	2.2	7.5	6.7	19.9
Egalitarian	34.3	31.4*	3.1*	7.5	9.0#	21.4*

*Significant at $p < .01$.
**Significant at $p < .05$.
#Significant at $p < .10$ (using "traditional" as the reference category).

[a] Gender role attitudes were measured by responses to the following statement: "It is much better for everyone if the man earns the main living and the woman takes care of the home and family." Respondents were classified as egalitarian if their responses were "disagree" or "strongly disagree," neutral if responses were "neither agree nor disagree," and traditional if responses were "agree" or "strongly agree." The estimated coefficients above are controlling for all the covariates shown in table 7.6.

role attitudes of either spouse, the greater the proportion of the housework that is done by the husband. This is so both because wives' household task hours decrease *and* because husbands' task hours increase. Not surprisingly, husbands' own attitudes are more strongly related to their behavior than are those of their wives: husbands' shares of tasks increase from 20 to 26 percent from the least to the most egalitarian husband and from 19 to 21 percent when related to their wives' attitudes.

Conclusion

This chapter has addressed the time that spouses spend on household tasks, as well as combined workload of employment and housework. The latter is based on the recognition that work in both spheres contributes to joint household production. Further, our analysis uses data on both spouses, rather than simply on men and women separately.

Wives are similar in Japan and the U.S. with respect to the time they spend on housework and employment, but husbands' housework time and employment hours differ considerably. Japanese husbands spend much less time on housework than their U.S. counterparts but work considerably longer hours in paid employment. Consequently, the average combined workload is similar between the two countries.

In both Japan and the U.S., when housework and employment hours are considered jointly, gender contributions to the combined workload become very similar. Gender equality in the average combined workload, however, masks an extremely large differential in wives' workload depending on their employment hours. In both countries, combined workload doubles as their employment time increases from zero to sixty or more hours per week, clearly revealing the "second shift" experienced by wives in both countries who are employed full-time.

In multivariate analyses, we find that the time constraints of their own employment hours reduce the household task efforts of both husbands and wives in the U.S. and of wives in Japan. Further, husbands in both countries respond to the increased time pressure on their working wives by increasing their own contributions to household tasks. As a result, the gender division of household labor is altered in the predicted direction. However, the effect of wives' employment hours on husbands' housework contribution differs somewhat in Japan: husbands' housework time and share increases only when wives are employed full-time and earn high incomes.

The presence of others in the household affects the amount of work done by husbands and wives as expected, but the underlying factors are different in the two countries. In the U.S., the presence of preschool children decreases husbands' share in housework because while such presence increases the housework time of both spouses, the increase is larger for wives than for husbands. In Japan, husbands' housework share decreases because wives' housework time increases significantly when there are small children at home but that of husbands does not. The presence of school-aged children reduces husbands' share in housework in both countries (especially in Japan) by increasing wives' time on housework while decreasing husbands' contributions. School-age children create extra housework, which is shouldered mostly by their mothers; at the same time, they may contribute to housework by substituting for some of their fathers' household responsibilities.

Coresidence with parents also decreases husbands' share in Japan, suggesting that parents help with household chores, allowing husbands to do less. Contrary to our expectations, however, having adult daughters or daughters-in-law in the house has little effect on housework in either country.

We find some support for the relative resource hypothesis in explaining the gender division of household labor in both countries. Among wives employed full-time, wives with higher incomes do less housework and their husbands do more. However, the results by husbands' income are more mixed, with the major effect being the reduction of household effort among American husbands who earn high incomes.

In both countries, the effects of education are consistent with the gender role hypothesis in that in couples with more highly educated husbands, and also in those with more highly educated wives, husbands do a higher proportion of the housework. Age of husbands (and therefore of wives) is negatively related to husbands' share in housework in the U.S., implying the cohort change in gender role attitudes that has taken place in postwar American society. To the extent that age indexes differences in gender ideology and socialization, gender role attitudes seem to play an important role in explaining the gender division of household labor in the U.S., but this is clearly not the case in Japan.

Furthermore, the direct measure of gender role attitudes has only a minor effect on the gender division of household labor in Japan, whereas egalitarian attitudes significantly increase husbands' share in housework in the U.S. This difference may reflect the more recent changes in gender roles in Japan (see chapter 2) and also the tendency for attitudes to lag behind (even as they may then become causally relevant to subsequent behavior).[14]

Our analysis of the combined workload expanded our perspective on the gender division of labor beyond the customary focus on female household tasks. At the same time, the latter remains important for its symbolic importance to the gender division of labor, as well as for the sharing of effort in a home. Men do less at home, in part because they spend more hours on their jobs; hence, their overall contribution to the collective family work effort is much larger than generally acknowledged in studies of gender inequality at home. At the same time, the gender *division* of labor is reinforced, and as employment hours increase for women, the proportion of women carrying a heavy double burden will increase as well. The gender gap is large and changes may be slow, especially in the context of Japan's more patriarchal cultural heritage.

Chapter Eight

The Family in Comparative Perspective

Ronald R. Rindfuss

This volume explores family life in Japan, Korea, and the United States. The institution of the family is clearly important to both individuals and society at large. It provides context within which individuals may find support, nourishment, protection, shelter, and comfort. As a crucial social institution, the family mediates between individuals and other institutions and plays a major role in the transfer of values from one generation to the next. As such, it provides the crucible within which social change is accommodated. All three countries are undergoing significant social change in the family, as well as in other institutions that affect the family (chapter 1), and the various chapters in this volume examine how social change has affected family life as filtered through the countries' respective cultural backgrounds.

Recognizing that the causal relationship between attitudes and behavior is complex and reciprocal, this volume began with an examination of responses to attitudinal items (chapters 2 and 3), including many that relate directly to the behaviors analyzed in the following chapters. Information on attitudes makes it possible to explore areas that cannot be observed directly, such as approval or disapproval of emerging family patterns or perceptions of the costs and benefits of a mother's employment.

Both horizontal and vertical components of family life are examined in the volume, with particular attention to differences by age and gender. Vertically, several analyses focus on the parent-child relationship, including relationships between married adults and their parents and the education of the young (chapters 4 and 5). Horizontally, the employment patterns of both spouses are examined, as well as the relationship between employment and the sharing of household tasks (chapters 6 and 7).

Methodologically, the sociological and social demographic literature on the family has followed two approaches: either inquiring about respondents' attitudes toward relevant family topics or attempting to observe family behavior. Both approaches have their strengths and weaknesses, and both are represented in the chapters in this volume. Studying attitudes allows the researcher to explore areas that might not be observable, as well as to obtain indicators of the norms and values of a society. On the other hand, the utility of studying attitudes is related to the salience of the topical area to respondents. Similarly, certain behaviors have a public aspect (e.g., a marriage) and hence are easier to inquire about than others that tend to take place within the confines of the private side of the family and that go on more or less continuously (e.g., the socialization of children).

Family Boundaries and "Packages"

The collection of findings in this volume can be placed in perspective by considering the domains of behavior that fall within family boundaries and the "packages" that come with various aspects of the family. Family boundaries are not constant across cultures or over time, and it is the differences in these boundaries that are frequently illuminated by cross-cultural and historical family research. As noted in in chapter 1, under the expansion of market economies, the historical trend has been a reduction of the roles confined within the family. For example, numerous aspects of the education of children are now under the purview of educational institutions rather than the family, and economically productive aspects of men's and women's lives have moved out of the family and to businesses, small and large, or to government jobs.

Family boundaries differ considerably across Japan, Korea, and the U.S., reflecting the different cultural heritages and histories of these countries. For the sake of discursive simplicity, consider a fairly standard census definition of the family, which would include coresidence—that is, family members are those who live within the same dwelling unit and are related by blood or marriage. Other relatives not living within this dwelling unit might be kin, but they are not family. Japan and Korea, with their strong influence of Confucianism and the relative homogeneity of both populations, have a strong paternalistic emphasis, including a norm for the eldest adult son to coreside with his parents. In contrast, the U.S., with its multiracial and multiethnic heritage, has evolved a value for the independence of the elderly, coupled with the understanding that sons and daughters should provide help as needed. Hence, the residential family tends to be broader in Japan and Korea than in the U.S., more frequently including three generations.

This difference in intergenerational residence patterns is important not only from the perspective of contact between parents and their adult children, but also because it ripples throughout the topics covered in this book. For example, as seen in chapter 6, married women in Japan and Korea who coreside with parents are more likely to be in the labor force. And as shown in chapter 7, married Japanese men who coreside with parents spend fewer hours on household tasks. Further, chapter 3 reports that among unmarried young adults in Japan, those who coreside with parents have less favorable views toward marriage. (This is also the case to a lesser degree among unmarried young adults in the U.S.—with roughly one-half of single persons aged 20–27 living with parents.) Too few married couples live with parents in the U.S. for us to examine whether similar relationships exist, but our hunch is that they do not. As an approved and expected pattern in Korea and Japan, intergenerational coresidence appears to facilitate wives combining work and family roles while simultaneously allowing men to do less around the house, making marriage, as a concept and institution, appear less attractive to unmarried women who are living with their parents.

This raises the issue of the "packages" implied by the various family concepts cross-culturally. Concepts like "marriage," "mother," and "son" are not constant across time or societies. We use the word "package" here to highlight the idea that associated with each of these terms is a culturally and temporally specific set of norms and expectations that define the term and give it meaning to those involved. This is not to say that all members of a society agree to these norms and expectations, nor is it to say that all members of the society follow them. Rather, these packages set the stage for the attitudes and behaviors of members of the society.

Consider marriage, a topic of central importance throughout this volume. The package associated with marriage is quite different in the U.S. in comparison to Japan and Korea. There is less expectation that marriage is permanent in the U.S., as indicated by high divorce rates, cohabitation, and public discussion about prenuptial agreements. In Japan and Korea, marriage tends to be expected to last for life, divorce rates are relatively low (albeit rising), and cohabitation is almost absent as a living arrangement among the unmarried (chapter 1). Unmarried young people in the U.S. are much more likely to be living on their own, whereas in Korea and Japan they are likely to be living with their parents. After marriage, coresidence with parents is still an expected pattern in Japan and Korea, especially for the eldest son (chapter 4). In contrast, very few married couples live with parents in the U.S., and even then coresidence is usually triggered by a crisis in either the senior or junior generation (Bumpass 1994).

In Japan and Korea, marriage, childbearing, and child rearing are tightly linked. Childbearing ought not, and rarely does, occur prior to marriage; childbearing should, and typically does, occur soon after marriage (Rindfuss, Morgan, and Swicegood 1988; National Institute of Population and Social Security Research 1998: 146, 2002: 65). In the two East Asian countries, when marriage is considered, the link to childbearing and child rearing is understood by all parties. In the U.S., the link is not nearly as strong and has been weakening over time. In the 1990s, about one-third of all births occurred to women who were not currently married (Bianchi and Casper 2000), and disapproval of unmarried childbearing has declined rapidly (Pagnini and Rindfuss 1993). The high rates of nonmarital childbearing and divorce have resulted in a substantial fraction of children experiencing repeated changes in family contexts

(Bumpass and Lu 2000). Because divorce rates are still relatively low in Japan and Korea, child rearing occurs mostly within marriage.

In all three countries, marriage and family formation have little effect on men's employment, only marginally increasing the number of hours worked. The opposite is true for women, however, as marriage and family tend to reduce their employment. The extent of this negative effect varies considerably across the three countries, as seen in chapter 6. In the U.S., the relationship of family formation to female labor force participation has declined markedly in recent generations, to the point where the classic "M-shaped" relationship with age is no longer seen. The percent employed by age no longer declines during the prime childbearing years. In Japan the M-shaped pattern is still discernable.

The division of household tasks is also very different in Japan and the U.S. (chapter 7). Married men in the U.S. spend much more time on household tasks than Japanese husbands, who do very little of them indeed. While we do not have an exactly comparable measure for Korea, Korean men also contribute very little to household tasks—as expected from both their patriarchal cultural heritage and long hours of employment (Tsuya and Bumpass 1998). In the U.S., as the number of hours worked outside the household by the wife increases, the number of hours the husband spends on housework also increases, and the number of hours the wife spends on housework decreases. Nonetheless, American wives who work full-time still spend more than twice as many hours on housework as their husbands. The overall image that emerges from the U.S. data is one of trade-offs and bargaining.

There is little change in the number of hours a Japanese husband spends on housework unless his wife works many hours in the labor market and earns a relatively high wage. On the other hand, Japanese wives do reduce their housework hours as their employment time increases and parents (his and/or hers) increase the amount of time they contribute to household tasks. It is as if in Japan the bargaining involves the wife and his (or her) parents, with the husband on the sidelines. Actually, the husband may be participating in the bargaining, but as a mediator rather than as someone who will change his behavior.

In summary, the marriage package differs markedly between the two East Asian countries and the U.S., and this East-West difference reflects, at least in part, the different cultural heritages. At the risk of oversimplification, the marriage package is still a permanent commitment in Japan and Korea and is much more favorable toward men and their parents. Wives' roles are defined in terms of the family; the mother role is constrained to marriage; and husbands provide very little help with household chores, even when wives are working full-time. The marriage package is more flexible in the U.S. on virtually all dimensions. The behavioral footprints we observe are consistent with husband-wife bargaining that is governed, in part, by rules of fairness—that is, consideration of the balance of husband's and wife's work inside and outside the household. From the perspective of women, it would appear that the U.S. marriage package is more attractive than the Japanese package. For men, the Japanese package may be more attractive than the American, but this is not as clear-cut as is the case for women.

These differences in the nature of the marriage packages across the three countries illuminate some of our results regarding marriage-related attitudes. As documented in chapter 2, men in all three countries hold more traditional attitudes toward marriage than women, and the marriage packages tend to be more favorable from a male perspective than from a female one. Not surprisingly, respondents in the U.S. tend to be substantially less negative toward divorce than in either Korea or Japan. Chapter 3 shows that among never-married young adults, the Japanese hold less favorable attitudes toward marriage than Americans. Further, among these young Japanese, women are less favorable toward marriage than men. This pattern also is consistent with the nature of the marriage packages in both countries and the particularly unattractive nature of the Japanese marriage package from the perspective of a young unmarried woman. Thinking about marriage packages helps us to understand the seeming paradox that even though Japan has relatively low rates of marital dissolution, it also has a young population that is less favorably oriented toward marriage. The package facing young Japanese men and women is not as attractive as that facing young American men and women, and indeed we find marked country differences in what is expected in marriage.

While there is considerable evidence that the marriage package in the U.S. has changed substantially over the past two generations, the evidence is far less clear for Japan. For example, the percent of all births that were nonmarital was 1.2 and 1.6 in 1960 and 2000 respectively (National Institute of Population and Social Security Research 2002: 69). Divorces have been increasing, but they are still rare compared to the U.S. Coresidence of parents and adult children is still much more common in Japan than in the U.S., especially for the eldest son and his parents.

All the same, there have been changes in many other aspects in the lives of Japanese women and men. For example, while women's labor force participation was relatively stable between 1960 and 1999, fluctuating at around 50 percent, the percent of employed women who were unpaid family workers declined from 43 to 11 percent over this period (Rodosho Joseikyoku 2000). Thus, there has been a substantial change in *paid* employment among Japanese women, and this in turn could provide an awareness of potential economic independence. This may have large effects on their personal consumption while they are still unmarried and living with parents and hence create a further contrast between marriage and their present circumstances. In addition, this signals an important change in the environment in which women are working, as it is progressively less an environment controlled by family members. Concomitant with this change in women's employment has been a substantial increase in the numbers of women delaying marriage. Indeed, the attitudes of young unmarried women suggest that many would not be opposed to remaining unmarried.

So has the marriage package been changing in Japan? We have only indirect evidence on a number of components of this package. My current read of the evidence is that the marriage package is changing—but slowly. Japanese young people, women in particular, are ambivalent about buying that package, marriage is increasingly delayed, and nonmarriage is probably on the rise.

Cross-National Family Studies

This volume compares family patterns in three countries using individual-level survey data. Doing cross-national work at the individual or household level presents both exciting opportunities and frustrations, some of which are endemic to cross-national work and some of which are unique to the enterprise reported in this volume.

Perhaps the most exciting opportunity presented by cross-national work is that issues and concepts that might not be apparent in research within a country are highlighted when comparisons are made across countries. A number of examples emerge from this volume. Family support for after-school education is one. As noted in chapter 5, a salient aspect of the formal education systems in Japan and Korea is entrance examinations that sort students into schools with well-known rankings. This, in turn, has led to a collection of after-school and weekend programs that, for a fee, prepare students for these exams.

In contrast, the U.S. does not have entrance exams, except for a few connected with private schools. The closest equivalents are standardized tests used in the college and graduate school admissions process. Courses on how to take these exams can be purchased, but these are of relatively short duration. Similarly, some American families will hire tutors on occasion for a child having problems in a specific subject. In both instances, however, the practices are not nearly as pervasive as after-school education in Japan and Korea. In the present case, the U.S. survey did not inquire about after-school programs designed to either prepare children in test-taking skills or to teach them materials they somehow are not learning in school. The cross-national work suggests that asking about family inputs into children's education would be worthwhile in the future in the U.S. The questions would have to be framed differently than in Japan and Korea, but American families undoubtedly differ in their interest, willingness, and ability to put resources into programs outside of school that would give their children advantages in the educational system.

Despite the important gains from comparing countries, a difficulty repeatedly faced throughout this volume is the "small N" problem. At most we had data from three countries, and frequently it was two. Major differences across these three countries involve the following: (1) the presence or absence of a strong, historical Confucian influence; (2) the recency of the economic switch from agriculture to manufacturing to service; and (3) the recency and tempo of demographic transition, including mortality and fertility declines. Korea, Japan, and the U.S. also differ on a wide range of other dimensions, many of which have been discussed in the individual chapters. Examples include geographic size, transportation infrastructure, the usual working days per week, and both formal and informal aspects of the education system. With three countries, it is clearly impossible to sort out what differences at the country level might be associated with differences at the household or individual level. This is, however, a generic problem with most cross-national research. By statistical standards, there are very few countries in the world, and even fewer appropriate to address particular theoretical issues. This is a variant on a problem frequently encountered by those doing contextual or multilevel analysis—there are more contextual variables than contexts.

This volume exploits a unique opportunity presented by three sets of large-scale, nationally representative survey data. The comparability of these surveys was enhanced through the collaboration of researchers across the three countries: (a) researchers at the University of Wisconsin conducted the NSFH; (b) researchers at Nihon University, having already planned a national survey of the family, adapted this survey to include items comparable to some of those in the NSFH; and (c) researchers at KIHASA, who were conducting a period survey examining aspects of family and fertility, included a number of items from both the NSFH and the Japanese survey.

At the same time, however, there was no single funding agency for all three studies, as there was for the countries in the World Fertility Survey or the Demographic and Health Survey. Not having a single funding source, and hence a common set of protocols, meant that at a number of crucial junctures we could not include all three surveys in the analysis. For example, the Korean survey was based on a sample of household heads and their spouses. Hence, the Korean sample was not well suited to studying unmarried men and women, and Korea was excluded from the examination in chapter 3 of views about marriage held by young unmarried adults. The Korean survey also did not ask about the allocation of time to household tasks, so it could not be included in the analyses in chapter 7. The U.S. survey was excluded from chapter 5 because it did not have information on the after-hours schooling of children.

Not having complete comparability was frustrating at times, but this should not overshadow the value of analyses in this volume that were made possible by the data that are comparable. Family sociology has enjoyed a renaissance in the past twenty years, and this body of work often calls for cross-country comparisons. Yet comparable surveys across countries tend to occur around problem areas that attract the attention of international donors and are frequently confined to developing countries. In the absence of funding for large-scale family studies that are comparable across countries, the approach taken here is likely the best we can do. Collaboration among scholars with different, but coordinated, designs can substantially enhance our understanding of family relations within and across these countries.

We have based this volume largely on two cross-sectional surveys (Korea and Japan) and the first wave of a two-wave longitudinal study (U.S.). Yet the aspects of the family being examined are temporally dynamic. This has produced a bit of underlying consternation. Interest in many of these topics is motivated by what is known about changes in these three countries, as well as by speculation on what might be changing. Of particular importance are the changes in women's roles that have occurred or are anticipated in each of these countries. Clearly, a next step is to obtain time depth on these issues through retrospective data, longitudinal data, and/or repeated cross-sections. It is perhaps fitting to conclude this volume with speculation on women's roles and their likely change.

Family, Gender, and the Future

The tension between women's work and family roles was apparent in this volume in myriad ways, as was the contrast between the ways women and men solve the work/family conflict. For example, as shown in chapter 6, work hours for employed men and women are the longest in Korea and shortest in the U.S. Korean men work on the average fifty-two hours a week, and the comparable figure for women is fifty. Korea also has the longest commuting time, and the U.S. the shortest. Working on Saturdays, in addition to Monday through Friday, is normal for Korean full-time workers; this is changing in Japan and unusual in the U.S. Put differently, it would appear that the work and job structures in these three countries vary in a way that makes it more difficult for women to combine work and family roles in Korea than in Japan, and that this juggling act is easiest in the U.S., though by no means easy. Given this situation, perhaps it is not surprising that Korean women are least likely to be in the paid labor force and that Japanese women hold the most negative attitudes toward marriage.

There is also considerable evidence that the tension between work and family roles is far more acute for women than for men. For example, in all three countries, a number of family and life-course variables are correlated with whether or not the wife works and the number of hours she works (chapter 6). For men, however, the only factor related to the number of hours they work is the number of hours their wives work, and even then the relationship is relatively weak. With only slight exaggeration, it would appear that men simply work, and women make the adjustments dictated by family circumstances. There are also large differences in the time allocated to household chores such as cleaning, cooking, doing laundry, and grocery shopping (chapter 7). Even when both the wife and the husband are working full-time, the wife does many more of these household chores than the husband does.

What does all of this portend for the future? Clearly the answers are likely to be different for each of the three countries, reflecting their different histories of economic transformation and cultural background. The U.S. has an advanced, postindustrial economy, coupled with a pluralistic cultural heritage. Rapid and dramatic change has occurred in a number of areas in the American society. Educational levels have risen faster among women than among men (National Center for Education Statistics 2002: table 8). Female labor force participation rates have increased, with especially dramatic increases for mothers of preschool children (Bianchi 2000; Oppenheimer 1994). A variety of child-care arrangements has become available and widely used (Bianchi and Casper 2000). Hours devoted to housework have declined among women and increased somewhat among men (Bianchi et al. 2000). Marital dissolution rates rose very rapidly and then leveled off (Cherlin 1992; Goldstein 1999; Raley and Bumpass 2002). Nonmarital childbearing has increased substantially, and levels of fertility are among the highest in the developed world (Morgan 1996). Attitudes toward many of these changes in women's and family roles have also changed in concert with these behavioral changes (e.g., Pagnini and Rindfuss 1993; Rindfuss and Brewster 1996), and it is all but impossible to sort out cause and effect. These changes have at times involved substantial struggle and anguish and have fueled considerable religious and political discourse, but they have occurred nonetheless. It seems most likely that we will see more change in the future. The family institution in the U.S. has been remarkably resilient in accommodating to such rapid transformations.

There has been less empirical research on related behavioral and attitudinal changes in Japan. However, the chapters in this volume suggest that pressures are increasing that are likely to precipitate critical changes in the future. To use the terminology of meteorologists, the conditions seem ripe for some type of change. Before we ask which type, let us review some of the evidence about the conditions. A large fraction of Japanese wives is employed, even though the hours they work have little effect on the amount of housework their husbands do (chapters 6 and 7). Roughly one-third of married couples in the middle generation live with parents, and hence complex, three-generation households are relatively common (especially when the husband is the eldest son), as we saw in chapter 4. In essence, there are virtually no births occurring to unmarried women (about 1–2 percent since 1960), and Japan is the only country among those that had achieved low fertility by 1960 that has not had an increase in nonmarital fertility (Rindfuss, Benjamin, and Morgan 2000). At many points in this volume, the attitudinal evidence has suggested considerable dissatisfaction with the current marital package, particularly on the part of women (chapters 2 and 3). Behaviorally, Japanese women are delaying marriage (with hints that for the first time a significant fraction will remain unmarried), and they now have a fertility rate that is among the lowest in the world.

If the conditions are ripe for change, in the near term two different types of change are possible. Indeed, a combination of both is likely. On the one hand, the marriage package could remain essentially unchanged, with the consequence that Japanese women who want to get married and have children would do so and those who do not like the package would remain single and childless. On the other hand, the package itself could change in such a way that the tensions that now exist could be eased. Among the possibilities would be an increase in household help by husbands, increased availability of a variety of child-care options, lower levels of intergenerational coresidence, and greater flexibility in terms of work hours and schedules. Which is more likely? Although this is difficult to predict, we may well see substantially more delay in marriage and childbearing before there are fundamental changes in the nature of the marriage package itself. This, in turn, will likely generate more policy discussion about "solutions" for the delayed marriage and low fertility problems.

Korea, of the three countries examined, has experienced the industrial revolution most recently. With such a recent transition, work hours are long, part-time jobs are scarce, few married women are in the paid labor force, and the senior generation very often lives in rural areas while adult children live in Seoul and other urban areas. As these words are being written, Korea is about to emerge from a major economic downturn, making speculation about its future economy somewhat difficult. However, it seems most likely that the economy will recover and continue to grow and evolve. The nature of its evolution will likely have a profound effect on a variety of family issues. To the extent that work hours and commuting times remain long, little change in the marriage package would be expected. On the other hand, there is the intriguing possibility that Koreans are closely watching the changes in Japan with respect to women's family roles and employment. As the struggle between these domains continues in Japan, Korea may benefit from the Japanese experience.

Notes

Chapter 1: Introduction

1. The TFR is the average number of children that a cohort of women would have if they were to survive until age fifty and follow the age-specific fertility rates of a given year.

2. By "traditional," we refer to the family system that prevailed in Japan from the late nineteenth century to the end of World War II in 1945 and in Korea from the late seventeenth century (the latter half of the Yi dynasty) to the end of the Korean War in 1953. During the Koryo period (918–1392), which preceded the Yi dynasty, and even during the early period of the Yi dynasty, the institution of marriage and family was quite different from that defined here as "traditional." Similarly, the *ie* system in Japan had originally been dominant among the samurai (warrior) class in the Tokugawa period (1603–1868). Upon the fall of the Tokugawa regime through the Meiji Restoration in 1868, the system was adapted to and developed in the commoner population, taking the form of the civil code. For details on the traditional family system and ideals pertaining to marriage, family, and gender roles in Japan and Korea, see Choi (1970), Deuchler (1977), Taeuber (1958: 100– 104), Tsuya and Choe (1991), and Wagner (1983).

3. While the traditional *ie* and *jib* systems have many similarities, there are also differences. Although the rule of descent was basically patrilineal in both countries, the Korean system put far more emphasis on paternal consanguinity (i.e., biological continuity of the male bloodline) through succession of the family headship (Choi 1970; Lee 1978). This strong emphasis on a biological male heir is argued to have formed the basis for the strong son preference that still exists in Korea today (Cho, Arnold, and Kwon 1982; B.-M. Chung, Cha, and Lee 1977). In contrast, even when a biological son was available in Japan, adoption was possible if the son was judged incompetent or unworthy. An adopted son or son-in-law was given all the authority and obligations pertaining to the future head of the family. (On the *ie* system, see Aruga 1960; Yonemura and Nagata 1998.) Hence, the basic function of the Korean system was to preserve the bloodline, whereas that of the Japanese system was to preserve the social institution of the *ie*.

4. Because of the readily available option of adopting a son or son-in-law, one may argue that the Japanese *ie* was bilateral. However, the *ie* and the *jib* were both patrilineal in the sense that succession of family headship and inheritance of family property occurred through the male line—biologically through reproduction or socially through adoption.

5. Furthermore, by bearing and rearing an heir, a woman belonged to the heir's descent line as an ancestor after death, thereby ensuring a resting place for her soul (Greenhalgh 1985).

6. This is not to say that the relationships in the two systems were not affectionate. They had to be if the systems were to continue to be viable social institutions. However, an essential characteristic of the systems in the two countries was a for-

mal structure that dictated the lives of individual family members for the continuity of the family as a whole.

7. Describing the situation of the Japanese marriage market for women before the recent decade, Brinton (1992) introduces a popular Japanese riddle: "Why are women like Christmas cakes? Because they are popular and sell like hot cakes up until 25 and after that you have a lot of trouble getting rid of them." To the best of our knowledge, this was a widely popular notion on the "appropriate" age for women to marry in Japan before the 1980s. For more details, see Tsuya (1994).

Chapter 2: Attitudes Relating to Marriage and Family Life

1. While there is a substantial gulf between those raised during the Great Depression and those who grew up in the much more prosperous postwar environment, the earlier of these cohorts is beyond the upper age limit of our analysis.

2. This similarity in emphasis on traditional family systems in Japan and Korea is important, even though there are differences in traditional cultural norms, the assumption of family headship, and about the responsibilities and privileges of the eldest and younger sons. For more details, see chapter 1; see also Choi (1970) and Tsuya and Choe (1991).

3. In Japan the "traditional" norms against sexual activity of unmarried young adults, especially young women, apply primarily to the period after the Meiji Restoration in 1868. Sexual indulgence appears to have been quite prevalent among young unmarried men and women in rural areas during the preceding Tokugawa period. For more details, see Tsuya (1993).

4. This item appeared only in NSFH1.

5. Under the prewar family system in these two countries, the rules of divorce were applied very differently to men and women. Women were not allowed by law or social custom to divorce (or obtain a separation from) their husbands, whereas men could divorce their wives easily, especially during the early years of marriage. For example, in Korea, a man was legally allowed to divorce his wife if she did not show enough filial piety to her parents-in-law, failed to bear a son, was unchaste or jealous, contracted a severe disease, was too talkative, or committed a crime (Lee 1978: 114; Cho, Arnold, and Kwon 1982: 88). Though these legal grounds for divorce were often not strictly enforced, procreation and filial piety seem to have been important because infecundity and conflicts of a wife with her in-laws (especially her mother-in-law) were the most frequently cited reasons for divorcing or deserting a wife in prewar Korea and Japan (Cho, Arnold, and Kwon 1982: 98; Lee 1978: 114–123; Tsuya and Choe 1991; Vogel 1971: 204–205).

Chapter 3: Views of Marriage among Never-Married Young Adults

1. Both surveys also asked about relations with parents, but we omit this dimension because it seems less central and, in fact, is not related to our outcomes of interest. Each survey also included at least one dimension not asked about in the other survey—for example, respect from others in Japan and sex life and friendships with others in the U.S.

2. In the context of the wording of this question in the Japanese survey, "don't know" is interpreted as a respondent's being uncertain about *whether or not* he/she wanted

to marry, rather than about when he/she wanted to marry, since a prior response category was "eventually."

3. In NSFH2, there are also questions about the desires of the unmarried to be married now, within the next year, or someday. Because the lowest age for single persons in the NSFH2 is twenty-four, however, we decided to use the data from the original survey.

4. We also examined gender role attitudes, but these were unrelated to any of the dependent variables.

5. We omitted the personal freedom question because responses to it did not correlate well with responses to the other marriage perception questions, and, as a single item, it was unrelated to marriage desires. Therefore, the questions on standard of living, emotional security, and overall happiness were formed into a marriage perception scale by summing responses to the three items.

6. Also, separating the responses of the never-married and currently married by age in the U.S. suggests a more complex story than mere selection for positive outlooks toward marriage among those who marry early. For example, on the standard of living question, younger men (ages 20–23) are less likely than older men to view marriage as beneficial *regardless* of marital status, and within each age group, there is no difference between the never-married and the currently married. Thus, the age pattern for this question is not entirely consistent with supposing that early marriage selects those who are most positive in their views of marriage.

7. As mentioned above, cohabitors are excluded from this table because the NSFH did not ask cohabiting persons whether they would *like* to get married. They are, however, asked about whether they expected to marry their partner and, if not, whether they expected ever to marry. Most who expect to marry undoubtedly also want to do so, and the same proportion as reported in table 3.3 (90 percent) think that they will eventually get married. Hence, the omission of cohabitors does not affect our results.

8. The ordered logistic regression model estimates the coefficients of the effects of covariates on an ordered categorical variable (McCullagh and Nelder 1989). We estimated final equations containing only gender and other predictors that are statistically significant at the 10 percent level or better. We tested for interactions of gender with the other covariates and found no significant effects.

9. Note that the results for the U.S. pertain only to individuals who are not currently cohabiting.

10. Although it is too soon to be certain, there are hints of a rapid decline in cohort fertility in Japan in recent years. The cumulative cohort TFR at age thirty-five is around 1.9–2.0 children per woman for those who were born in 1957 or earlier, whereas the corresponding figure for those born in 1960 is 1.7 and for those born in 1965 it is 1.5 (National Institute of Population and Social Security Research 2002: 61–63).

Chapter 4: Intergenerational Relations

1. If it is an in-law relationship, it begins with the marriage and typically ends with the death of the parents-in-law. If a marriage is terminated by dissolution, the relationship with the parents-in-law may or may not end. Further, stepparent-stepchild

relationships vary over the life course, depending on the age of the child when the stepfamily was formed.

2. Because of high levels of unmarried childbearing and union disruption in the U.S., half of all children will have an absent father for at least part of their childhood. For many of these, the father-child relationship becomes much more tenuous.

3. "Interaction" here refers to interaction between *living* parents and their *living* children. In planning the project that resulted in this volume, the topic of obligations toward deceased ancestors arose. Issues involved can range from religiously or culturally mandated ceremonies to the high cost of obtaining proper burial sites in Japan. However, no questions were included on these topics in any of the three national surveys—our major data sources—and these topics will not be addressed in this chapter.

4. To see the difference, consider a simple hypothetical example. Imagine a country where every couple has four children, equally divided between boys and girls, all of whom survive to adulthood and marry. Further assume that there is a strong and effective norm for the parents and eldest son to coreside, but not the others, and that all the parents have survived up to the time when the data were collected. Then a data collection effort focusing on the parents might show that all members of the senior generation are living with their sons, but only 50 percent of the adult sons are living with their parents.

5. Although not germane to this chapter, it is worth noting that the Japanese *koseki* and the Korean *hojeok* systems of record keeping create problems for an out-of-wedlock child and may be a contributing factor to the low level of nonmarital childbearing in both countries.

6. A colloquial Japanese term for marriage is *seki wo yireru,* which literally means to list one's *koseki* in the spouse's *koseki.*

7. We should also note that the nature of the Korean data might have led to somewhat higher levels of couples without living parents. As noted in chapter 1, in the Korean survey, only heads of households or spouses of heads of households were chosen as respondents. If a married adult child and his/her parents are living together in the same household and if there is a tendency to designate someone from the senior generation as head of the household, then one would have fewer in the middle generation with living parents. However, this aspect of the Korean data does not seem to be a major problem. First, if this were an important factor, then one would expect greater differences in the distributions between Japan and Korea; instead they are reasonably close, especially for husband's parents. Second, based on data from the 1994 National Fertility and Family Health Survey—a nationally representative sample of 10,255 households and 34,836 individuals conducted by KIHASA—the proportions of ever-married men by age who are reported to be heads of household are as follows: 95 percent for ages 30–34, 97 percent for ages 35–39, 99 percent for ages 40–44, 98 percent for ages 45–54, and 97 percent for ages 55–59.

8. For example, the expectation of life at birth in the three countries in 1960 is seen in the following table.

Sex	Japan	Korea	U.S.
Male	65.3	53.0	66.6
Female	70.2	57.8	73.1

9. Korea has a land mass of 98,480 square kilometers. Japan and the U.S. are 377,835 and 9,372,610 square kilometers respectively. When we consider the relative sizes of the three countries, it is important to remember that the population is not evenly distributed across the landscape. For example, in the U.S., the population tends to be heavily concentrated up and down the East and West Coasts, with vast expanses across the plains with very few people.

10. There is also urban-to-urban migration in all three countries that reflects the nature of the job markets and affects intergenerational relations. In our data sets, we know about respondents' rural-urban upbringing, but we do not know the specific places where they and their spouses grew up.

11. Note that relatively high proportions in both Korea and the U.S. have missing data on husband's father's education. This is not surprising for a number of reasons. First, in approximately one-half of the cases, the respondent was the wife, and she simply might not have known her father-in-law's educational attainment. Further, parental mortality or a marital dissolution occurring when the respondent was relatively young might make it more likely that the respondent would not know the father's education.

12. Using the data from the 1988 national family survey in Japan, Martin and Tsuya (1991) found that the likelihood of coresidence of middle-aged couples with the wife's parents was determined solely by demographic factors—such as the wife being the only child, the husband being a younger son, or a parent having no spouse.

13. There is a fourth dummy variable for the U.S. to indicate whether there is missing data on the husband's education. In NSFH1, information on respondents came from an interview with them, whereas spouses of respondents were asked to fill out and return a self-administered questionnaire (Sweet 1989). While this procedure has certain advantages, it created more missing data on spouse characteristics because some of the spouse questionnaires were not completed.

14. This variable is not available for Japan.

15. To be certain, the continuation of the family name through adoption of a son-in-law (wife's husband) does not have to be accompanied by actual coresidence with the wife's parents. By the same token, even if the husband is not adopted, couples can and do live with the wife's parents, especially when the wife is the only child or has no male sibling while the husband is not the eldest or only son (Martin and Tsuya 1991; Tsuya 1990).

16. We should note that this is the general approach used in collecting information on intergenerational interactions. It would be possible to design a questioning sequence that asked about contact with each parent by each spouse, but the time investment on extra data collection would be substantial and the respondent burden would be high.

17. Specifically, the turning point is age 53 for seeing wife's parents and age 49 for seeing husband's parents.

18. Costs for telephone usage do vary across the three countries, as well as within the U.S. For example, in Japan, local calls are charged in three-minute units, but in the U.S. unit charges for local calls do not exist in most locations. Also note that these surveys were conducted about 1994, when e-mail was to be found in few homes. As a side note, it will be interesting to see how the penetration of e-mail

into more and more homes will change patterns of intergenerational contact. Anec-dotal evidence suggests that the increasingly widespread use of e-mail might pro-foundly influence these patterns by reducing the friction of space. The third wave of the NSFH (NSFH3)—to be conducted in 2002–2003—includes a question about the frequency of intergenerational contact via phone, written correspon-dence, or e-mail.

19. This inflection point ranges from a low of age 50 for telephoning with wife's par-ents in the U.S. to a high of age 59 for telephoning husband's parents, also in the U.S.

Chapter 5: Investments in Children's Education, Desired Fertility, and Women's Employment

1. The one exception, to our knowledge, is an essay by Rohlen (1980). In the essay, Rohlen discusses characteristics of cram schools in the cultural context of Japan. Ogawa and Retherford (1993b) also note the salience of educational costs, espe-cially those for after-school programs, in Japan's fertility decline in recent years.

2. There is, however, concern in some segments of the U.S. population with invest-ing in other kinds of children's after-school activities such as music or dance lessons. These activities are often costly, and mothers may become employed to pay for them. Similar nonacademic after-school activities exist in Japan and Korea, and they too tend to be costly and often include elements of status competition. However, we do not have comparative data for these activities.

3. For specifics of the educational system in Japan, Korea, and the U.S., see Brinton (1992), Dore (1976: 35–50), Y.-H. Kim (1993), Rohlen (1980), and Turner (1960).

4. Though increasing over the years, the proportion of Japan's elementary and mid-dle schools that are private remains extremely small—0.8 percent and 5.3 percent respectively in 1995 (Monbusho 1997: 48, 51).

5. Information on recent changes in the Korean government's educational policy was obtained through personal communications with Young-Chan Byun at KIHASA and Jong-Kun Choi, a visiting fellow at the East-West Center in 1998.

6. In August 1998, *Asahi Newspaper,* one of the largest dailies in Japan, reported (on the basis of findings from a 1998 national household expenditures survey by the Economic Planning Agency) that despite the current economic slump, Japanese parents were still eager to invest heavily in children's after-school programs. According to the survey, whereas the average expenses for eating out and leisure activities had declined by 15 percent from the previous year, the average expenses for children's supplementary education were estimated to have *increased* by 5 percent.

7. This survey was based on a nationally representative sample of 3,013 ever-married women aged 15–64. A multistage stratified probability sample was used in which ever-married women under age 65 were selected for face-to-face interviews. Out of the 3,022 sampled ever-married women, interviews were conducted with 2,838, a response rate of 94 percent.

8. We also analyzed the likelihood of children's enrollment in after-school programs, using the data on the mothers of school-aged children. However, we decided to approach this issue from the perspective of children rather than that of mothers

in order to avoid complications pertaining to mothers with multiple school-aged children.

9. For specifics of the WTMFR, see Kulkarni and Choe (1998).

10. The estimate of TMFR$_{ppr}$ for Japan is drawn from Ogawa and Retherford (1993b) and that for Korea from Choe et al. (1995). For specifics on calculations of the TMFR$_{ppr}$, see Feeney and Yu (1987).

11. For Japan, we also computed the percentages enrolled in after-school programs by sex of children. Since we found only small differences between boys and girls, we decided not to present the data.

12. We also tested the effect of father's education in Japan. Because father's education and income are correlated, the effects of these variables disappeared when included in the same model. When the model included only father's education (but not his income), the effect was positive but not statistically significant.

13. A study based on a small-scale survey in the Taegu area in Korea found that household income was positively associated with the costs of children's cram schools or private tutoring (Y. S. Chung 1996). With the same data, when household income was replaced by spouses' income, wife's income was found to be positively associated with children's enrollment in expensive after-school programs but husband's income did not have a significant effect (Y. S. Chung and Choe 2001). We are uncertain why wife's income, rather than husband's income, matters.

14. In Japan the population at age 18 is estimated to have peaked in 1991 with 2,068,000. After 1991, it was estimated that the size of the 18-year-old population would continue to decline steadily and rapidly until 2008–2009. In Korea, according to the 1995 census report, the population at age 18 is projected to peak in 1999 and decline rapidly afterward. For details, see Institute of Population Problems (1992: 63–98) and National Statistical Office (1996: 71–106).

Chapter 6: Employment

1. We employed different multivariate models as appropriate to the dependent variables. Wives' employment status (employed or not) and preferences concerning wives' employment were both examined using binary logistic regression models; hours of employment of wives and husbands were examined with ordinary least squares (OLS) multiple regressions, and satisfaction with marital relationship with ordered logistic regression. Of the three project surveys, only the Japanese sample is self-weighting. In the other two, all cross-tabulations used weights, but multivariate analyses were done without weights.

2. Yoshio Okunishi of Hosei University provided us the results of microdata from the 1993 Japanese wage structure survey.

3. According to the 1995 census in the Republic of Korea, 92 percent of women employed in nonagricultural sectors were employed full-time (T.-H. Kim and Yang 1997: 101). Based on data from Korea's monthly labor statistics for nonagricultural enterprises with ten or more employees, the average for those with regular employment was 5.68 days per week in 1994 and 5.54 days per week in 1998 (National Statistical Office 1999: 111–112). Assuming that many of those in agriculture (or small businesses) work on a full-time basis, we chose the multiplier of 5.5 days per week.

4. The Japanese and U.S. surveys asked all respondents (both employed and not employed) of both sexes to answer the two following questions: (1) "If you could work just the number of hours in paid employment that you would like, how many hours per week would that be?" (2) "If your spouse could work just the number of hours in paid employment that *you* would like, how many hours per week would that be?" To these questions, the Japanese survey provided (identical) sets of pre-coded categories from which respondents were to choose an answer. In the U.S. survey, respondents were to choose between zero (not at all) and some hours. For the latter, the survey further asked the respondent to specify a number.

5. Ogawa (1990) also found a negative relationship between education of married women of reproductive ages and their employment in Japan, using data from the 1990 national opinion survey on family planning.

6. In Japan this negative relationship remains, net of factors pertaining to wives themselves (such as their age and education) and their family/household characteristics (such as age of youngest child or coresidence with or nearness to parents). When husband's income is added, however, the relationship becomes statistically insignificant, though the overall inverse relationship still persists. We also tested interactions of wife's education with age of youngest child and with husband's income (because highly educated wives tend to be older when they bear children and consequently more likely to have small children and because highly educated women tend to have husbands with higher earnings). However, we found none of these interactions statistically significant.

7. In the Japanese survey, the questions on commuting time were addressed to those who "work outside the home." Respondents who were self-employed, family workers, or farmers were not asked to answer these questions because these were presumed to be applicable only to persons who were employees of organizations that were geographically away from their residence. Thus, most self-employed persons, small business proprietors, and farmers did not answer these questions as they live in (or near) the place where they work.

Chapter 7: Gender and Housework

1. The Korean survey (NSQL) asked a question about time spent on "housework as a whole, including, in addition to traditionally female tasks, such other tasks as child care, helping children with homework, other work related to the education of children, visiting relatives, and all other activities required in running a household."

2. A comparative study by Kamo (1994) found that wives' employment status did not have a significant effect on the gender division of household labor in either Japan or the U.S. However, this analysis was based on small, nonrepresentative data.

3. An exception is Bergen (1990), who found that the presence of young children *significantly increases* husbands' contributions to housework.

4. Though child care was asked about as well in the Japanese and U.S. surveys, we have excluded child-care time because it is almost impossible to assign unique hours to the time spent on child care, especially among mothers of young children. Parents (especially mothers) are likely to do other tasks while caring for their children. It is also difficult to separate the work dimension of child care (e.g., feeding and bathing the child) from general oversight (simply keeping an eye out for

needed intervention) or the leisure dimension (e.g., playing with the child). Measuring and analyzing spouses' hourly contributions to different dimensions of child care and housework, Ishii-Kuntz and Coltrane (1992) indicated that child care and housework are distinct but interrelated activities.

NSFH1 also collected information on the time spent in male tasks such as household maintenance or auto repair, as well as such gender-neutral tasks as paying bills and keeping household financial records. However, these areas were not covered in the Japanese survey. Although not germane to this chapter, wives' perceptions of the fairness of the division of household tasks are found to be affected by husbands' participation in traditionally female tasks but not in male or gender-neutral tasks (Benin and Agostinelli 1988; Blair and Johnson 1992). This is probably so because a husband's help with female tasks is more salient and therefore more deeply appreciated.

5. Yoshio Okunishi provided us the results of computations of microdata of the survey.

6. There is also a difference between the two countries in the combined workload when considered by husbands' income. In the U.S. the average combined workload for wives of high-income husbands is considerably lower than that of other wives, whereas there is little differential in Japan in terms of husbands' income. This suggests a "leisure-time effect" of household financial resources on American wives' time—that is, wives of high-income husbands can afford not to work in the labor market and can also hire outside help in household maintenance.

7. Based on an analysis of demographic and socioeconomic profiles of husbands who work less than thirty-five hours per week, many of these husbands seem to be older men who are retired from previous full-time employment.

8. We do not present the results of multivariate analyses of combined workload because there is not much information added by these analyses. Because husbands' employment hours constitute a vast majority of husbands' combined workload in both countries (95 percent for Japan and 83 percent for the U.S.), husbands' combined workload and their share in combined work are determined largely by their employment hours. As for wives' combined workload, our earlier analysis showed that whereas the average total hours are similar in Japan and the U.S., the underlying factors are somewhat different. Nonetheless, once the effects of wives' employment hours are controlled for, the remaining variations are explained mostly by the factors affecting wives' housework time.

9. We also attempted to measure the effect of relative resources by using two continuous variables: the log of husband's income and the log of the ratio of husband's income to wife's income. However, we eventually decided to use categorical variables, primarily because our multivariate analyses showed the nonlinearity of the effects of husband's and wife's income on the time spouses spend on housework, as well as on husbands' share of housework.

10. Among the covariates in our model, men's income has the highest number of missing cases: 70 (4 percent of the sample) for Japan and 254 (7 percent of the sample) for the U.S. The number of missing cases on wives' income is not as high as that on husbands' income. Further, we use income information only for women who work full-time, and the number of missing cases on income for these women is quite small: 16 for Japan and 82 for the U.S.

11. To examine whether this composite measure of women's income (conditional on their employment hours) captures the effect of their economic resources, we also analyzed patterns of employment hours for the higher and lower income groups of full-time employed women and found little difference between these two groups in both countries.

12. The Japanese and U.S. surveys also had comparable attitude measures with respect to husbands' contribution to household tasks—in the former: "If the wife is employed, the husband should help with the household chores substantially"; in NSFH1: "If a husband and a wife both work full-time, they should share household tasks equally." Because of obvious simultaneity between these items and actual household task hours, we did not include these statements in our scale.

13. For the analysis of husbands' housework hours, we employ tobit regression because around 43 percent of Japanese husbands (and 9 percent of U.S. husbands) have zero housework hours. Tobit models are limited dependent variable models that allow the dependent variable to be censored or truncated at a certain value (Greene 1991: 565–602).

14. We argue this in the context of the strong patriarchal tradition in Japan rooted in Confucianism. Retherford, Ogawa, and Sakamoto (1996) provide an example of value change in Japan lagging behind fertility change, then evolving more rapidly in accommodation to changed social and economic conditions.

References

Abelmann, Nancy. 1997. "Women's Class Mobility and Identities in South Korea: A Gendered, Transnational, Narrative Approach." *Journal of Asian Studies* 56 (2): 398–420.

Aquilino, William, and Kahlil Supple. 1991. "Parent-Child Relations and Parents' Satisfaction with Living Arrangements When Adult Children Live at Home." *Journal of Marriage and the Family* 53: 999–1010.

Arnold, Fred. 1987. "The Effect of Sex Preference on Fertility and Family Planning: Empirical Evidence." *Population Bulletin of the United Nations* No. 23/24: 44–55.

Aruga, Kizaemon. 1960. "Kazoku to ie" [Family and the *ie* in Japan]. *Testugaku* 38: 79–110.

Asahi Newspaper. 1998. "Gaishoku ya goraku hikaetemo, kyoiku ewa oshimazu" [Even if reducing expenses for eating out or leisure, Japanese consumers do not spare expenses for children's education]. *Asahi Newspaper* 15 August (http://www.asahi.com/flash/fnational/html).

Atoh, Makoto. 1988. "Changes in Family Patterns in Japan." Paper presented at IUSSP seminar on Theories of Family Change, Tokyo, 29 November–2 December.

———. 1992. "Family Policy in the Age of Below-Replacement Fertility." In *Summary of the Twenty-first National Survey on Family Planning*. Ed. Population Problems Research Council, 171–194. Tokyo: Mainichi Shimbun.

Axinn, William, and Arland Thornton. 1996. "The Influence of Parent's Marital Dissolution on Children's Attitudes toward Family Formation." *Demography* 33 (1): 66–81.

Becker, Gary S. 1981. *A Treatise on the Family.* Cambridge, Mass.: Harvard University Press.

Bellah, Robert N. 1964. *Values and Social Change in Modern Japan.* Tokyo: International Christian University. Studies in Modernization of Japan by Western Scholars, Asian Cultural Studies, vol. 3.

Benin, Mary Holland, and Joan Agostinelli. 1988. "Husbands' and Wives' Satisfaction with the Division of Labor." *Journal of Marriage and the Family* 50: 349–361.

Bergen, E. 1990. "The Multidimensional Nature of Domestic Labor." Paper presented at the annual meeting of the National Council on Family Relations, Seattle, November.

Bernard, Jessie. 1973. *The Future of Marriage.* New York: Bantam Books.

Bianchi, Suzanne M. 2000. "Maternal Employment and Time with Children: Dramatic Change or Surprising Continuity?" *Demography* 37 (4): 401–414.

Bianchi, Suzanne M., and Lynne M. Casper. 2000. "American Families." *Population Bulletin* 55 (4): 1–52.

Bianchi, Suzanne M., and Daphne Spain. 1986. *American Women in Transition.* New York: Russell Sage Foundation.

———. 1996. "Women, Work, and Family in America." *Population Bulletin* 51 (3): 1–48.

Bianchi, Suzanne M., Melissa Milkie, Liana Sayer, and John Robinson. 2000. "Is Anyone Doing the Housework?" *Social Forces* 79: 191–228.

Blair, Sampson Lee. 1992. "Children's Participation in Household Labor: Child Socialization versus the Need for Household Labor." *Journal of Youth and Adolescence* 21: 241–258.

Blair, Sampson Lee, and Michael P. Johnson. 1992. "Wives' Perceptions of the Fairness of the Division of Household Labor: The Intersection of Housework and Ideology." *Journal of Marriage and the Family* 54: 570–581.

Blood, Robert O., and Donald M. Wolfe. 1960. *Husbands and Wives: The Dynamics of Married Living.* Glencoe, Ill.: Free Press.

Bongaarts, John. 1990. "The Measurement of Wanted Fertility." *Population and Development Review* 16 (3): 487–506.

Brinton, Mary C. 1988. "The Social-Institutional Bases of Gender Stratification: Japan as an Illustrative Case." *American Journal of Sociology* 94 (2): 300–334.

———. 1990. "Intrafamilial Markets for Education in Japan." In *Social Institutions: Their Emergence, Maintenance and Effects.* Ed. Michael Hechter, Karl-Dieter Opp, and Reinhard Wippler, 307–330. New York: Aldine de Gruyter.

———. 1992. "Christmas Cakes and Wedding Cakes: The Social Organization of Japanese Women's Life Course." In *Japanese Social Organization.* Ed. Takie Sugiyama Lebra, 79–107. Honolulu: University of Hawai'i Press.

———. 2001. "Married Women's Labor in East Asian Economies." In *Women's Working Lives in East Asia.* Ed. Mary C. Brinton, 1–37. Stanford, Calif.: Stanford University Press.

Brinton, Mary C., Yean-Ju Lee, and William L. Parish. 1995. "Married Women's Employment in Rapidly Industrializing Societies: Examples from East Asia." *American Journal of Sociology* 100 (5): 1099–1130.

Bumpass, Larry L. 1982. "Employment among Mothers of Young Children: Changing Behavior and Attitudes." Madison: Center for Demography and Ecology, University of Wisconsin–Madison. *CDE Working Paper* 26.

———. 1990. "What's Happening to the Family? Interactions between Demographic and Institutional Change." *Demography* 27 (4): 483–498.

———. 1994. "A Comparative Analysis of Coresidence and Contact with Parents in Japan and the United States." In Cho and Yada, eds., *Tradition and Change,* 221–246.

———. 1998. "The Changing Significance of Marriage in the United States." In Mason, Tsuya, and Choe, eds., *The Changing Family in Comparative Perspective,* 63–79.

———. 2002. "Family-Related Attitudes, Couple Relationships, and Union Stability." In *Meaning and Choice: Value Orientations and Life Cycle Decisions.* Ed. Ron Lesthaeghe, 161–164. The Hague: Netherlands Interdisciplinary Demographic Institute.

Bumpass, Larry L., and Hsien-Hen Lu. 2000. "Trends in Cohabitation and Implications for Children's Family Contexts in the U.S." *Population Studies* 54 (1): 29–41.

Bumpass, Larry L., and R. Kelly Raley. 1999. "Divorce: Estimates of Trends, Differentials, and Data Quality." Madison: Center for Demography and Ecology, University of Wisconsin–Madison. *CDE Working Paper* 99–25.

Bumpass, Larry L., and James A. Sweet. 1992. "Family Experiences across the Life Course: Differences by Cohort, Education, and Race/Ethnicity." In *Proceedings: The Peopling of the Americas.* Ed. International Union for the Scientific Study of Population, 3:313–350. Liege: IUSSP.

Bumpass, Larry L., James Sweet, and Andrew Cherlin. 1991. "The Role of Cohabitation in Declining Significance of Marriage." *Journal of Marriage and the Family* 53 (4): 913–927.

Byun, Yong-Chan. 1996. "Economic Development and Changes in Family Structure in Korea." Paper presented at the Nihon University International Symposium on the Contemporary Family in Comparative Perspective, Tokyo, 4–7 March.

Caldwell, John C. 1976. "Toward a Restatement of Demographic Transition Theory." *Population and Development Review* 2 (2): 321–366.

———. 1982. *Theory of Fertility Decline.* London: Academic Press.

Carter, Wendy Y. 1993. "Non-Marital Childbearing, Cohabitation, and Marriage among Blacks and Whites." Madison: Center for Demography and Ecology, University of Wisconsin–Madison. *NSFH Working Paper* 61.

Casper, Lynn, Mary Hawkins, and Martin O'Connell. 1991. "Who's Minding the Kids?" *Current Population Survey Reports* P70-36. Washington, D.C.: U.S. Department of Commerce.

Casterline, John B., Ronald D. Lee, and Karen A. Foote, eds. 1996. *Fertility in the United States: New Patterns, New Theories.* Supplement to *Population and Development Review* 22. New York: Population Council.

Chamratrithirong, Aphichat, S. Philip Morgan, and Ronald R. Rindfuss. 1988. "Living Arrangements and Family Formation." *Social Forces* 66 (4): 926–950.

Chang, H.-S., H.-O. Kim, and H. O. Bae. 1994. *Kajok yongyok ui sam ui chil kwa chongchaek yonku* [The quality of family life and policy implications]. Seoul: Korea Institute for Health and Social Affairs.

Cherlin, Andrew J. 1981. *Marriage, Divorce, Remarriage.* Cambridge, Mass.: Harvard University Press.

———. 1992. *Marriage, Divorce, Remarriage.* Revised and enlarged edition. Cambridge, Mass.: Harvard University Press.

Cherlin, Andrew J., and Frank F. Furstenberg Jr. 1986. *The New American Grandparent.* New York: Basic Books.

Chesnais, Jean-Claude. 1996. "Fertility, Family and Social Policy in Contemporary Western Europe." *Population and Development Review* 22 (4): 729–739.

Cho, Lee-Jay, Fred Arnold, and Tai Hwan Kwon. 1982. *The Determinants of Fertility in the Republic of Korea.* Washington, D.C.: National Academy Press.

Cho, Lee-Jay, and Moto Yada, eds. 1998. *Tradition and Change in the Asian Family.* Honolulu: East-West Center.

Cho, Namhun, Seungkwon Kim, Aejŏ Cho, Yongsik Chang, and Yŏnghi Oh. 1997. *Chŏnkuk ch'ulsanyŏk mit kajok pogŏn silt'ae chosa pogosŏ* [The report of the 1997 Korean national survey on fertility and family health]. Seoul: Korea Institute for Health and Social Affairs.

Choe, Minja Kim. 1998. "Changing Marriage Patterns in South Korea." In Mason, Tsuya, and Choe, eds., *The Changing Family in Comparative Perspective,* 43–62.

Choe, Minja Kim, and Insook Han Park. 1989. "Patterns and Covariates of Contraceptive Method Choice in the Republic of Korea." In *Choosing A Contraceptive: Method Choice in Asia and the United States.* Ed. R. A. Bulatao, J. A. Palmore, and S. E. Ward, 105–125. Boulder, Colo.: Westview.

Choe, Minja Kim, Sae-Kwon Kong, and Karen Oppenheim Mason. 1994. "Korean Women's Labor Force Participation: Attitude and Behavior." In *Korean Studies: New Pacific Currents.* Ed. Dae Sook Suh, 283–298. Honolulu: Center for Korean Studies.

Choe, Minja Kim, Lee-Jay Cho, Robert D. Retherford, and Norman Y. Luther. 1995. "Fertility Transition in the Republic of Korea." Document prepared for the poster session at the annual meeting of the Population Association of America, San Francisco, 6–8 April.

Choi, Jai-Seuk. 1970. "Comparative Study on the Traditional Families in Korea, Japan, and China." In *Families in East and West: Socialization Processes and Kinship Ties.* Ed. Reuben Hill and Rene Konig, 202–210. Paris: Mouton.

Chung, Bom-Mo, J. H. Cha, and S. J. Lee. 1977. *Boy Preferences and Family Planning in Korea.* Seoul: Korea Institute for Research in the Behavioral Sciences.

Chung, Young Sook. 1996. "Household Expenditure on After-School Education and Screening Hypothesis." (In Korean.) *Journal of Consumer Studies* 7 (2): 207–221.

Chung, Young Sook, and Minja Kim Choe. 2001. "Sources of Family Income and Expenditure on Children's Private, After-School Education in Korea." *International Journal of Consumer Studies* 25 (3): 193–199.

Cogner, Rand D., and Glen H. Elder Jr. 1994. "Families in Troubled Times: The Iowa Youth and Families Project." In *Families in Troubled Times: Adapting to Change in Rural America.* Ed. R. D. Cogner and G. H. Elder Jr., 3–19. New York: Aldine de Gruyter.

Coverman, Shelley. 1985. "Explaining Husbands' Participation in Domestic Labor." *Sociological Quarterly* 26: 81–97.

Coverman, Shelley, and Joseph F. Sheley. 1986. "Changes in Men's Housework and Child-Care Time, 1965–1975." *Journal of Marriage and the Family* 48: 413–422.

DaVanzo, Julie, and M. Omar Rahman. 1993. *American Families: Trends and Policy Issues.* Santa Monica, Calif.: RAND.

Deuchler, Martina. 1977. "The Tradition: Women during the Yi Dynasty." In *Virtues in Conflict: Tradition and the Korean Women Today.* Ed. Sandra Mattielli, 1–47. Seoul: Samhwa.

Dore, Ronald Philip. 1976. *The Diploma Disease: Education, Qualification and Development.* Berkeley: University of California Press.

England, Paula, and George Farkas. 1986. *Households, Employment, and Gender: A Social, Economic, and Demographic View.* New York: Aldine de Gruyter.

Farkas, George. 1976. "Education, Wage Rates, and the Division of Labor between Husband and Wife." *Journal of Marriage and the Family* 38: 473–483.

Feeney, Griffith, and Jingyuan Yu. 1987. "Period Parity Progression Measures of Fertility in China." *Population Studies* 41 (2): 77–102.

Ferree, M. M. 1991. "The Gender Division of Labor in Two-Earner Marriages: Dimensions of Variability and Change." *Journal of Family Issues* 12: 158–180.

Forrest, J. D., and S. Singh. 1992. "The Sexual and Reproductive Behavior of American Women, 1982–1988." *Family Planning Perspectives* 22: 206–214.

Freedman, Ronald. 1975. *The Sociology of Human Fertility: An Annotated Bibliography.* New York: Irvington.

Fukuzawa, Rebecca Erwin. 1994. "The Path to Adulthood according to Japanese Middle Schools." *Journal of Japanese Studies* 20 (1): 61–86.

Gecas, Victor. 1987. "Born in the USA in the 1980's: Growing up in Difficult Times." *Journal of Family Issues* 8: 434–436.

Gershuny, Jonathan, and John P. Robinson. 1988. "Historical Change in the Household Division of Labor." *Demography* 25: 537–552.

Goldscheider, Frances K., and Linda J. Waite. 1991. *New Families, No Families? The Transformation of the American Home*. Berkeley: University of California Press.

Goldstein, Joshua R. 1999. "The Leveling of Divorce in the United States." *Demography* 36 (3): 409–414.

Goode, William J. 1963. *World Revolution and Family Patterns*. New York: Free Press.

Greene, William H. 1991. *LIMDEP User's Manual and Reference Guide*. Version 6.0. Bellport, N.Y.: Econometric Software.

Greenhalgh, Susan. 1985. "Sexual Stratification: The Other Side of 'Growth with Equity' in East Asia." *Population and Development Review* 11: 265–314.

Han, S., M. K. Choe, M.-S. Lee, and S.-H. Lee. 2001. "Risk-Taking Behavior among High School Students in South Korea." *Journal of Adolescence* 24 (4): 571–574.

Hanley, Susan B., and Kozo Yamamura. 1975. "*Ichi hime, ni taro*: Educational Aspirations and the Decline in Fertility in Postwar Japan." *Journal of Japanese Studies* 2 (1): 83–125.

Harevan, Tamara. 1982. *Family Time and Industrial Time: The Relationship between the Family and Work in a New England Industrial Community*. New York: Cambridge University Press.

Hochschild, Arlie. 1991. *The Second Shift*. New York: Penguin.

Hong, Munsik, Sangyong Yi, Yŏngsik Chang, and Yŏnghi Oh. 1994. *1994 chŏnkuk ch'ulsanyŏk mit kajok pogŏn silt'ae chosa pogosŏ* [The 1994 Korean national survey on fertility and family health]. Seoul: Korea Institute for Health and Social Affairs.

Huber, Joan, and Glenna Spitze. 1983. *Sex Stratification: Children, Housework, and Jobs*. New York: Academic Press.

Inglehart, Ronald. 1990. *Culture Shift in Advanced Industrial Society*. Princeton, N.J.: Princeton University Press.

Institute of Population Problems. 1989a. *Marriage Dissolution Tables for Japanese Couples, 1935–1985*. (In Japanese.) Tokyo: Institute of Population Problems, Japan Ministry of Health and Welfare.

———. 1989b. *Showa-62-nen dokushin seinenso no kekkonkan to kodomokan* [Attitudes of young, single Japanese toward marriage and children in 1987]. Tokyo: Institute of Population Problems, Japan Ministry of Health and Welfare.

———. 1992. *Population Projection for Japan: 1991–2090*. Tokyo: Institute of Population Problems, Japan Ministry of Health and Welfare.

———. 1993. *Tenth Japanese National Fertility Survey, 1992. Volume 1: Marriage and Fertility in Present-Day Japan*. (In Japanese.) Tokyo: Institute of Population Problems, Japan Ministry of Health and Welfare.

Ishii-Kuntz, Masako, and Scott Coltrane. 1992. "Predicting the Sharing of Household Labor: Are Parenting and Housework Distinct?" *Sociological Perspectives* 35: 629–647.

Jolivet, Muriel. 1997. *Japan: The Childless Society*. New York: Routledge.

Kamo, Yoshinori. 1988. "Determinants of Household Division of Labor: Resources, Power, and Ideology." *Journal of Family Issues* 9: 177–200.

———. 1994. "Division of Household Work in the United States and Japan." *Journal of Family Issues* 15: 348–378.

Kim, Seung-Kwon. 1992. "Sexual Behavior among Single Men and Women in Korea." In *Special Report on 1991 National Fertility Survey*. Ed. Korea Institute for Health and Social Affairs, 1–39. Seoul: Korea Institute for Health and Social Affairs.

Kim, Tae-Hong, and Seung-Joo Yang. 1997. *Women's Characteristics and Their Changes: Comprehensive Analysis of the 1995 Population and Housing Census.* Report 7-3. Seoul: National Statistical Office.

Kim, Yong-Hwa. 1993. *Inequality of Education in South Korea: Expansion of Higher Education, Its Processes and Effects.* Seoul: Educational Sciences.

Kohn, Melvin. 1976. "Social Class and Parental Values: Another Confirmation of the Relationship." *American Sociological Review* 41: 538–545.

Kong, Sae-Kwon, and Minja Kim Choe. 1989. "Labor Force Participation of Married Women in Contemporary Korea." *Journal of Population and Health Studies* 9 (2): 117–136.

Kong, Sae-Kwon, A.-J. Cho, S.-K. Kim, and S.-H. Son. 1992. *Hanguk esŏ-ui kajok hyŏng-sŏng kwa ch'ulsan haengt'ae* [Family formation and fertility behavior in Korea]. Seoul: Korea Institute for Health and Social Affairs.

Kong, Sae-Kwon, A.-J. Cho, J.-S. Kim, H.-S. Chang, and M.-K. Suh. 1990. *Changing Family Functions and Role Relations in the Republic of Korea.* (In Korean.) Seoul: Korea Institute for Health and Social Affairs.

Kulkarni, Sumati, and Minja Kim Choe. 1998. "Unwanted Fertility in Selected States of India." *National Family Health Survey Reports,* no. 6. Honolulu: East-West Center Program on Population.

Kuo, Hsiang-Hui, and Robert M. Hauser. 1996. "Gender, Family Configuration, and the Effect of Family Background on Educational Attainment." *Social Biology* 43 (1–2): 98–131.

Kurosu, Satomi. 1994. "Who Lives in the Extended Family and Why? The Case of Japan." In Cho and Yada, eds., *Tradition and Change,* 179–198.

Kwon, Tai-Hwan. 1993. "Exploring Socio-cultural Explanations of Fertility Transition in South Korea." In *The Revolution of Asian Fertility.* Ed. Richard Leete and Iqbal Alam, 41–53. Oxford: Clarendon Press.

Lawton, L., M. Silverstein, and V. Bengston. 1994. "Affection, Social Contact, and Geographic Distance between Adult Children and Their Parents." *Journal of Marriage and the Family* 56: 57–68.

Lebra, Takie Sugiyama. 1984. *Japanese Women: Constraints and Fulfillment.* Honolulu: University of Hawai'i Press.

Lee, Kwang-Kyu. 1972. "The Korean Family in a Changing Society." *East Asian Cultural Studies* 11: 28–43.

———. 1978. *Kankoku kazoku no kozo bunseki* [The structural analysis of the Korean family]. (In Japanese.) Translated from the Korean by Tamio Hattori. Tokyo: Tosho Kanko Kai.

Lesthaeghe, Ron. 1983. "A Century of Demographic and Cultural Change in Western Europe: An Exploration of Underlying Dimensions." *Population and Development Review* 9: 411–435.

Lesthaeghe, Ron, and Dominique Meekers. 1986. "Value Changes and the Dimensions of Familism in the European Community." *European Journal of Population* 86: 225–268.

Lesthaeghe, Ron, and Johan Surkin. 1988. "Cultural Dynamics and Economic Theories of Fertility Change." *Population and Development Review* 14: 1–45.

Lesthaeghe, Ron, and Chris Wilson. 1986. "Modes of Production, Secularization, and the Pace of the Fertility Decline in Western Europe, 1870–1930." In *The Decline in Fertility in Europe*. Ed. Ansley J. Coale and Susan C. Watkins, 261–292. Princeton, N.J.: Princeton University Press.

Logan, John, and Glenna Spitze. 1996. *Family Ties: Enduring Relations between Parents and Their Grown Children*. Philadelphia: Temple University Press.

Maeda, Masako. 1997. *Hoikuen wa ima* [Day-care centers in Japan today]. Tokyo: Iwanami Shoten.

Mainichi Shimbun Jinko Mondai Chosakai. 1992. *Kiroku Nihon no jinko: Shousan eno kiseki kaitei-ban* [Japan's Population: Paths to Low Fertility]. Revised edition. Tokyo: Mainichi Shimbun.

Maret, Elizabeth, and Barbara Finlay. 1984. "The Distribution of Household Labor among Women in Dual-Earner Families." *Journal of Marriage and the Family* 46: 357–364.

Martin, Linda G. 1990. "Changing Intergenerational Family Relations in East Asia." *Annals of the American Academy of Political and Social Science* 510: 102–114.

Martin, Linda G., and Noriko O. Tsuya. 1991. "Interactions of Middle-Aged Japanese with Their Parents." *Population Studies* 45: 299–311.

———. 1992. "Japanese Women in the Middle: Work and Family Responsibilities." Paper presented at the annual meeting of the Population Association of America, Denver, 30 April–1 May.

Mason, Karen Oppenheim. 1993. "The Impact of Women's Position during the Course of Development." In *Women's Position and Demographic Change*. Ed. N. Federici, K. O. Mason, and S. Sogner, 19–42. Oxford: Clarendon Press.

Mason, Karen Oppenheim, Noriko O. Tsuya, and Minja Kim Choe, eds. 1998. *The Changing Family in Comparative Perspective: Asia and the United States*. Honolulu: East-West Center.

McCullagh, P., and J. A. Nelder. 1989. *Generalized Linear Models*. 2d edition. London: Chapman and Hall.

McDonald, Peter. 2000. "Gender Equity in Theories of Fertility Transition." *Population and Development Review* 26 (3): 427–439.

Monbusho. 1985. *Jido seito no gakkogai katsudo ni kansuru jittai chosa* [Survey on extracurricular activities of elementary and secondary school students]. Tokyo: Ministry of Education, Science, Sports, and Culture.

———. 1997. *Monbu tokei yoran heisei-9-nendo* [Educational statistical abstract 1997]. Tokyo: Ministry of Finance Printing Office.

———. 1998. *Monbu tokei yoran heisei-10-nenban* [Handbook on educational statistics 1998]. Tokyo: Ministry of Finance Printing Office.

Moon, Okpyo. 1990. "Urban Middle Class Wives in Contemporary Korea: Their Roles, Responsibilities and Dilemma." *Korea Journal* 30 (11): 30–44.

Morgan, S. Philip. 1982. "Parity-Specific Fertility Intentions and Uncertainty: The United States, 1970–1976." *Demography* 19 (3): 315–334.

———. 1996. "Characteristic Features of Modern American Fertility." In Casterline, Lee, and Foote, eds., *Fertility in the United States*, 19–63.

Morgan, S. Philip, and Kiyoshi Hirosima. 1983. "The Persistence of Extended Family Residence in Japan: Anachronism or Alternative Strategy?" *American Sociological Review* 48 (2): 269–281

National Center for Education Statistics. 2002. "Digest of Education Statistics, 2000." Washington, D.C.: National Center for Education Statistics (http://www.nces.ed.gov/pubs2001/digest/).

National Institute of Population and Social Security Research. 1998. *Eleventh Japanese National Fertility Survey, 1997. Volume 1: Marriage and Fertility in Present-Day Japan.* (In Japanese.) Tokyo: National Institute of Population and Social Security Research.

———. 1999. *Eleventh Japanese National Fertility Survey, 1997. Volume 2: Attitudes toward Marriage and the Family among Unmarried Japanese Youth.* (In Japanese.) Tokyo: National Institute of Population and Social Security Research.

———. 2002. *Latest Demographic Statistics 2001/2002.* (In Japanese.) Tokyo: National Institute of Population and Social Security Research.

National Statistical Office. 1995. *Advance Report of 1995 Population and Housing Census.* Seoul: National Statistical Office, Republic of Korea.

———. 1996. *Population Projection.* (In Korean.) Seoul: National Statistical Office, Republic of Korea.

———. 1997a. *1995 Population and Housing Census Report.* Volume 1. Seoul: National Statistical Office, Republic of Korea.

———. 1997b. *1995 Population and Housing Census Report.* Volume 5. Seoul: National Statistical Office, Republic of Korea.

———. 1998. *Social Indicators in Korea 1998.* Seoul: National Statistical Office, Republic of Korea.

———. 1999. *Monthly Statistics of Korea.* Vol. 41, no. 6. Taejon: National Statistical Office, Republic of Korea.

———. 2000. *Social Indicators in Korea 2000.* Daejon: National Statistical Office, Republic of Korea.

Nihon Daigaku Sogo Kagaku Kenkyusho. 1994. *Gendai-kazoku ni kansuru zenkoku-chosa hokokusho* [Report of the 1994 survey on work and family life in Japan]. Tokyo: University Research Center, Nihon University.

Oakley, Ann. 1976. *Women's Work: The Housewife, Past and Present.* New York: Vintage Books.

Ogawa, Naohiro. 1990. "Labor Supply and Earning Power of Married Japanese Women of Childbearing Age." In *Summary of the Twentieth National Survey on Family Planning.* Ed. Population Problems Research Council, 163–202. Tokyo: Mainichi Shimbun.

Ogawa, Naohiro, and Robert D. Retherford. 1993a. "Care of the Elderly in Japan: Changing Norms and Expectations." *Journal of Marriage and the Family* 55: 585–597.

———. 1993b. "The Resumption of Fertility Decline in Japan: 1973–92." *Population and Development Review* 19 (4): 703–741.

———. 1997. "Shifting Costs of Caring for the Elderly Back to Families in Japan." *Population and Development Review* 23 (1): 59–94.

Ogburn, William F. 1964. *On Culture and Social Change.* Chicago: University of Chicago Press.

Oppenheimer, Valerie Kincade. 1994. "Women's Rising Employment and the Future of the Family in Industrial Societies." *Population and Development Review* 20 (2): 293–342.

Pagnini, Deanne L., and Ronald R. Rindfuss. 1993. "The Divorce of Marriage and

Childbearing: Changing Attitudes and Behavior in the United States." *Population and Development Review* 19 (2): 331–347.

Pleck, Joseph H. 1977. "The Work-Family System." *Social Problems* 24: 417–427.

———. 1985. *Working Wives/Working Husbands*. Beverly Hills, Calif.: Sage Publications.

Population Problems Research Council. 1996. *Toward a New Century of Equality and Symbiosis: Summary of Twenty-third National Survey on Family Planning*. Tokyo: Mainichi Shimbun.

Presser, Harriet B. 1994. "Employment Schedules among Dual-Earner Spouses and the Division of Household Labor by Gender." *American Sociological Review* 59: 348–364.

Preston, Samuel H. 1976. *Mortality Patterns in National Populations with Special Reference to Recorded Causes of Death*. New York: Academic Press.

Raley, R. Kelly, and Larry L. Bumpass. 2002. "The Topography of the Divorce Plateau: Differences in Rates and Trends after 1980." Paper submitted for journal publication.

Raley, R. Kelly, and Ronald R. Rindfuss. 1999. "Intergenerational Contact in the United States and Japan: The Effect of the Kinship Position of the Respondent." *Population Research and Policy Review* 18: 279–298.

Retherford, Robert D., and Minja Kim Choe. 1993. *Statistical Models for Causal Analysis*. New York: John Wiley and Sons.

Retherford, Robert D., Naohiro Ogawa, and Rikiya Matsukura. 2001. "Late Marriage and Less Marriage in Japan." *Population and Development Review* 27: 65–102.

Retherford, Robert D., Naohiro Ogawa, and Satomi Sakamoto. 1996. "Values and Fertility Change in Japan." *Population Studies* 50 (1): 5–25.

Rexroat, C., and C. Shehan 1987. "The Family Life Cycle and Spouses' Time in Housework." *Journal of Marriage and the Family* 49: 737–750.

Rindfuss, Ronald R., and Karin L. Brewster. 1996. "Childrearing and Fertility." In Casterline, Lee, and Foote, eds., *Fertility in the United States*, 259–289.

Rindfuss, Ronald R., and R. Kelly Raley. 1998. "Intergenerational Contact in the United States and Japan." In Mason, Tsuya, and Choe, eds., *The Changing Family in Comparative Perspective*, 194–213.

Rindfuss, Ronald R., and Elizabeth H. Stephen. 1990. "Marital Non-Cohabitation: Separation Does Not Make the Heart Grow Fonder." *Journal of Marriage and the Family* 52: 259–270.

Rindfuss, Ronald R., Karen Benjamin, and S. Philip Morgan. 2000. "How Does Marriage and Female Labor Force Participation Affect Fertility in Low-Fertility Countries?" Paper presented at the annual meeting of the Population Association of America, Los Angeles, 23–25 March.

Rindfuss, Ronald R., Karin L. Brewster, and Andrew L. Kavee. 1996. "Women, Work, and Children: Behavioral and Attitudinal Change in the United States." *Population and Development Review* 22 (3): 457–482.

Rindfuss, Ronald R., S. Philip Morgan, and Gary Swicegood. 1988. *First Births in America: Changes in the Timing of Parenthood*. Berkeley: University of California Press.

Rodosho Joseikyoku [Bureau on Women, Japan Ministry of Labour]. 1999. *Heisei-10-nen-ban josei rodo hakusho* [White paper on female labor 1998]. Tokyo: 21-seiki Shokugyo Zaidan.

———. 2000. *Heisei-11-nendo-ban josei rodo hakusho: Hataraku jyosei no jitujyo* [White paper on female labor 1999: The situation of working women in Japan]. Tokyo: 21-seiki Shokugyo Zaidan.

Rohlen, Thomas P. 1980. "The *Juku* Phenomenon: An Exploratory Essay." *Journal of Japanese Studies* 6 (2): 207–242.

Ross, Catherine E. 1987. "The Division of Labor at Home." *Social Forces* 65: 816–833.

Rossi, A., and P. Rossi. 1990. *Of Human Bonding: Parent-Child Relationships over the Life Course.* New York: Aldine de Gruyter.

Saluter, Arlene. 1996. "Marital Status and Living Arrangements, March 1995 (Update)." *Current Population Reports: Population Characteristics,* P20-491. Washington, D.C.: U.S. Bureau of the Census.

"Share of Educational Expenses in South Korea Double That in Japan." *Digital Chosunilbo,* 5 August (h).

Shimada, Haruo, and Yoshio Higuchi. 1985. "An Analysis of Trends in Female Labor Force Participation in Japan." *Journal of Labor Economics* 3: 335–374.

Smith, Robert J. 1987. "Gender Inequality in Contemporary Japan." *Journal of Japanese Studies* 13: 1–25.

Spitze, Glenna. 1986. "The Division of Task Responsibility in U.S. Households: Longitudinal Adjustments to Change." *Social Forces* 64: 689–701.

Spitze, Glenna, and John Logan. 1991. "Sibling Structure and Intergenerational Relations." *Journal of Marriage and the Family* 53: 871–884.

Spitze, Glenna, and Russell Ward. 1995. "Household Labor in Intergenerational Households." *Journal of Marriage and the Family* 57: 355–361.

Stafford, Rebecca, Elaine Beckman, and Pamela Dibona. 1977. "The Division of Labor among Cohabiting and Married Couples." *Journal of Marriage and the Family* 39: 43–56.

Steinhoff, Patricia G. 1994. "A Cultural Approach to the Family in Japan and the United States." In Cho and Yada, eds., *Tradition and Change,* 29–44.

Sweet, James A. 1970. "Family Composition and the Labor Force Activity of American Wives." *Demography* 7 (2): 195–209.

———. 1989. "Response Rates for Secondary Respondents." Madison: Center for Demography and Ecology, University of Wisconsin–Madison. *NSFH Working Paper* 7.

Sweet, James A., and Larry L. Bumpass. 1996. "The National Survey of Families and Households—Waves 1 and 2: Data Description and Documentation." Madison: Center for Demography and Ecology, University of Wisconsin–Madison (http://www.ssc.wisc.edu/nsfh/home.htm).

Sweet, James, Larry L. Bumpass, and Vaughn Call. 1988. "The Design and Content of the National Survey of Families and Households." Madison: Center for Demography and Ecology, University of Wisconsin–Madison. *NSFH Working Paper* 1.

Taeuber, Irene B. 1958. *The Population of Japan.* Princeton, N.J.: Princeton University Press.

Thornton, Arland. 1989. "Changing Attitudes Towards Family Issues in the United States." *Journal of Marriage and the Family* 51: 873–895.

Thornton, Arland, and Deborah Freedman. 1983. "The Changing American Family." *Population Bulletin* 38: 1–44.

Tsuya, Noriko O. 1990. "Coresidence with Parents at Different Stages of Life." In *Sum-*

mary of Twentieth National Survey on Family Planning. Ed. Population Problems Research Council, 101–161. Tokyo: Mainichi Shimbun.

———. 1992. "Work and Family Life in Japan: Changes and Continuities." Paper presented at the 1992 annual meeting of the American Sociological Association, Pittsburgh, 20–24 August.

———. 1993. "Sexual Activity and Contraceptive Use of Young Unmarried Japanese Women." Paper presented at the 1993 annual meeting of the Population Association of America, Cincinnati, 1–3 April.

———. 1994. "Changing Attitudes toward Marriage and the Family in Japan." In Cho and Yada, eds., *Tradition and Change,* 91–119.

———. 2000. "Women's Empowerment, Marriage Postponement, and Gender Relations in Japan: An Intergenerational Perspective." In *Women's Empowerment and Demographic Processes: Moving Beyond Cairo.* Ed. Harriet B. Presser and Gita Sen, 319–348. Oxford: Oxford University Press.

Tsuya, Noriko O., and Larry L. Bumpass. 1998. "Time Allocation between Employment and Housework in Japan, South Korea, and the United States." In Mason, Tsuya, and Choe, eds., *The Changing Family in Comparative Perspective,* 83–104.

Tsuya, Noriko O., and Minja Kim Choe. 1991. "Changes in Intrafamilial Relationships and the Roles of Women in Japan and Korea." Tokyo: Nihon University Population Research Institute. *NUPRI Research Paper Series* 58.

———. 1994. "Nuptiality Change in Asia: Patterns, Causes, and Prospects." Paper prepared for presentation at the Twenty-Fifth Summer Seminar on Population, Distinguished Lecturers Series, East-West Center, Honolulu, 20 June.

Tsuya, Noriko O., and Karen Oppenheim Mason. 1995. "Changing Gender Roles and Below-Replacement Fertility in Japan." In *Gender and Family Change in Industrialized Countries.* Ed. Karen Oppenheim Mason and An-Magritt Jensen, 139–167. Oxford: Clarendon Press.

Turner, Ralph. 1960. "Sponsored and Contested Mobility and the School System." *American Sociological Review* 25 (6): 855–867.

United Nations. 1996. *World Population Prospects 1996.* New York: United Nations.

U.S. Bureau of the Census. 1973. *1970 Census of Population: Detailed Characteristics, United States Summary.* Washington, D.C.: U.S. Bureau of the Census.

———. 1975. *Historical Statistics of the United States, Colonial Times to 1970, Bicentennial Edition, Part 2.* Washington D.C.: U.S. Bureau of the Census.

———. 1980. *Statistical Abstract of the United States: 1980.* Washington, D.C.: U.S. Bureau of the Census.

———. 1998. *Statistical Abstract of the United States: 1998.* Washington, D.C.: U.S. Bureau of the Census.

———. 2000. *Educational Attainment in the United States, March 2000, Detailed Tables.* Washington, D.C.: U.S. Bureau of the Census (http://www.census.gov/population/www/socdemo/education/p20-536.html).

Ventura, S. J. 1995. "Births to Unmarried Mothers, United States, 1980–92. *Vital and Health Statistics* 21 (53). Washington, D.C.: National Center for Health Statistics.

Ventura, S. J., J. A. Martin, S. C. Curtin, and T. J. Mathews. 1998. "Report of Final Natality Statistics, 1996." *Monthly Vital Statistics Report* 46, no. 11, supplement. Hyattsville, Md.: National Center for Health Statistics.

Vogel, Ezra F. 1971. *Japan's New Middle Class: The Salary Man and His Family in a Tokyo Suburb.* 2d ed. Berkeley: University of California Press.

Wagner, Edward, W. 1983. "Two Early Genealogies and Women's Status in Early Yi Dynasty Korea." In *Korean Women: View from the Inner Room.* Ed. Laurel Kendall and M. Peterson 23–32. New Haven, Conn.: East Rock Press.

Waite, Linda J. 1981. "U.S. Women at Work." *Population Bulletin* 36 (2): 1–43.

Wolf, D. A., and B. J. Soldo. 1994. "Married Women's Allocation of Time to Employment and Parental Care." *Journal of Human Resources* 29: 1259–1276.

World Bank. 1991. *World Tables 1991 Update.* Baltimore: Johns Hopkins University Press.

———. 1997. *World Development Indicators 1997.* Washington, D.C.: World Bank.

Yamazaki, Hirotoshi, Hiroshi Shimada, Hiroaki Urata, Masashi Fujimura, and Takeo Kikuchi. 1983. "Gakureki kenkyu no doko [The trend of studies on educational credentialism]." *Kyoiku shakaigaku kenkyu* 38: 94–109.

Yi, Hyŏn-Song, Kyŏng-Hi Chŏng, Kyŏng-Hye Han, Hye-Kyŏng Yi, and Hye-Kyu Kang. 1996. *Yŏsŏng yi kyŏngje hwaldong kwa kajok pokji* [Women's economic activities and family welfare]. Seoul: Korea Institute for Health and Social Affairs.

Yonemura, Chiyo, and Mary Louise Nagata. 1998. "Continuity, Solidarity, Family and Enterprise: What Is an *Ie?*" In *House and the Stem Family in Eurasian Perspective.* Ed. Antoinette Fauve-Chamoux and Emiko Ochiai, 193–214. Kyoto: International Research Center for Japanese Studies.

Contributors

Larry L. Bumpass is N. B. Ryder Professor Emeritus of Sociology at the University of Wisconsin–Madison.

Yong-Chan Byun is director of the Department of Social Affairs Research at the Korea Institute for Health and Social Affairs, Seoul.

Minja Kim Choe is a senior fellow in the Population and Health Studies Research Program at the East-West Center, Honolulu.

Karen Oppenheim Mason is director of Gender and Development at the World Bank.

Ronald R. Rindfuss is Robert Paul Ziff Professor in the Department of Sociology at the University of North Carolina–Chapel Hill.

Noriko O. Tsuya is a professor in the Department of Economics at Keio University, Tokyo.

Index

attitudes toward sex: extramarital, *28, 29,*
29–30; premarital, 20, 26–28, 27

behavior: and attitudes, relations between, 19,
38, 118, 133, 134, 154n14; nontraditional,
tolerance of, 22; and the study of the
family, 135
benefits of marriage. *See* attitudes toward
marriage; marriage, costs and benefits of
bias due to selectivity in data on never-
married adults, 45, 147n6
bilateral family system in U.S., 4–5, 56, 66;
and contact with parents, 66. *See also*
cultural backgrounds; patrilineal relationships
birth order. *See* eldest son

Caldwell, John: theory of fertility decline, 54
childbearing: linkage to marriage, 50–51, 136;
nonmarital, 7–8, 136–137, 138, 142, 148n5
child care, time spent on, not included in
analysis, 115, 120, 152n4
children: ages of (*See* ages of children);
number of, and after-school programs, 90;
possibility of a full life without, 24, 25,
25–26; quality of, *vs.* quantity, 92
children, costs of, 76; and fertility, 16. *See also*
education costs
children, presence of: and employment of
women, 100–103, *101, 102*; and household
tasks, 116–117; and household tasks, time
spent on, 121–123, *122, 123*
city size. *See* residence
cohabitation, 7–8, 24, 38, 42, 136, 147n7
cohort differences and age differences, 21
combined workload in household, 17, 116,
118–121, *119, 120,* 132; data on, *119*; and
income of men, 153n6; measuring, 118
commuting time, 17, 107–109, *108,* 112; measuring, 96, 152n7; missing data on, 107
Confucianism: and family obligations, 2, 3,
20, 36–37; and filial piety, 20, 38, 146n5;
and importance of education, 77; influence of, on family, 2, 3, 20, 36–37, 61, 135;
and interactions of adults with parents,
56–57; and marriage, 52; and power within
the family, 61; and relationships between
employment and family, 114; and responsibilities of mothers, 92–93. *See also* cultural backgrounds
constraints on interactions of adults with
parents, 58–61, 74–75

contact between adults and parents. *See*
coresidence; e-mail contact; personal contact; telephone contact
coresidence of adults with parents, 16, 57,
74–75; and age, 63, 65; and allocation of
household tasks, 127, *128,* 132, 135; attitudes toward, 35–36, *36;* and conflict
between work and family roles, 96–97, 136;
cultural expectations regarding, 61–62; and
education, 63, 65; and eldest son, 56, 57,
62, 63, 64, 65, 72, 135, 136, 138, 148n4; and
employment of women, *101,* 135; factors
affecting, 42, 62–64, 65, 149n12; and family systems, 3–4; and fertility decline, 62,
75; and gender, 51, 63, 64, 65; and gender
division of household tasks, 117; and hours
worked by men, *106;* and hours worked by
women, *101;* and household tasks, 117, *124;*
and household tasks, share of, 127, *128,*
132, 135; and household tasks, time spent
on, *122, 123,* 123–125, 127, *128,* 136; and *ie*
(traditional family system in Japan), 75;
levels and trends of, 61–62, *62,* 138, 142;
and marriage, costs and benefits of, *47,*
48; and marriage desires, *49,* 135–136;
as a norm, *42, 135;* and patrilineal inheritance, 4, 16, 56–57, 75, 135; and personal
contact with parents, 67; and rural-urban
origins, 63, 65; and values, 58. *See also*
proximity to parents
coresidence with adult daughters, *124;* and
allocation of household tasks, 127–129; and
household tasks, share of, 117, *128;* and
household tasks, time spent on, *122, 123,*
123, 128, 132
costs: of education (*See* education costs); of
marriage (*See* marriage, costs and benefits
of)
costs of children, 76; and fertility, 16. *See also*
children, costs of; education costs
country differences in measures, 139–140,
See also *specific measures*
country size, 149n9; effect of, on personal
contact, 67
cram schools. *See* after-school programs
credentialism in education, 77–78
cross-national research and analysis on family,
139–141
cultural backgrounds: and attitudes, 19–20,
38; differences and similarities in, 2, 3–5,
20, 56–57, 142; and divorce, 34; and gender roles, 37; and intergenerational rela-

128–129, 131, 131–132; and gender, 129; and hours worked, 121, 122, 123, 128, 132; and income, 128, 129, 132; levels and patterns of, 17, 118–119, 119, 142; measuring, 118, 152n1, 154n13; and mode effect, 126–127; and presence of children, 121–123, 122, 123; and time availability, 115, 116; and time returned home from work, 109

household tasks and gender, 114–133; and coresidence with adult daughters, 127–129; and coresidence with parents, 127, 128, 132, 135; and employment of women, 17, 102, 112–113, 116, 118–121, 119, 152n2; factors affecting, 115–118, 125, 127–131, 128–129, 133, 135, 153n8 (See also attitudes toward gender roles; resources of spouses; time availability); factors affecting, measuring, 127; and hours worked, 98, 107; levels and patterns of, 4–5, 52–53, 118–119, 119; and resources of spouses, 117–118, 132, 133; and traditional attitudes, 118

housework. See household tasks

husbands. See men under specific topics

ie (traditional family system in Japan), 3–4, 143n3, 145nn2,4,6; and coresidence, 75

illegitimacy. See childbearing, nonmarital

income: and cohabitation, 42; dual, and intergenerational interactions, 61; and household tasks, 17; and household tasks, share of, 17, 126, 127, 128, 129, 132; and marriage costs and benefits, 47, 48; and marriage desires, 49, 50; missing data on, 81, 125, 126, 127, 153n10; pooling of, 42, 43; and resources, 125–126

income of men: and after-school programs, 87, 88–89, 94, 151n13; data on, 93; and household tasks, share of, 128, 129; and household tasks, time spent on, 128, 132

income of women, 125; and after-school programs, 89; fully-employed, 124, 126; and hours worked, 129; and household tasks, share of, 127, 128, 129, 132; and household tasks, time spent on, 128, 129; measuring, 126

independence of elderly, 36, 57, 135

independent households. See coresidence; living arrangements

industrial development. See economic development

inequality: gender, 17, 20

inheritance, patrilineal. See patrilineal inheritance

interactions of adults with parents, 16, 54–75; and Confucianism, 56–57; constraints on, 58–61, 74–75; culture's effects on, 16, 74–75; and distance between residences, 58–59, 59, 67; measuring, 55–56, 65–66; normative and cultural expectations of, 56–57, 62, 74–75; and rural-urban origins, 70, 71, 72–74; types of, 55; and urbanization, 60, 62. See also coresidence; personal contact; telephone contact

interactions with ancestors, 148n3

intercourse, extramarital, 38; attitudes toward, 28, 29, 29–30

intercourse, premarital, 7–8; attitudes toward, 20, 26–28, 27; in earlier Japan, 146n3; levels of, 29

intergenerational relations. See interactions of adults with parents

investments in children's education: measuring, 80–81. See also after-school programs

Japanese women and benefits of marriage, 15–16, 17, 42–45, 46, 51, 52–53, 110, 138–139, 141–143

jib (traditional family system in Korea), 3–4, 145nn3,4,6

joint economic response hypothesis, 100

juku (Japanese cram schools), 77. See also after-school programs

ka-jeong kyosa (private tutoring in Korea), 77. See also after-school programs

katei-kyoshi (private tutoring in Japan), 77. See also after-school programs

koseki (individual register in Japan), 57, 148nn5,6

kwa-oe (Korean cram schools), 77. See also after-school programs

labor force participation rate. See under employment of women

life expectancy, levels of, 148

living arrangements: independent, 4, 36, 42, 56, 57, 75, 135. See also coresidence

marital fertility. See fertility

marriage, 27, 27, 39, 76, 139, 142–143; age at (See marriage, delay in); arranged, 20; attitudes toward (See attitudes toward mar-

in family systems of Japan and Korea, 4; integenerational, and marital stability, 34–38; of mothers, for raising children, 83, 100; of mothers, in Confucianism, 92–93; to one's family, historically, 1; of parents, to invest in children's education, 79, 91; to parents and children, 26; to stay married for sake of children, 35; toward deceased ancestors, 148n3. *See also* attitudes, *especially* attitudes toward obligations

origins. *See* rural-urban origins

pa-ato, 109. *See also* employment of women, part-time

package of concepts relating to: the family (*See under* family; marriage package); marriage (*See* marriage package)

parental survival status, 58, *58,* 61

parity and fertility desires, 81–83, *82*

parity progression ratio, and wanted family size, 80, 83

paternal contact, 16, 56, 75, 135. *See also* coresidence; interactions of adults with parents; personal contact; telephone contact

paternal lines and linkages, 4, 56–57, 72, 145n3

patriarchal family systems, 2, 3, 117; and allocation of household tasks, 117–118, 133, 137

patriarchal heritage, 18, 33, 114, 133, 137, 154n14

patrilineal family systems, 3, 4, 145n4

patrilineal inheritance, 145nn3,4; and coresidence of adults with parents, 4, 16, 56–57, 75, 135

patrilineal relationships, 56, 66, 74

patrilocal family systems, 3, 16. *See also* cultural backgrounds

perceptions of marriage. *See* marriage, perceptions of

personal contact between adults and parents, 64–74; and coresidence, 67; and education, 75; effect of country size on, 67; effort required for, 58–59; factors affecting, 67–70, *68, 69, 71,* 75; levels of, 64–67, *66. See also* coresidence; interactions of adults with parents; telephone contact

personal freedom. *See under* attitudes toward marriage

phone contact with parents. *See* telephone contact with parents

power within the family, in Confucian tradition, 61

preference: for number of hours worked, 96; for wife's employment, 110–112, *111*

preindustrial societies, families and households in, 1

premarital sex. *See* intercourse

prenuptial agreements, 136

primary industries: decreasing importance of, 9. *See also* agriculture

proximity to parents: and employment of women, *101,* 103, 112–113; and hours worked by women, *101,* 103–104; measuring, 97; and preferences for wife's employment, *111;* and residence, 97, *101. See also* distance between residences

psychological well-being of elderly, 54–55

research and analysis, cross-national, 139–141

residence (urban-rural, city-size). *See also* coresidence; distance; living arrangements; rural-urban origins: data on, 93; and employment of women, *101,* 105; and hours worked by men, *106;* and hours worked by women, *101;* measuring, 81, 97; and after-school programs, 84, 85, 86, 87, 92, 94; and preferences for wife's employment, *111;* proximity of adults to parents, 97, *101*

resources and assistance, intergenerational flows of, 54–55

resources of spouses: and allocation of household tasks, 117–118, 132, 133; and marriage desires, 40; measuring, 125–126, 153n9; relative resource hypothesis, 117, 129, 132. *See also* income

roles. *See* gender roles

rural-urban origins, 149n10; and coresidence, 63, 65; and interactions between adults and parents, 70, 71, 72–74

sample size: and cross-national research on the family, 139–140; effect of, on personal contact, 67

schooling: data on, 93; measuring, 81. *See also* education

schools, competition for, 77, 78

seki wo yireru (colloquial Japanese term for marriage), 148n6 selectivity bias in data on never-married adults, 45, 147n6

sex. *See* gender; intercourse

sibling composition: and after-school programs, 87, 88, 94; data on, 93; measuring, 81

single adults. *See* never-married adults

size of city. *See* residence

size of country. *See* country size

size of sample. *See* sample size

small N problem and cross-national research on the family, 139–140

socioeconomic status. *See* income

sons: eldest (*See* eldest son); importance of, 20; preference for, 88, 145

stakeholders in children's lives, parents as, 77

standard of living. *See under* attitudes toward marriage

structural constraints on interactions of adults with parents, 58–61, 74

Survey on Family Life Cycle (Korea), 79, 150n7

surveys described, xiii, 12–14, 140–141

survival status of parents, 58, 58, 61

telephone contact with parents, 70–74, 72, 73, 75; cost of, 149n18. *See also* coresidence; personal contact

TFR (Total Fertility Rate). *See* fertility

time availability: and employment, 61; and household tasks, time spent on, 115, 116; measuring, 125. *See also* hours worked by men; hours worked by women

time returned home from work, and household tasks, 109, *109*

time spent: on household tasks (*See under* household tasks); on travel, and interactions of adults with parents, 58–59, 59, 67

Total Fertility Rate (TFR). *See* fertility

traditional attitudes. *See* attitudes; values

traditional family system, 4, 145nn2,3,6, 146n2, See also *ie, jib*

transportation system and interactions of adults with parents, 59

travel time and interactions of adults with parents, 58–59, 59, 67

unfaithfulness. *See* intercourse, extramarital

urbanization, 9, 74; and interactions of adults with parents, 60, 62

urban-rural origins. *See* rural-urban origins

values: egalitarian, 130; intergenerational transfer of, 134; US and Confucian, 20. *See also* attitudes; cultural backgrounds; cultural expectations

values, traditional: and coresidence of adults with parents, 58; shift from, 21; and urban background, 74

values about: eldest sons, 88; the family, 1, 3, 74

visits between adults and parents. *See* personal contact

wanted family size, 80, 83

Wanted Total Marital Fertility Rate (WTMFR): defined, 80; levels and patterns of, 83, *84*. *See also* fertility desires

women: double shift among (*See* double shift); in preindustrial societies, 1; in traditional family systems, 4

women's education. *See* education of women

women's employment. *See* employment of women

women's hours worked. *See* hours worked by women

women's income. *See* income of women

women's roles. *See* gender roles

work-family interface, 3, 114

WTMFR. *See* Wanted Total Marital Fertility Rate

Production Notes for
Tsuya and Bumpass / *Marriage, Work, and Family Life*

Cover and interior designed by Deborah Hodgdon

Text and display type in Fairfield and Agenda Black

Composition by Josie Herr

Printing and binding by The Maple-Vail Book Manufacturing Group

Printed on 60# Text White Opaque, 426 ppi